_Betty Crocker_

# Christmas
## COOKBOOK

Houghton Mifflin Harcourt
Boston • New York • 2017

## GENERAL MILLS

Owned Media and Publishing Director:
Amy Halford

Owned Media and Publishing Manager:
Danielle Andrews

Senior Editor: Cathy Swanson

Recipe Development and Testing: Betty
Crocker Kitchens

Photography: General Mills Photography
Studios and Image Library

## HOUGHTON MIFFLIN HARCOURT

Editorial Director: Deb Brody

Executive Editor: Anne Ficklen

Managing Editor: Marina Padakis

Production Editor: Helen Seachrist

Cover Design: Tai Blanche

Interior Design and Layout: Tai Blanche

Senior Production Coordinator:
Kimberly Kiefer

**Inspiring America to Cook at Home™**

The Betty Crocker Kitchens seal guarantees
success in your kitchen. Every recipe has been
tested in America's Most Trusted Kitchens™ to
meet our high standards of reliability, easy
preparation and great taste.

FIND MORE GREAT IDEAS AT
*BettyCrocker*.com

**Merry Christmas from the photo and editorial teams!**

www.hmhco.com

**Library of Congress Cataloging-in-Publication Data**

Names: Crocker, Betty, author.
Title: Betty Crocker Christmas cookbook.
Other titles: Christmas cookbook.
Description: Boston : Houghton Mifflin Harcourt, 2017. | Includes index.
Identifiers: LCCN 2017019017 (print) | LCCN 2017018470 (ebook) |
ISBN 9781328710383 (ebook) | ISBN 9781328710291 (trade paper)
Subjects: LCSH: Christmas cooking. | LCGFT: Cookbooks.
Classification: LCC TX739.2.C45 (print) | LCC TX739.2.C45 C74 2017 (ebook) |
DDC 641.5/686—dc23
LC record available at https://lccn.loc.gov/2017019017

Manufactured in China

SCP 10 9 8 7 6 5 4 3 2 1

Cover photos: Raspberry-Apple Stocking Coffee Cake (page 136); Bûche de Noël (page 232);
Mango-Ginger Snowdrift Mimosas (page 39); Beer- and Rosemary-Roasted Turkey (page 89);
Elf-Tinis (page 37); Onion- and Pepper-Braised Brisket (page 98); Cake Ball Ornaments (page
236); Balsamic Kale-and-Strawberry Salad (page 130); Peppermint Cupcake Tree (page 243)

# Dear Friends,

When we look back at Christmases past, what is it we remember most? It's the laughter, time spent together and the food! During the holiday season, is it possible to find the balance between making things special for your family and friends while keeping your sanity? Is it possible to have total enjoyment without all the rushing?

Yes! We've got great solutions for anything that happens during the month of December. Inside you'll find quick, wow appetizers for a Friday night holiday party, elfishly-cute foods to give as gifts and drool-worthy recipes for your BIG holiday meal. Look to the icons to help you choose recipes to maximize your time in the kitchen:

| | |
|---|---|
| **SLOW COOKER** | Slow Cooker recipe |
| **MAKE AHEAD** | Make-Ahead recipe |
| **QUICK FIX** | Quick-Fix recipe (prep in 15 minutes or less) |

Take a peek at the special features throughout the book to help make your December merry and bright. *Bring On the Beverages* (page 40) shows you how much liquor you'll need for your party, how to stock a bar and special ways to garnish your drinks. Entertain like you have a workshop full of helpers with our great ideas for hosting memorable get-togethers in *Host a Fondue Party* (page 100) and *Start a New Tradition* (page 244).

Let's make great Christmas memories together!

*Betty Crocker*

# CONTENTS

## FEATURES

# More Jolly, Less Humbug Tips

**Try these tips to help with the craziness of the holiday season.**

**Entertain with Dust Bunnies:** Give yourself permission to not be perfect. People will remember good food and conversation—not the dust. If you're not ready to completely embrace this idea, dim the lights and add some candles—no one will see the imperfections.

**Savor the Moment:** Allow yourself to be in the moment—not thinking about the next thing you can cross off your list. Make it easy on yourself by serving foods you've made ahead, a combination of premade and store-bought foods and recipes that are simple yet "wow."

**Do Something That Brings You Joy:** It might seem counterintuitive, but adding an event that brings you joy might just be the thing that makes your to-do list seem doable. Go caroling, enjoy a nighttime walk around your neighborhood to see the holiday light displays or give back to the community.

**Ask for Help:** Even Santa doesn't do it all by himself—he has elves. Assign tasks to everyone in the house—whether they're family members or guests, everyone (except for the occasional scrooge) will love the team spirit of working together.

**Focus on Events from a Wide Angle:** Plan the events you want to host in December, and then "zoom out"—what things can you do now to prepare so that there isn't that last-minute rush? Shop ahead for nonperishables (and when stores aren't busy), pull out serving dishes and buy the wine or chill the ingredients for your drinks.

**Have a Secret Stash:** Keep some presents ready for last-minute gifts or hostess gifts. Or keep the ingredients on hand for a gift from the kitchen (starting on page 262) to make up a fresh gift in a jiffy.

**Prep Your Pantry:** Stock up on baking supplies early (and when on sale) to avoid having to make emergency runs during the month. Have flour, both granulated sugar and brown sugar, butter, vanilla, baking soda and baking powder on hand.

**Take a Breather:** Schedule in some much-needed breaks throughout the month. Whether it's coffee with a friend, a bubble bath or a holiday show, the breaks will help sustain your energy for all of the month's festivities.

**Bake Smart:** Homemade cookies and bread most times can be made in advance and frozen until needed, taking a lot of last-minute stress off your plate. See Storing and Gifting Cookies (page 196) or individual recipes with the **MAKE AHEAD** symbol for how they can be made ahead.

**Share the Fun:** With so many events to host and so little time, why not cohost an event with another couple or family? Whether it's family or friends, you can share the work and the cost, making the event more enjoyable for everyone.

**Dance Your Way Through Chores:** Turn on your favorite Christmas music while you clean and prepare. Upbeat melodies will help the tasks seem more enjoyable and will go more quickly when you have a soundtrack.

**Express Gratitude:** Take the time to look out the window at nature, and try to count as many things, big and small, that you're grateful for. The act of expressing gratitude will calm the craziness of the season.

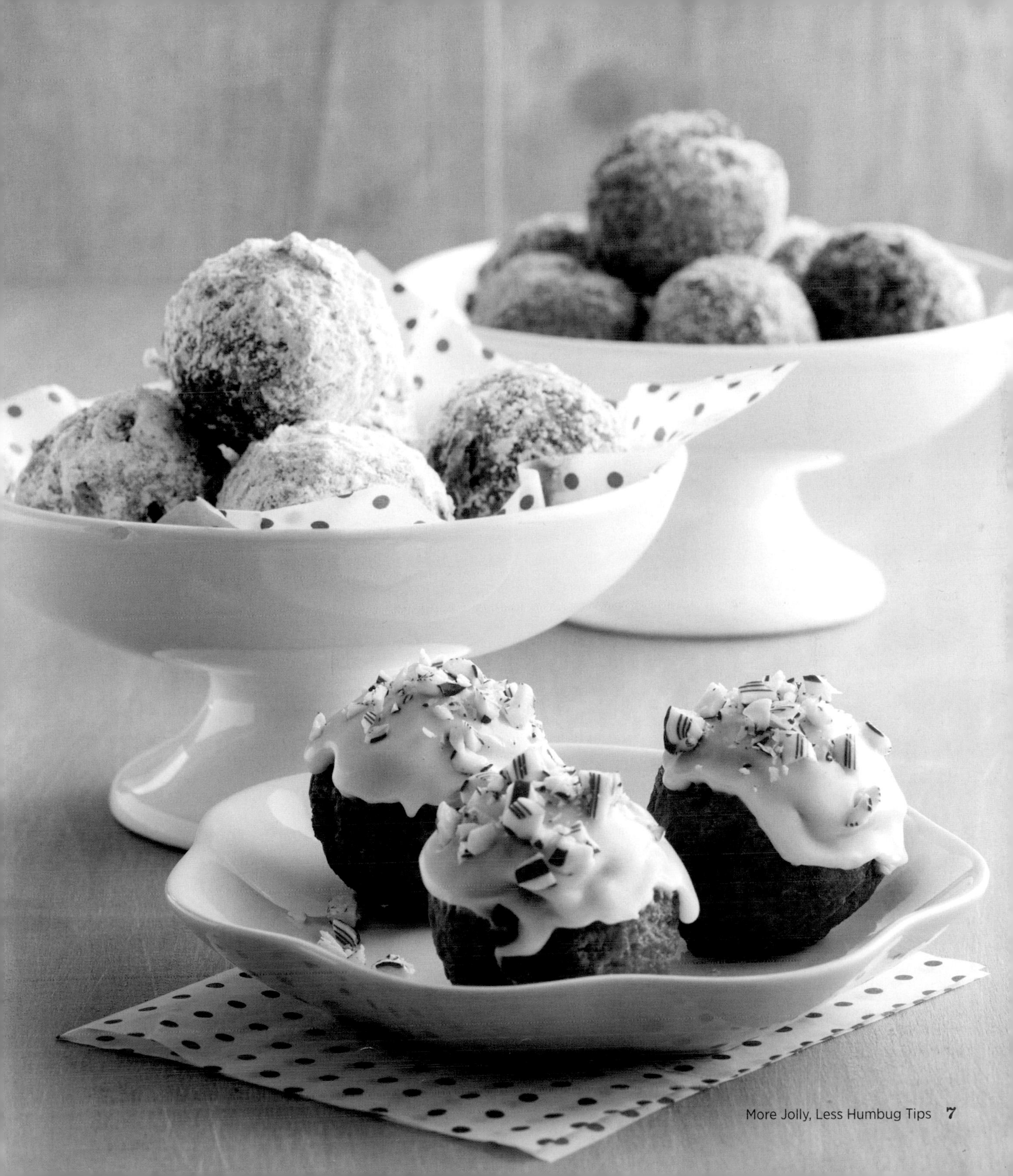

# Appetizers & Beverages

# Holiday Tree–Shaped Cheese Balls

**PREP TIME:** 20 Minutes  **START TO FINISH:** 4 Hours 20 Minutes  *56 servings*

- 3 packages (8 oz each) cream cheese, softened
- 4 cups shredded Cheddar cheese (16 oz)
- 2 tablespoons basil pesto
- 1 tablespoon grated onion
- ¼ teaspoon yellow mustard
  Red pepper sauce
- ¼ cup finely chopped fresh parsley or cilantro
- ¼ cup sliced almonds or pine nuts
- 2 tablespoons chopped red bell pepper
  Assorted crackers and raw vegetables, if desired

1 In large bowl, stir together cream cheese and Cheddar cheese; divide in half. Stir pesto into one portion; stir onion, mustard and 2 or 3 drops pepper sauce into other portion. Cover; refrigerate about 4 hours or until firm enough to shape.

2 Place cheese mixtures on large plate. Shape each into cone shape to look like a pine tree.

3 Just before serving, roll trees in parsley, pressing it evenly onto trees. Press almonds onto trees in string form for garland. Press bell pepper pieces onto trees for ornaments. Serve with crackers and vegetables.

**1 Serving (2 Tablespoons):** Calories 80; Total Fat 8g (Saturated Fat 4g, Trans Fat 0g); Cholesterol 20mg; Sodium 100mg; Total Carbohydrate 0g (Dietary Fiber 0g); Protein 2g **Exchanges:** ½ High-Fat Meat, 1 Fat **Carbohydrate Choices:** 0

## Make-Ahead Magic After shaping the trees, wrap tightly and freeze up to 1 month. Thaw in wrapper in refrigerator 12 hours before serving. Continue as directed in Step 3.

## Festive Touch Cut a star shape from a piece of lemon peel to place atop the tree. Place the tree in the middle of a platter covered with a cloth napkin "tree skirt," and surround it with crackers of all shapes and sizes for the "gifts."

# Creamy Brussels Sprout Party Dip

**PREP TIME:** 15 Minutes  **START TO FINISH:** 40 Minutes  *16 servings*

- 2 boxes (10 oz each) frozen baby Brussels sprouts and butter sauce
- 1 package (8 oz) ⅓-less-fat cream cheese (Neufchâtel), softened
- ½ cup reduced-fat sour cream
- ¼ cup plus 2 tablespoons shredded Parmesan cheese
- ¼ cup fat-free (skim) milk
- 1 tablespoon spicy brown or stone-ground mustard
- 2 teaspoons fresh lemon juice
- ¼ cup finely chopped bell pepper (any color)
  Multigrain sea salt–sweet potato chips, if desired
  Assorted raw vegetables, if desired

1 Heat oven to 350°F. Spray 1½-quart shallow glass baking dish or 9½ inch deep-dish glass pie plate with cooking spray.

2 Cook Brussels sprouts as directed on box. Meanwhile, in large bowl, with an electric mixer, beat cream cheese on medium speed until smooth. Beat in sour cream, ¼ cup of the Parmesan cheese, the milk, mustard and lemon juice on low speed until well blended. Stir in bell pepper.

3 Chop Brussels sprouts; stir Brussels sprouts with butter sauce into cream cheese mixture until well blended. Spread evenly in baking dish. Sprinkle with remaining 2 tablespoons Parmesan cheese.

4 Bake uncovered 20 to 25 minutes or until thoroughly heated. Serve with chips and raw vegetables.

**1 Serving (¼ Cup):** Calories 80; Total Fat 5g (Saturated Fat 3g, Trans Fat 0g); Cholesterol 15mg; Sodium 230mg; Total Carbohydrate 4g (Dietary Fiber 1g); Protein 3g **Exchanges:** 1 Vegetable, 1 Fat **Carbohydrate Choices:** 0

## Make-Ahead Magic Cover and refrigerate the unbaked dip up to 24 hours. Uncover and bake as directed.

## Festive Touch Use both red and green bell peppers in the dip for a holiday look. Garnish with additional red and green peppers after baking.

# Hot Artichoke and Spinach Dip

**PREP TIME:** 15 Minutes   **START TO FINISH:** 2 Hours 15 Minutes   *20 servings*

- 1 can (14 oz) artichoke hearts, drained, chopped
- 1 box (9 oz) frozen chopped spinach, thawed, squeezed to drain
- ½ cup Alfredo pasta sauce
- ½ cup mayonnaise
- ¾ teaspoon garlic salt
- ¼ teaspoon pepper
- 1 cup shredded Swiss cheese (4 oz)
- 1 loaf (20 inch) baguette, cut into 40 slices

**1** Spray 1- to 1½-quart slow cooker with cooking spray. In slow cooker, mix all ingredients except bread.

**2** Cover; cook on Low heat setting 2 to 4 hours. Serve dip with bread.

**1 Serving (2 Tablespoons Dip and 2 Slices Bread):** Calories 130; Total Fat 8g (Saturated Fat 3g, Trans Fat 0g); Cholesterol 15mg; Sodium 230mg; Total Carbohydrate 11g (Dietary Fiber 2g); Protein 4g **Exchanges:** ½ Starch, ½ Medium-Fat Meat, 1 Fat **Carbohydrate Choices:** 1

## Make-Ahead Magic
You can make the dip ahead of time in a bowl; cover and refrigerate up to 2 days before serving. When ready to heat, transfer the dip to the slow cooker and heat as directed.

## Festive Touch
For an extra holiday "pop," serve this dip with red and green tortilla chips instead of bread. Look for them near the deli at your grocery store during the holiday season.

# Layered Greek Dip

**PREP TIME:** 25 Minutes   **START TO FINISH:** 25 Minutes
*8 servings*

- 1 container (6 oz) Greek lemon or plain yogurt
- ¼ cup crumbled feta cheese (1 oz)
- 1 tablespoon chopped fresh parsley
- 1 teaspoon fresh lemon juice
- ⅛ teaspoon salt
- 1 cup plain hummus (from 7-oz container)
- 3 medium plum (Roma) tomatoes, seeded, chopped (½ cup)
- ½ cup finely chopped seeded cucumber
- ½ cup pitted kalamata olives, coarsely chopped
- 2 tablespoons chopped green onions (2 medium)
  Pita chips, if desired
  Sliced cucumbers and bell pepper strips, if desired

**1** In small bowl, mix yogurt, cheese, parsley, lemon juice and salt.

**2** Into each of 8 (2- to 3-oz) glasses or jars, layer 2 tablespoons hummus, 1 heaping tablespoon yogurt mixture, 1 tablespoon tomato, 1 tablespoon chopped cucumber, 1 tablespoon olives and slightly less than 1 teaspoon green onions.

**3** Serve with pita chips, sliced cucumbers and bell peppers.

**1 Serving:** Calories 130; Total Fat 7g (Saturated Fat 2.5g, Trans Fat 0g); Cholesterol 15mg; Sodium 310mg; Total Carbohydrate 13g (Dietary Fiber 2g); Protein 5g **Exchanges:** 1 Starch, 1½ Fat **Carbohydrate Choices:** 1

## Make-Ahead Magic
You can prep this recipe ahead to make it a breeze to put together. Mix the ingredients in Step 1; cover and refrigerate up to 24 hours in advance of serving. Everything but the tomatoes can be chopped and refrigerated in small bags or containers up to 24 hours ahead as well. When ready to serve, chop the tomatoes and layer the dip as directed.

## Festive Touch
These individual dips are perfect for a buffet—no worries about double dipping! But you can also do a platter presentation if you like: Spread the hummus on a serving platter, and spoon the yogurt mixture over the hummus. Arrange the toppings in rows over the yogurt mixture.

# Easy Spinach Dip Wreath

**PREP TIME:** 25 Minutes    **START TO FINISH:** 4 Hours 25 Minutes    *12 servings*

1 round uncut loaf (16 oz)
Hawaiian or sourdough bread

### SPINACH DIP

1 box (9 oz) frozen chopped
spinach, thawed

1 cup mayonnaise or salad
dressing

1 cup sour cream

1 package (1.8 oz) vegetable soup
and dip mix

1 can (8 oz) water chestnuts,
drained, chopped

1 medium green onion, chopped
(1 tablespoon)

### GARNISHES

Rosemary sprigs, if desired

Red bell pepper pieces,
if desired

**1** Cut and hollow out 3-inch-wide ring on top of bread loaf to within ½ inch of bottom, leaving center of loaf intact. Reserve scooped-out bread.

**2** Squeeze thawed spinach to drain; spread on paper towels and pat dry. In large bowl, stir spinach, mayonnaise, sour cream, soup mix (dry), water chestnuts and onion until well mixed. Cover and refrigerate at least 4 hours to blend flavors and soften soup mix.

**3** Spoon about 1½ cups of the spinach dip into hollowed-out ring. (Cover and refrigerate remaining spinach dip for another use.) Arrange rosemary and bell pepper pieces on dip to look like sprigs of holly.

**4** Tear remaining bread into bite-size pieces. Use torn bread and reserved scooped-out bread for dipping.

**1 Serving:** Calories 180; Total Fat 8g (Saturated Fat 2g, Trans Fat 0g); Cholesterol 20mg; Sodium 240mg; Total Carbohydrate 21g (Dietary Fiber 1g); Protein 4g **Exchanges:** 1½ Starch, 1½ Fat **Carbohydrate Choices:** 1½

## Make-Ahead Magic
Make it easy by prepping this festive appetizer the night before. Make the spinach dip (or purchase already made dip from the refrigerated section of the produce department) and cut the bread. When ready to serve, simply spoon the dip into the bread ring and arrange the garnishes and dippers.

## Festive Touch
Stir about 1 cup dried cranberries into the spinach dip for a jolly touch of sweetness and color. You can also decorate the "wreath" or serving platter with yellow or red cherry or grape tomatoes.

## Kitchen Secrets
You can easily adapt this recipe to suit your taste! Just substitute another flavor of dip for the spinach dip, and serve with cut-up veggies along with the bread pieces.

# Cheese Fondue

**PREP TIME:** 15 Minutes   **START TO FINISH:** 45 Minutes
*5 servings*

- 2  cups shredded Swiss cheese (8 oz)
- 2  cups shredded Gruyère or Swiss cheese (8 oz)
- 2  tablespoons all-purpose flour
- 1  clove garlic, cut in half
- 1  cup dry white wine or nonalcoholic white wine
- 1  tablespoon lemon juice
- 3  tablespoons kirsch, dry sherry, brandy or nonalcoholic white wine
- 1  loaf (1 lb) French bread, cut into 1-inch pieces

1  In resealable food-storage plastic bag, place cheeses and flour. Shake until cheese is coated with flour; let stand 30 minutes at room temperature.

2  Rub garlic on bottom and side of fondue pot, saucepan or skillet; discard garlic. Add wine. Heat over low temperature setting in fondue pot or over low heat in saucepan or skillet just until bubbles rise to surface (do not boil). Stir in lemon juice.

3  Gradually add cheese mixture, about ½ cup at a time, gently stirring constantly with whisk over low heat until melted. If the mixture is stirred too vigorously, the cheese could become stringy. (To keep fondue creamy and smooth, it's important to make sure all cheese is melted before each new addition of cheese.)

4  Stir in kirsch. Keep warm over simmer setting. If made in saucepan or skillet, pour into a fondue pot or heatproof serving bowl and keep warm over low heat. Fondue must be served over heat to maintain its smooth, creamy texture. Spear bread pieces with fondue forks; dip and swirl in fondue with stirring motion. If fondue becomes too thick, stir in ¼ to ½ cup heated dry white wine or nonalcoholic white wine.

**1 Serving (2 Tablespoons Fondue and 4 Bread Pieces):** Calories 630; Total Fat 28g (Saturated Fat 16g, Trans Fat 1g); Cholesterol 85mg; Sodium 860mg; Total Carbohydrate 58g (Dietary Fiber 2g); Protein 35g **Carbohydrate Choices: 4**

## Festive Touch
This recipe makes a great partner to Herbed IPA Fondue (page 102). After you cook the meat and veggies as directed in that fondue, dunk them in the cheese of this one. Delicious!

# Crostini with Caramelized Onion Jam

**PREP TIME:** 25 Minutes   **START TO FINISH:** 1 Hour 5 Minutes
*24 appetizers*

- 2  tablespoons olive or vegetable oil
- 2  medium sweet onions, thinly sliced (about 2 cups)
- 2  teaspoons finely chopped garlic
- 1  teaspoon coarse (kosher or sea) salt
- 2  tablespoons packed brown sugar
- ¼  cup red wine vinegar
- ½  cup chicken or vegetable broth
- 24  slices (¼ inch thick) baguette
   Cooking spray
- 2  oz cream cheese or chèvre (goat) cheese, softened (½ cup)
- 1  tablespoon chopped fresh thyme or oregano leaves

1  In 2-quart saucepan, heat oil over medium-high heat. Cook onions and garlic in oil 10 minutes, stirring every 3 to 4 minutes. Add salt, brown sugar, vinegar and broth. Heat to boiling; reduce heat. Cover; simmer 30 minutes.

2  Uncover; increase heat to medium-high. Cook 2 to 5 minutes, stirring frequently, until most of the liquid is reduced and the mixture is the consistency of jam. Remove from heat; set aside.

3  Heat oven to 325°F. Place baguette slices on ungreased cookie sheet; spray lightly with cooking spray. Bake 6 to 9 minutes or until crispy.

4  Spoon 1 teaspoon caramelized onion jam on each toasted baguette slice; top with 1 teaspoon cream cheese. Sprinkle with thyme.

**1 Appetizer:** Calories 40; Total Fat 2g (Saturated Fat 0.5g, Trans Fat 0g); Cholesterol 0mg; Sodium 95mg; Total Carbohydrate 5g (Dietary Fiber 0g); Protein 0g **Exchanges:** ½ Other Carbohydrate, ½ Fat **Carbohydrate Choices:** ½

## Make-Ahead Magic
You can cook the caramelized onion jam and toast the bread up to a day in advance. Cover and refrigerate the jam (allow it to come to room temperature before using, 1 to 2 hours). Store the cooled toasts in a resealable food-storage plastic bag.

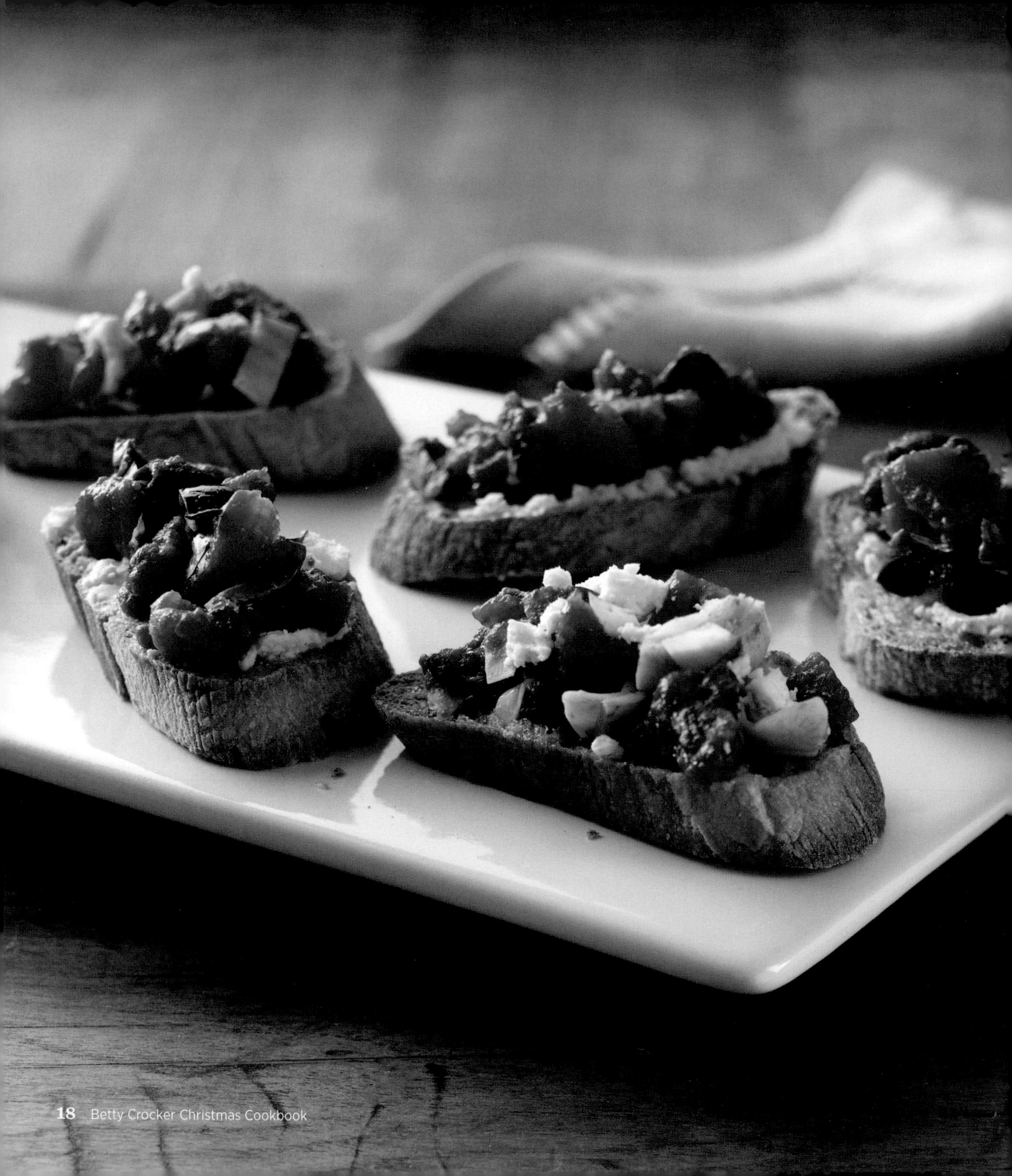

# Fire-Roasted Tomato and Olive Bruschetta

**PREP TIME:** 20 Minutes  **START TO FINISH:** 20 Minutes  *24 appetizers*

24 slices (½ inch thick) baguette

1 can (14.5 oz) fire-roasted diced tomatoes, drained

¼ cup pitted kalamata olives, quartered

¼ cup coarsely chopped drained roasted red bell peppers (from a jar)

2 tablespoons chopped fresh basil leaves

1 tablespoon olive oil

2 oz chèvre (goat) cheese, softened (½ cup)

**1** Heat oven to 425°F. On ungreased cookie sheet, place baguette slices. Bake 4 to 5 minutes or until light golden brown.

**2** Meanwhile, in medium bowl, mix tomatoes, olives, roasted peppers, basil and oil.

**3** Spread 1 teaspoon cheese onto each toasted baguette slice; top evenly with tomato mixture. Serve immediately.

**1 Appetizer:** Calories 40; Total Fat 1.5g (Saturated Fat 0.5g, Trans Fat 0g); Cholesterol 0mg; Sodium 90mg; Total Carbohydrate 5g (Dietary Fiber 0g); Protein 1g **Exchanges:** ½ Other Carbohydrate, ½ Fat **Carbohydrate Choices:** ½

**Festive Touch** You can replace the kalamata olives with sliced pimiento-stuffed olives for a touch of red and green.

# How to Host an Appetizer Party

Throwing a festive appetizer party during the holidays is a great way to get friends or relatives together, enjoy each other's company and celebrate the season! Here are our favorite tips and tricks to pull it off with ease:

**Invite Guests Early** It's a busy time of year—get on people's calendars before they make other plans.

**Make It or Make It Easy** Decide what you will provide: do you want to provide everything or provide the beverages and ask guests to bring an appetizer? To ensure you get a variety (and to make it more fun), designate the type of appetizer guests bring with the invitation.

You can designate the type of appetizer (see types below) guests bring by the first letter of their last name such as A–E bring a dip, F–H bring chips, I–L bring meat apps such as chicken wings or meatballs, etc. Or think of something more creative, such as the number of years they've known you.

**Choose Variety** The bigger the crowd, the more types of appetizers you'll want to offer your guests:

*10 to 12 guests:* 4 to 5 appetizer choices

*13 to 25 guests:* 5 to 9 appetizer choices

*26 to 50 guests:* 10 to 13 appetizer choices

**Select Appetizer Types** Pick a variety of appetizers for your get-together:

*Dips and Spreads:* Chip and vegetable dips, salsa, spreadable cheeses, tapenades, relishes

*Dippers:* Veggies, breadsticks, crackers, pretzels

*Protein-Based:* Meatballs, chicken wings, sushi, eggs or egg dishes, cheese or tofu

*Hearty:* Mini sandwiches, sliders, pizza, bruschetta

*Garden:* Veggies or fruit that are served raw, cooked or stuffed

**Decorate Elfishly** No need to buy special decorations for your party. Gather a few of your holiday decorations as a centerpiece between the platters of appetizers.

**Plan to Be a Guest** Create a to-do list, knocking things off your list as early as possible. So when the day arrives, you're organized, rested and ready to party!

**Enlist Your Phone** Keep track of when appetizers need to go into the oven or come out by using your phone to set a timer. Keep the phone volume on low or vibrate and in your pocket so it won't be distracting to guests.

# Christmas Tree Roll-Ups

**PREP TIME:** 20 Minutes    **START TO FINISH:** 2 Hours 20 Minutes    *64 appetizers*

- 1 package (8 oz) cream cheese, softened
- ½ cup chopped drained roasted red bell peppers (from a jar)
- ¼ cup chopped ripe olives
- ¼ cup chopped fresh basil leaves
- ¼ cup shredded Parmesan cheese (1 oz)
- 4 spinach-flavor flour tortillas (8 to 10 inch)
  Additional ripe olive pieces

1 In medium bowl, mix cream cheese, roasted peppers, chopped olives, basil and Parmesan cheese. Spread mixture evenly over tortillas, spreading to edges; roll up tightly.

2 Press each tortilla roll into triangle shape, using fingers. Wrap in plastic wrap. Refrigerate at least 2 hours but no longer than 24 hours.

3 To serve, cut rolls into ½-inch slices. Place olive piece at bottom of each triangle to look like tree trunk; secure with toothpick.

**1 Appetizer:** Calories 25; Total Fat 1.5g (Saturated Fat 1g, Trans Fat 0g); Cholesterol 0mg; Sodium 50mg; Total Carbohydrate 2g (Dietary Fiber 0g); Protein 0g **Exchanges:** ½ Fat **Carbohydrate Choices:** 0

## Kitchen Secrets
**Short on time? Or making this appetizer for an occasion other than Christmas? Don't shape the rolls into triangles. Simply cut into round slices and serve, skipping the olive pieces and toothpicks. This recipe can also easily be cut in half for a smaller group.**

# Stuffed Mini Sweet Peppers

**PREP TIME:** 20 Minutes    **START TO FINISH:** 50 Minutes    *32 appetizers*

- 16 mini sweet peppers (red, yellow and orange)
- ¾ cup refried beans (from 16-oz can)
- ¾ cup shredded Monterey Jack cheese (3 oz)
- ¼ cup sour cream
- 2 teaspoons taco seasoning mix (from 1-oz package)
- ¾ cup corn chips, crushed
  Chopped fresh cilantro, if desired

1 Heat oven to 375°F. Line large cookie sheet with cooking parchment paper; set aside.

2 Cut each sweet pepper in half lengthwise, leaving stem intact. Remove seeds and membranes. Place halved sweet peppers on cookie sheet, cut side up.

3 In medium bowl, mix refried beans, cheese, sour cream and taco seasoning until well blended. Place mixture in resealable food-storage plastic bag. Cut ½ inch off one corner of bag. Pipe mixture into pepper halves.

4 Top each pepper half with crushed corn chips. Bake 15 to 20 minutes or until peppers are crisp-tender. Cool on cookie sheet 10 minutes. Top with cilantro.

**1 Appetizer:** Calories 40; Total Fat 2g (Saturated Fat 1g, Trans Fat 0g); Cholesterol 0mg; Sodium 60mg; Total Carbohydrate 4g (Dietary Fiber 1g); Protein 1g **Exchanges:** ½ Other Carbohydrate, ½ Fat **Carbohydrate Choices:** 0

## Make-Ahead Magic
**To speed up the final prep, make as directed through Step 3. Cover with plastic wrap, and refrigerate up to 6 hours until ready to bake. Top with corn chips, and bake as directed.**

## Festive Touch
**Take these over the top by sprinkling a couple pieces of crisply cooked, crumbled bacon on top of the peppers along with the corn chips.**

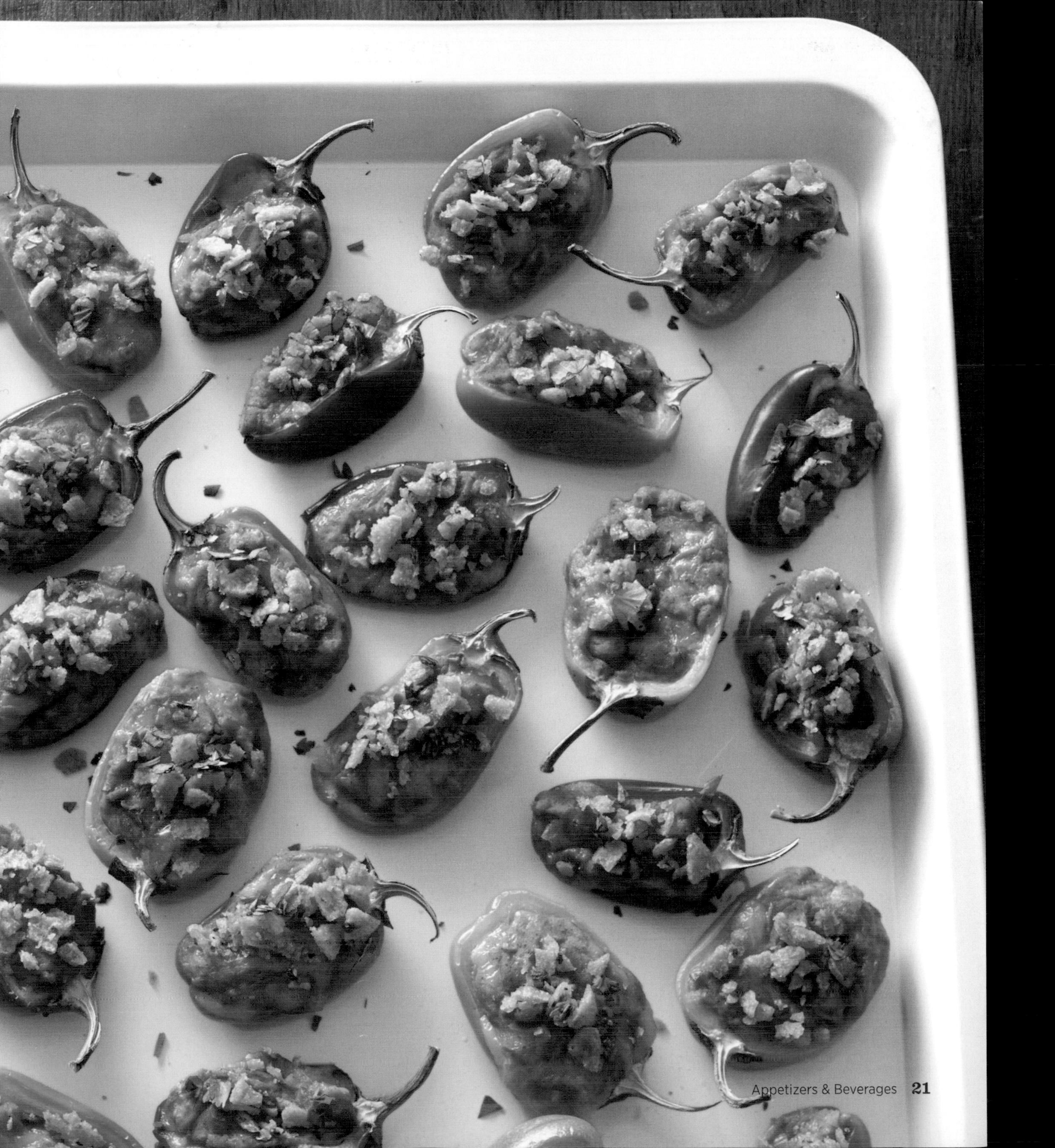

# Cranberry, Pomegranate and Caramelized Onion Flatbread

**PREP TIME:** 30 Minutes    **START TO FINISH:** 45 Minutes    *12 servings*

3 tablespoons butter

1 large onion, cut in half, thinly sliced

½ teaspoon salt

¼ teaspoon crushed red pepper flakes

1 package (10 oz) prebaked thin Italian pizza crust (12 inch)

1 cup whole-berry cranberry sauce

⅓ cup pomegranate seeds

¾ teaspoon grated orange peel

½ cup crumbled chèvre (goat) cheese (2 oz)

1 tablespoon chopped fresh chives

**1** In 10-inch skillet, melt butter over medium heat. Add onion, salt and pepper flakes; cook about 20 minutes, stirring occasionally, until onion is browned and caramelized. Remove from heat.

**2** Heat oven to 400°F. Place pizza crust on ungreased cookie sheet. In small bowl, mix cranberry sauce, pomegranate seeds and orange peel. Spread over crust. Sprinkle cheese over cranberry mixture; spread onions over top.

**3** Bake about 12 minutes or until cheese is melted. Sprinkle with chives.

**1 Serving:** Calories 150; Total Fat 6g (Saturated Fat 3g, Trans Fat 0g); Cholesterol 10mg; Sodium 270mg; Total Carbohydrate 23g (Dietary Fiber 1g); Protein 3g **Exchanges:** 1 Starch, ½ Other Carbohydrate, 1 Fat **Carbohydrate Choices:** 1½

## Make-Ahead Magic

**To get a jump-start on this appetizer pizza, cook the onions, then transfer to a microwavable bowl. Cover and refrigerate up to three days in advance. When you're ready to make the pizza, microwave the onions on High about 30 seconds or until warm. Assemble the pizza and bake as directed.**

## Kitchen Secrets

**Use your favorite thin pizza crust in this recipe. Or if you have time, make your own flatbread dough from scratch.**

# Cheesy Broccoli Puffs with Sriracha Mayonnaise

**PREP TIME:** 20 Minutes    **START TO FINISH:** 45 Minutes    *12 servings*

1 bag (12 oz) frozen broccoli and cheese sauce

¾ cup Original Bisquick™ mix

½ teaspoon crushed red pepper flakes

⅛ teaspoon salt

½ cup milk

2 eggs

¼ cup grated Parmesan cheese

6 slices packaged precooked bacon (from 2.1-oz package), chopped

½ cup mayonnaise

2 teaspoons Sriracha sauce

Sliced green onions, if desired

1 Heat oven to 375°F. Generously grease 24 mini muffin cups with shortening or cooking spray. Cook broccoli & cheese sauce as directed on bag for minimum time. Chop broccoli.

2 In medium bowl, stir Bisquick mix, pepper flakes, salt, milk and eggs with whisk or fork until blended. Stir in broccoli & cheese sauce, Parmesan cheese and bacon. Divide mixture evenly among muffin cups (cups will be full).

3 Bake 16 to 18 minutes or until toothpick inserted in center comes out clean and tops are light brown. Cool 5 minutes. With thin knife, loosen sides of puffs from pan; remove to cooling rack.

4 In small bowl, mix mayonnaise and Sriracha sauce until smooth. Top each warm puff with 1 teaspoon mayonnaise mixture; garnish with onion.

**1 Serving (2 Appetizers):** Calories 120; Total Fat 7g (Saturated Fat 2g, Trans Fat 0g); Cholesterol 40mg; Sodium 460mg; Total Carbohydrate 9g (Dietary Fiber 0g); Protein 5g **Exchanges:** ½ Starch, ½ Medium-Fat Meat, 1 Fat **Carbohydrate Choices:** ½

## Kitchen Secrets

**Satisfy your vegetarian guests by substituting either ¼ cup finely chopped red or green bell pepper or 2 tablespoons sliced green onions for the bacon.**

# Gluten-Free Bacon-Wrapped Figs

**PREP TIME:** 15 Minutes    **START TO FINISH:** 25 Minutes    *30 appetizers*

1 package (12 oz) fully cooked gluten-free cottage or Canadian bacon

2 packages (8 oz each) dried whole Calimyrna figs, stems removed

30 pistachio nuts

30 small fresh basil leaves

**1** Heat oven to 425°F. Spray 15x10x1-inch pan with cooking spray (without flour).

**2** Cut each bacon slice in half. Cut slit in each fig; stuff with nut. Place basil leaf on bacon strip; wrap around fig. Place seam side down in pan.

**3** Bake 8 to 10 minutes or until bacon is browned. Serve warm with toothpicks.

**1 Appetizer:** Calories 70; Total Fat 1.5g (Saturated Fat 0g, Trans Fat 0g); Cholesterol 5mg; Sodium 180mg; Total Carbohydrate 10g (Dietary Fiber 1g); Protein 3g **Exchanges:** ½ Starch, ½ Fat **Carbohydrate Choices:** ½

## Make-Ahead Magic

Assemble appetizers 3 to 4 hours ahead of your party and refrigerate. You may need to add 1 to 2 minutes to the bake time.

## Kitchen Secrets

Calimyrna figs are large, squat, green-skinned, white-fleshed figs grown in California. Instead of the figs, you can use dried apricot or peach halves, folding them in half around the nut.

## Cooking Gluten Free?

Always read labels to make sure each recipe ingredient is gluten free. Products and ingredient sources can change.

# Crab Bites

**PREP TIME:** 15 Minutes   **START TO FINISH:** 40 Minutes   *45 appetizers*

3 packages (2.1 oz each) frozen mini fillo shells (15 shells each)

¾ cup mayonnaise or salad dressing

¾ cup grated Parmesan cheese

½ teaspoon finely chopped garlic

8 medium green onions, finely chopped (½ cup)

1 can (14 oz) artichoke hearts, drained, finely chopped

1 can (6.5 oz) special white crabmeat, drained*

**1** Heat oven to 375°F. Line cookie sheet with foil or cooking parchment paper. Place fillo shells on cookie sheet.

**2** In large bowl, mix remaining ingredients until well blended. Spoon about 1 tablespoon crab mixture into each fillo shell.

**3** Bake 20 to 25 minutes or until puffed and golden brown. Serve warm.

*Refrigerated pasteurized or imitation crabmeat can be substituted for the canned crabmeat.

**1 Appetizer:** Calories 60; Total Fat 4.5g (Saturated Fat 1g, Trans Fat 0g); Cholesterol 5mg; Sodium 95mg; Total Carbohydrate 3g (Dietary Fiber 0g); Protein 1g **Exchanges:** 1 Fat **Carbohydrate Choices:** 0

## Make-Ahead Magic

**Save yourself some time on hectic days by making the crab filling up to 24 hours in advance. Then just fill the shells and bake right before serving. You may need to bake them a minute or two longer.**

## Festive Touch
Garnish each crab bite with a cherry tomato half to add color.

# Bacon-Wrapped Chicken Wings with Bourbon Barbecue Sauce

**PREP TIME:** 25 Minutes **START TO FINISH:** 1 Hour 25 Minutes *35 to 40 appetizers*

### CHICKEN

- 3 lb chicken wings and drummettes*
- ¼ teaspoon freshly ground pepper
- 16 to 20 slices bacon, cut crosswise in half

### BARBECUE SAUCE

- ½ cup ketchup
- ½ cup bourbon
- ¼ cup packed brown sugar
- 2 tablespoons soy sauce
- 3 cloves garlic, finely chopped
- 1 teaspoon Dijon mustard
- ½ teaspoon crushed red pepper flakes

**1** Heat oven to 425°F. Line 2 cookie sheets with sides with heavy-duty foil; spray with cooking spray.

**2** Sprinkle chicken with pepper. Wrap each chicken piece with a half slice of bacon. Place on cookie sheets.

**3** Bake 30 minutes. Turn chicken pieces over; rotate placement of cookie sheets in the oven. Bake 20 to 30 minutes longer or until golden brown and juice of chicken is clear when thickest part is cut to bone (at least 165°F).

**4** Meanwhile, in 1-quart saucepan, mix sauce ingredients. Heat to boiling over medium heat, stirring frequently. Reduce heat; simmer uncovered, stirring frequently, until sugar is dissolved, about 5 minutes. Remove from heat; set aside.

**5** In large bowl, toss chicken with half of the sauce. Serve warm with remaining sauce on the side for dipping.

*Purchase already cut chicken wings in the meat or frozen foods section of your grocery store. They're sometimes called chicken drummies or wingettes and drummettes. You can use just wings or just drummettes if you prefer.

**1 Appetizer:** Calories 50; Total Fat 2g (Saturated Fat 0.5g, Trans Fat 0g); Cholesterol 20mg; Sodium 210mg; Total Carbohydrate 3g (Dietary Fiber 0g); Protein 5g **Exchanges:** 1 Lean Meat **Carbohydrate Choices:** 0

 **Festive Touch** Stick a holiday pick into each chicken wing after baking to make it easy on your guests to grab these irresistible appetizers.

# Meatballs in Tomato Chutney

**PREP TIME:** 30 Minutes   **START TO FINISH:** 4 Hours 30 Minutes   *36 appetizers*

3 cans (14.5 oz each) fire-roasted diced tomatoes with garlic, drained

2 cups chopped onions (2 large)

1 jalapeño chile, seeded, chopped

½ cup golden raisins

1 can (6 oz) tomato sauce

3 tablespoons tomato paste

½ cup cider vinegar

½ cup packed brown sugar

1 teaspoon curry powder

1½ teaspoons salt

1 lb bulk Italian pork sausage

1 lb ground beef round

¼ cup finely chopped fresh parsley

1 egg

Additional chopped fresh parsley, if desired

1 Spray 6-quart slow cooker with cooking spray. In slow cooker, stir together tomatoes, 1½ cups of the onions, the chile, raisins, tomato sauce, tomato paste, vinegar, brown sugar, curry powder and ½ teaspoon of the salt. Cook uncovered on High heat setting 3 hours or until thickened.

2 Meanwhile, heat oven to 400°F. Spray 15x10x1-inch pan with cooking spray. In large bowl, mix sausage, beef, ¼ cup parsley, the egg, remaining ½ cup onion and remaining 1 teaspoon salt. Shape mixture into 36 (1-inch) balls. Arrange in single layer in pan. Bake 15 minutes or until thoroughly cooked and no longer pink in center.

3 Add meatballs to slow cooker. Reduce heat setting to Low. Cover; cook 1 hour. Sprinkle with additional parsley.

**1 Appetizer:** Calories 200; Total Fat 11g (Saturated Fat 4g, Trans Fat 0g); Cholesterol 0mg; Sodium 620mg; Total Carbohydrate 16g (Dietary Fiber 1g); Protein 10g **Exchanges:** ½ Fruit, ½ Other Carbohydrate, 1 Vegetable, 1 Lean Meat, ½ High-Fat Meat, 1 Fat **Carbohydrate Choices:** 1

## Make-Ahead Magic
**You can make the sauce and meatballs up to 2 days ahead of time. Spoon cooled sauce and meatballs into large microwavable bowls; stir to combine. Cover and refrigerate. The day of serving, microwave bowls on High 3 to 4 minutes, stirring occasionally, until hot. Transfer hot meatballs and sauce to slow cooker. Cover; cook on Low heat setting 1 hour.**

# Maple Bacon-Wrapped Asparagus

**PREP TIME:** 30 Minutes   **START TO FINISH:** 30 Minutes
*14 to 16 appetizers*

- 14 to 16 fresh asparagus spears*
- 1 cup packed brown sugar
- 1 tablespoon dried sage leaves, crushed
- ¼ teaspoon pepper
- 1 package (16 oz) bacon
- 2 tablespoons real maple syrup

1  Set oven control to broil. Line broiler pan and broiler pan rack with foil; cut slits in foil on rack.

2  Snap off tough bottom ends of asparagus. In pie plate, mix brown sugar, sage and pepper. Dip bacon strips into mixture, turning to coat both sides. Wrap bacon slice around each asparagus spear.

3  Place asparagus on broiler pan with tips toward center. Broil with tops 6 inches from heat 13 to 15 minutes or until bacon is crisp, turning and brushing with syrup halfway through baking.

*Use the same amount of spears as slices of bacon. Depending on which brand you purchase, you will have 14 to 16 slices per pound of bacon.

**1 Serving:** Calories 120; Total Fat 3g (Saturated Fat 1g, Trans Fat 0g); Cholesterol 10mg; Sodium 160mg; Total Carbohydrate 18g (Dietary Fiber 0g); Protein 3g **Exchanges:** 1 Other Carbohydrate, ½ High-Fat Meat **Carbohydrate Choices:** 1

**Kitchen Secrets** If you like, try smoked bacon (such as applewood or mesquite) or, for a little extra heat, peppered bacon.

# Gorgonzola- and Hazelnut-Stuffed Mushrooms

**PREP TIME:** 25 Minutes   **START TO FINISH:** 45 Minutes
*36 appetizers*

- 36 medium whole mushrooms
- ⅓ cup crumbled Gorgonzola cheese
- ¼ cup seasoned bread crumbs
- ¼ cup chopped hazelnuts (filberts)
- ¼ cup finely chopped red bell pepper
- 4 medium green onions, chopped (¼ cup)
- ½ teaspoon salt

1  Heat oven to 350°F. Twist mushroom stems to remove from mushroom caps; reserve caps. Finely chop enough stems to measure about ½ cup; discard remaining stems.

2  In medium bowl, mix chopped mushroom stems and remaining ingredients until well blended. Spoon into mushroom caps, mounding slightly. Place in ungreased 15x10x1-inch pan.

3  Bake 15 to 20 minutes or until hot. Serve warm.

**1 Appetizer:** Calories 20; Total Fat 1g (Saturated Fat 0g, Trans Fat 0g); Cholesterol 0mg; Sodium 55mg; Total Carbohydrate 1g (Dietary Fiber 0g); Protein 1g **Exchanges:** Free **Carbohydrate Choices:** 0

**Festive Touch** Add whole hazelnuts and oregano or parsley sprigs to the serving platter for a dramatic flair.

**Kitchen Secrets** Italian Gorgonzola is rich and creamy with a mild, yet slightly pungent flavor and aroma. If you can't find Gorgonzola, use blue cheese instead. And walnuts or pistachios can be used in place of the hazelnuts.

# Cheddar-Stuffed Pretzel Nuggets

**PREP TIME:** 45 Minutes   **START TO FINISH:** 1 Hour 25 Minutes   *48 servings*

## PRETZELS

- 3¾ to 4¼ cups all-purpose flour
- 1 tablespoon sugar
- ½ teaspoon table salt
- 1 package regular active or fast-acting dry yeast (2¼ teaspoons)
- 1½ cups very warm water (120°F to 130°F)
- 1 tablespoon butter, melted
- ½ cup shredded Cheddar cheese (2 oz)
- 4 strips bacon, crisply cooked, crumbled
- 2 tablespoons finely chopped seeded jalapeño chiles (about 2 medium)
- 2 cans (16 oz each) American-style lager beer
- 2 tablespoons baking soda
- 1 egg, beaten
- 1 tablespoon coarse (kosher or sea) salt

## BEER CHEESE DIP

- 1 package (8 oz) cream cheese, cut into cubes, softened
- ¾ cup American-style lager beer (reserved from 1 can above)
- 2 cups shredded Cheddar cheese (8 oz)

**1** Line large cookie sheets with cooking parchment paper. In large bowl, mix 3¾ cups of the flour, the sugar, table salt and yeast. Add warm water and butter; beat with electric mixer on medium speed 3 minutes, scraping bowl frequently and adding additional flour, ¼ cup at a time, until dough is soft and leaves side of bowl. Divide dough into 4 equal portions.

**2** On lightly floured surface, roll each portion into 12x4-inch rectangle. On one long side of each rectangle, sprinkle 2 tablespoons Cheddar cheese, 2 teaspoons crumbled bacon and 1½ teaspoons chiles. Starting at one long side, roll up dough; firmly pinch edges to seal. Cut each roll into 12 (1-inch) pieces; pinch cut edges to seal. Place on cookie sheets. Cover with plastic wrap; let stand 30 minutes.

**3** Heat oven to 425°F. Reserve ¾ cup of the beer for dip. In 3-quart saucepan, heat remaining beer and the baking soda to boiling; reduce heat to low. Gently place 4 to 5 dough pieces in beer; cook about 20 seconds, turning once. Remove with slotted spoon; return to cookie sheets. Repeat with remaining dough pieces. Brush with egg; sprinkle with coarse salt. Bake 8 to 10 minutes or until golden brown.

**4** Meanwhile, in 2-quart saucepan, cook cream cheese and reserved beer over medium heat 6 to 7 minutes, stirring frequently, until cheese is melted. Stir in Cheddar cheese, a little at a time; cook about 4 minutes, stirring frequently, until all cheese is melted and sauce is smooth. Serve warm pretzel nuggets with warm dip.

**1 Serving (1 Pretzel Nugget and 2 Teaspoons Dip):** Calories 90; Total Fat 4.5g (Saturated Fat 2.5g, Trans Fat 0g); Cholesterol 15mg; Sodium 320mg; Total Carbohydrate 8g (Dietary Fiber 0g); Protein 3g **Exchanges:** ½ Starch, 1 Fat **Carbohydrate Choices:** ½

## Make-Ahead Magic

You can make these delicious party snacks well in advance. Place baked cooled pretzel nuggets in a resealable freezer plastic bag; freeze up to 2 weeks. To reheat, place on cookie sheets and bake at 350°F for 12 to 14 minutes or until hot. Make the Beer Cheese Dip while they bake.

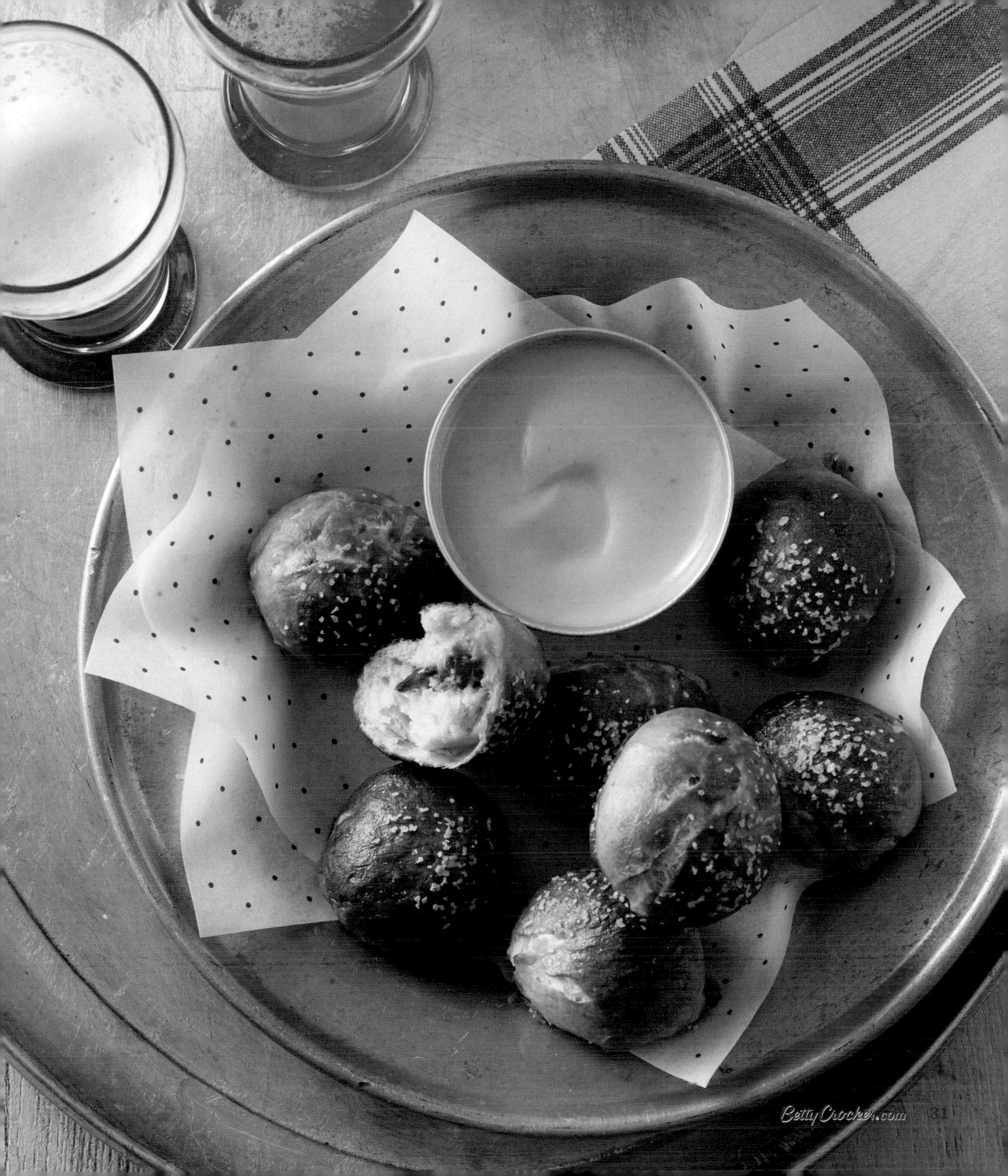

# Baked Sweet Potato–Zucchini Tots

**PREP TIME:** 25 Minutes   **START TO FINISH:** 55 Minutes   *6 servings*

## CITRUS-MUSTARD SAUCE

- ½ cup mayonnaise
- 2 tablespoons Dijon mustard
- ¼ teaspoon ground mustard
- 4 teaspoons honey
- 1 teaspoon grated orange or lemon peel
- 1 tablespoon orange or lemon juice

## SWEET POTATO–ZUCCHINI TOTS

- 1 cup packed grated zucchini (about 1 large)
- 1 teaspoon salt
- 1 cup cooked sweet potato (about 1 large)
- 2 eggs, slightly beaten
- ¼ cup panko crispy bread crumbs
- ⅓ cup shredded Gruyère or white Cheddar cheese
- 3 tablespoons grated Parmesan cheese
- ⅓ cup finely chopped onion
- ¼ teaspoon garlic powder
- 1½ teaspoons finely chopped fresh or ½ teaspoon dried thyme or oregano leaves
- 3 tablespoons finely chopped fresh Italian (flat-leaf) parsley
- ½ teaspoon pepper

1  Heat oven to 400°F. Line large cookie sheet with foil; spray foil with cooking spray.

2  In small bowl, mix sauce ingredients with whisk until smooth. Cover; refrigerate until serving time.

3  In colander, place zucchini and ½ teaspoon of the salt; gently toss. Place colander over bowl or sink; let drain 10 minutes. Place zucchini on cheesecloth or paper towel; wrap cheesecloth around zucchini and twist gently to remove as much remaining moisture as possible.

4  In large bowl, mix sweet potato and eggs with whisk until smooth. Add zucchini, bread crumbs, cheeses, onion, garlic powder, thyme, parsley, pepper and remaining ½ teaspoon salt; blend gently with fork.

5  For each tot, gently roll 1 tablespoon mixture in palm of hand into small oval or log shape. Place about 1 inch apart on cookie sheet.

6  Bake 15 to 18 minutes, turning once, until crisp and golden brown. Serve hot with sauce.

**1 Serving (About 5 Tots and 2 Tablespoons Sauce):** Calories 260; Total Fat 19g (Saturated Fat 4.5g, Trans Fat 0g); Cholesterol 80mg; Sodium 770mg; Total Carbohydrate 15g (Dietary Fiber 1g); Protein 7g **Exchanges:** 1 Starch, ½ Medium-Fat Meat, 3 Fat **Carbohydrate Choices:** 1

**Make-Ahead Magic** The **Citrus-Mustard Sauce** can be made up to 1 day ahead of time and stored in the refrigerator. It's also good with chicken nuggets or cooked shrimp.

**Make-Ahead Magic** The **Sweet Potato–Zucchini Tots** can be frozen up to 1 week before serving. Bake as directed, cool and place in resealable freezer plastic bag or freezer container. To reheat, place frozen tots on a cookie sheet. Bake at 350°F for 13 to 15 minutes or until thoroughly heated.

# Cheesy Ranch Chex Mix

**PREP TIME:** 10 Minutes  **START TO FINISH:** 10 Minutes  *26 servings*

9 cups Corn Chex™, Rice Chex™
   or Wheat Chex™ cereal (or
   a combination)

2 cups small pretzel twists

2 cups bite-size cheese crackers

3 tablespoons butter

1 package (1 oz) ranch dressing
   and seasoning mix

½ cup grated Parmesan cheese

1   In large microwavable bowl, mix cereal, pretzels and crackers; set aside.

2   In small microwavable bowl, microwave butter uncovered on High about 30 seconds or until melted. Pour over cereal mixture; stir until evenly coated. Stir in dressing mix and cheese until evenly coated.

3   Microwave uncovered on High 3 minutes, stirring after each minute. Spread on paper towels to cool. Store in airtight container for up to 5 days.

**1 Serving (½ Cup):** Calories 100; Total Fat 3g (Saturated Fat 1.5g, Trans Fat 0g); Cholesterol 5mg; Sodium 260mg; Total Carbohydrate 14g (Dietary Fiber 1g); Protein 2g **Exchanges:** 1 Starch, ½ Fat **Carbohydrate Choices:** 1

## Festive Touch Make it easy for guests to help themselves to this fun snack mix by serving it up in small decorative disposable cups.

# Tequila-Lime Chex Mix

**PREP TIME:** 10 Minutes   **START TO FINISH:** 10 Minutes   *24 servings*

9 cups Corn Chex, Rice Chex
  or Wheat Chex cereal (or
  a combination)

2 cups pretzels

1 cup peanuts

1 cup tortilla strips

¼ cup butter

3 tablespoons tequila

3 tablespoons
  Worcestershire sauce

1 tablespoon lime juice

2 teaspoons seasoned salt

1 teaspoon chili powder

1 teaspoon garlic powder
  Grated peel of 1 lime

**1** In large microwavable bowl, mix cereal, pretzels, peanuts and tortilla strips; set aside.

**2** In small microwavable bowl, microwave butter uncovered on High about 40 seconds or until melted. Stir in tequila, Worcestershire sauce, lime juice, seasoned salt, chili powder and garlic powder. Pour over cereal mixture; stir until evenly coated.

**3** Microwave uncovered on High 5 to 6 minutes, thoroughly stirring every 2 minutes. Spread on paper towels to cool. Sprinkle with lime peel. Store in airtight container for up to 5 days.

**1 Serving (½ Cup):** Calories 120; Total Fat 6g (Saturated Fat 1.5g, Trans Fat 0g); Cholesterol 5mg; Sodium 280mg; Total Carbohydrate 15g (Dietary Fiber 1g); Protein 3g **Exchanges:** 1 Starch, 1 Fat **Carbohydrate Choices:** 1

**Oven Directions:** Heat oven to 250°F. Line 15x10x1-inch pan with cooking parchment paper. Prepare recipe as directed in Steps 1 and 2. Spread mixture in even layer in pan. Bake 1 hour, stirring every 15 minutes.

**Kitchen Secrets** **Tortilla strips can usually be found in grocery stores near the salad dressings or in the produce department. If you can't find them, substitute coarsely crushed tortilla chips or you can make your own tortilla strips. To make your own, heat oven to 375°F. Place 2 teaspoons vegetable oil in small dish; stir in 2 to 3 drops red or green food color (or color of your choice). Brush oil mixture over tortillas, working the brush until color is even. Using pizza cutter, cut tortillas into thin strips. Place on ungreased cookie sheet. Bake about 8 minutes, stirring once, until crisp.**

# Pomegranate-Orange Sangria

**PREP TIME:** 10 Minutes  **START TO FINISH:** 4 Hours 10 Minutes  *16 servings*

2 bottles (750 ml each) red or rosé (blush) wine

1½ cups pomegranate juice

1½ cups fresh orange juice

⅔ cup pomegranate- or orange-flavored liqueur or apricot brandy (5 oz)

⅓ cup superfine sugar

2 limes, thinly sliced

1 medium navel or blood orange, cut in half, thinly sliced

1 ripe pear, cut into cubes

1 cinnamon stick (3 inch)

1 bottle (1 liter) club soda or ginger ale (4¼ cups), chilled

Additional cinnamon sticks, if desired

1  In large pitcher, mix wine, juices, liqueur and sugar until sugar is dissolved. Stir in limes, orange, pear and cinnamon stick. Cover; refrigerate at least 4 hours but no longer than 24 hours to chill thoroughly and blend flavors.

2  Add club soda to sangria mixture; stir to mix. Garnish with cinnamon sticks.

**1 Serving:** Calories 160; Total Fat 0g (Saturated Fat 0g, Trans Fat 0g); Cholesterol 0mg; Sodium 20mg; Total Carbohydrate 19g (Dietary Fiber 1g); Protein 0g **Carbohydrate Choices:** 1

**Festive Touch** Serve the sangria in a clear pitcher or punch bowl so the beautiful fruit takes center stage.

**Festive Touch** Like your sangria extra-cold? Fill 2 ice cube trays with distilled water. Cut 3 orange slices into 8 wedges each; add an orange wedge and several pomegranate seeds to each section of the tray. Place in freezer 1 to 2 hours or until frozen. Add ice cubes to glasses or punch bowl before serving.

# Elf-Tinis

**PREP TIME:** 10 Minutes **START TO FINISH:** 10 Minutes *2 servings*

2 oz white chocolate

Ice cubes

3 tablespoons crème de cacao
(1½ oz)

3 tablespoons green crème de
menthe (1½ oz)

2 tablespoons Irish whiskey (1 oz)

1 tablespoon vanilla-flavored
vodka (½ oz)

¼ cup half-and-half

2 miniature candy canes

**1** In small microwavable bowl, microwave white chocolate uncovered on High 30 to 40 seconds, stirring every 10 seconds, until melted and smooth. Immediately pour melted chocolate onto saucer. Holding martini glass by the base, immediately roll rim of glass through chocolate to create a snowy rim. Repeat with second glass. Place glasses upright in refrigerator until ready to use.

**2** Fill cocktail shaker or small pitcher with ice. Add crème de cacao, crème de menthe, whiskey, vodka and half-and-half; shake or stir to blend and chill. Pour into glasses, straining out ice. Garnish each glass with candy cane looped over rim.

**1 Serving:** Calories 390; Total Fat 13g (Saturated Fat 10g, Trans Fat 0g); Cholesterol 20mg; Sodium 95mg; Total Carbohydrate 44g (Dietary Fiber 0g); Protein 3g **Carbohydrate Choices:** 3

## Make-Ahead Magic The martini glasses can be rimmed with the melted white chocolate and refrigerated up to 4 hours ahead of time.

## Festive Touch Before the white chocolate has a chance to set, dip the glass rims into a small shallow bowl of grated white chocolate mixed with white sanding sugar, holiday sprinkles or crushed peppermint candies.

# Mango-Ginger Snowdrift Mimosas

**PREP TIME:** 10 Minutes   **START TO FINISH:** 3 Hours 40 Minutes   *4 servings*

1½ cups mango juice

1½ teaspoons grated gingerroot

3 tablespoons sugar

1 teaspoon grated lemon peel

1 bottle (750 ml) champagne
or prosecco

Fresh raspberries

**1** Chill 4 champagne flutes or wine glasses. In 1-quart saucepan, heat mango juice, gingerroot, sugar and lemon peel to boiling, stirring constantly, 3 to 4 minutes or until sugar is dissolved. Remove from heat; cool to room temperature, about 30 minutes.

**2** Pour mango mixture into 8-inch square pan. Freeze uncovered about 30 minutes or until icy around edges. Use a fork to scrape frozen edges toward center; freeze 25 to 30 minutes longer. Repeat the scraping process until all of mixture is frozen, about 2 hours 30 minutes total.

**3** Spoon 2 to 3 tablespoons of the mango "snow" into each chilled glass. Fill with champagne. Garnish with raspberries.

**1 Serving:** Calories 240; Total Fat 0g (Saturated Fat 0g, Trans Fat 0g); Cholesterol 0mg; Sodium 15mg; Total Carbohydrate 27g (Dietary Fiber 0g); Protein 0g **Carbohydrate Choices:** 2

## Make-Ahead Magic The scraped mango mixture can be kept covered in the freezer up to 1 week before using.

## Festive Touch Offer guests this unique beverage with a swizzle stick in each glass. That way, they can stir the sweet mango mixture into the champagne just before drinking.

## Kitchen Secrets Any leftover frozen mango mixture can be used in smoothies, added to punch or enjoyed on its own for a refreshing treat.

# Bring On the Beverages

If you're hosting a holiday party, nothing says "welcome" like a well-stocked bar! Here's everything you need for a lively gathering.

## How Much Do I Need?

For a 3-hour party and for every 6 guests, plan on:

| Alcohol Being Served | Amount Needed | | |
| --- | --- | --- | --- |
| | Beer (12-oz cans or bottles) | Bottles of Wine (750 ml) | Bottles of Liquor (1 liter) |
| Beer, wine and liquor | 9 | 2 | 1 |
| Beer and wine | 13 | 3 | |
| Beer | 20 to 24 | | |
| Wine | | 5 to 6 | |

## Garnishes to Have on Hand

For a fun display, arrange your garnishes in small containers or a bento box. It makes it easy to grab what you need so your guests can help themselves at a make-your-own drink bar.

- Stuffed cocktail olives
- Maraschino cherries
- Cocktail onions
- Fresh fruit (lemon, lime and orange wedges or slices; berries)
- Celery sticks
- Whole hazelnuts
- Granulated, coarse and powdered sugar
- Coarse salt
- Black pepper
- Fresh mint or basil

## Add a Little Jolly to Your Holiday Cheer

With a simple festive garnish, even water can look special. So don't limit these just to boozy concoctions—garnishes are also great with hot chocolate, eggnog or even juice.

- **Edgy Sparkle:** Use colored sugar, toasted coconut, sprinkles or even a coarse salt–seasoning mixture for savory drinks. Wet the glass edge by dipping it in water, or use a wedge of lemon or lime for sugar or salt rims. Or when using heavier sparkles like coconut or shaved chocolate, dip the edge in a heavier mixture like simple syrup (see below) or melted chocolate (see Elf-Tinis, page 37).

- **Frozen Beauty:** Fill ice cube trays with berries, herbs or edible green leaves before adding juice or water. Or for a punch bowl, create an eye-catching ice ring; see Spiced Tea Punch (page 48) for inspiration. It's beauty and function, all in one!

- **Whipped Cream Fun:** Spoon a dollop of whipped cream onto a drink, and then add a sprinkle of ground cinnamon, nutmeg, candy sprinkles or crushed candy canes. Or freeze the whipped cream, and cut it into shapes with small cookie cutters (see Chai Hot Chocolate with Cinnamon Cream, page 46).

- **Dazzle with Drizzle:** Before pouring eggnog or light-colored drinks like milkshakes into glasses, squirt the inside of the glass with thick chocolate or caramel ice-cream topping to make interesting shapes (see Eggnog-Toffee Milkshakes, page 50).

**Simple Syrup:** In a 2-quart saucepan, mix 2 cups water and 2 cups sugar. Heat over medium heat until sugar is dissolved. Cool before using. Use in cocktails or to rim glasses. Store covered in refrigerator up to 1 month. Makes 3 cups.

Appetizers & Beverages

# Sparkling Holiday Sippers

**PREP TIME:** 10 Minutes    **START TO FINISH:** 2 Hours 10 Minutes    *4 servings*

½ cup pomegranate juice

Ice cubes

½ cup vanilla-flavored or plain vodka (4 oz)

3 tablespoons orange-flavored liqueur (1½ oz)

¼ cup fresh lime juice

1 bottle (750 ml) champagne or prosecco

Fresh mint sprigs

1 Chill 4 stemmed glasses in freezer. Pour pomegranate juice into 8 sections of ice cube tray, 1 tablespoon in each; freeze until solid, about 2 hours.

2 Fill cocktail shaker or small pitcher with ice. Add vodka, liqueur and lime juice; shake or stir to blend and chill.

3 Place 2 pomegranate ice cubes in each chilled glass. Pour vodka mixture into glasses, straining out ice. Fill glasses with champagne. Garnish with mint.

**1 Serving:** Calories 270; Total Fat 0g (Saturated Fat 0g, Trans Fat 0g); Cholesterol 0mg; Sodium 15mg; Total Carbohydrate 14g (Dietary Fiber 0g); Protein 0g **Carbohydrate Choices:** 1

## Make-Ahead Magic With your pomegranate ice cubes in the freezer, all you have to do is shake these up to serve.

## Festive Touch To really make a splash, freeze the pomegranate ice cubes in a mini ice cube tray or specialty shaped ice cube tray. Stars and small balls are beautiful.

# Berry-Rosemary Margaritas

**PREP TIME:** 15 Minutes   **START TO FINISH:** 1 Hour 25 Minutes   *6 servings*

1 bag (15 to 16 oz) frozen mixed
  berries, thawed

¾ cup sugar

1¼ cups water

2 large sprigs rosemary

1 cup silver tequila (8 oz)

½ cup fresh lime juice

⅓ cup orange-flavored liqueur
  (2½ oz)

  Additional sugar

  Lime wedge

  Ice cubes or crushed ice

  Additional rosemary sprigs and
  lime wedges, if desired

**1** In 2-quart saucepan, mash berries with ¾ cup sugar. Stir in water and 2 rosemary sprigs. Heat to boiling; reduce heat. Simmer uncovered 15 minutes. Strain syrup; discard solids. Cover; refrigerate at least 1 hour.

**2** In large pitcher, stir together berry-rosemary syrup, tequila, lime juice and liqueur.

**3** On small plate, place additional sugar. Rub rims of 6 margarita glasses (or other stemmed glasses) with lime wedge; dip wet rims in sugar.

**4** Fill glasses with ice; pour margarita mixture over ice. Garnish with rosemary sprigs and lime wedges.

**1 Serving:** Calories 270; Total Fat 0g (Saturated Fat 0g, Trans Fat 0g); Cholesterol 0mg; Sodium 0mg; Total Carbohydrate 39g (Dietary Fiber 2g); Protein 0g **Carbohydrate Choices:** 2½

## Make-Ahead Magic
The berry-rosemary syrup can be refrigerated up to 1 week.

## Festive Touch
Some bartenders prefer using superfine sugar for coating the edges of glasses. This is available in many grocery stores, but if you want to make your own, simply blend granulated sugar in a blender or food processor about 30 seconds. The texture of superfine sugar dissolves quickly and lends sweetness without grittiness to the cocktail.

# Pomegranate-Ginger Prosecco Cocktails

**PREP TIME:** 10 Minutes    **START TO FINISH:** 2 Hours 25 Minutes    *2 servings*

### GINGER SIMPLE SYRUP

- 1 cup sugar
- 1 cup water
- 2 tablespoons finely chopped gingerroot

### GINGER SUGAR

- 2 tablespoons sugar
- ½ teaspoon finely chopped gingerroot
- 1 slice fresh gingerroot

### COCKTAIL

- Ice cubes
- ¼ cup gin (2 oz)
- ¼ cup pomegranate juice
- ¼ cup prosecco (2 oz)
- 1 tablespoon pomegranate seeds

**1** In 1-quart saucepan, heat simple syrup ingredients over low heat until sugar is dissolved. Let stand 15 minutes. Cover; refrigerate 2 hours until chilled. Strain syrup; discard solids.

**2** In small bowl, stir together 2 tablespoons sugar and ½ teaspoon gingerroot. Place mixture on small flat plate. Rub fresh gingerroot slice around rims of 2 martini glasses to moisten. Dip moistened rims of glasses in ginger-sugar mixture. Refrigerate until ready to use.

**3** Fill cocktail shaker or small pitcher with ice. Add gin, pomegranate juice and 2 tablespoons of the Ginger Simple Syrup. (Cover and refrigerate remaining simple syrup for another use.) Shake or stir to blend and chill. Pour into prepared glasses, straining out ice. Add prosecco. Garnish with pomegranate seeds.

**1 Serving:** Calories 210; Total Fat 0g (Saturated Fat 0g, Trans Fat 0g); Cholesterol 0mg; Sodium 0mg; Total Carbohydrate 30g (Dietary Fiber 0g); Protein 0g **Carbohydrate Choices:** 2

## Make-Ahead Magic
**You can make the ginger syrup up to one month in advance. Cover and refrigerate until ready to use. The extra-cold syrup will make the cocktail nice and frosty.**

# Cranberry Old-Fashioned

**PREP TIME:** 5 Minutes   **START TO FINISH:** 5 Minutes
*1 serving*

- 1  orange wedge
- 1  sugar cube
- Dash aromatic bitters
- Crushed ice
- ¼  cup bourbon (2 oz)
- 2  tablespoons whole-berry cranberry sauce
- Club soda
- Orange slice and fresh cranberries, if desired

1  Using muddler or wooden spoon, muddle orange wedge, sugar cube and bitters against bottom and side of 10-oz old-fashioned glass. Fill glass with ice.

2  Stir in bourbon, cranberry sauce and splash of club soda. Garnish with orange slice and cranberries.

**1 Serving:** Calories 210; Total Fat 0g (Saturated Fat 0g); Sodium 10mg; Total Carbohydrate 21g (Dietary Fiber 1g); Protein 0g **Carbohydrate Choices:** 1

**Festive Touch** **To make these drinks icy cold, rinse the glasses under the tap, shake off the excess water and place them in the freezer at least 15 minutes before using. When you take them out of the freezer, the magic happens—they turn frosty looking.**

# Alpine Mint Hot Chocolate

**PREP TIME:** 15 Minutes   **START TO FINISH:** 15 Minutes
*10 servings*

- 1  cup whipping cream
- 2  tablespoons powdered sugar
- 1  tablespoon unsweetened baking cocoa
- ¾  teaspoon peppermint extract
- 6  cups milk
- 3  cups white vanilla baking chips (about 18 oz)

1  In chilled small bowl, beat whipping cream, powdered sugar, cocoa and ¼ teaspoon of the peppermint extract with electric mixer on high speed until stiff peaks form. Cover; refrigerate until serving time.

2  In 2-quart saucepan, heat milk just to simmering over medium-low heat (do not boil). Reduce heat to low. Add baking chips; stir constantly with whisk until melted and smooth. Stir in remaining ½ teaspoon peppermint extract.

3  Pour hot chocolate into cups or mugs. Top each serving with cocoa-mint whipped cream.

**1 Serving:** Calories 410; Total Fat 24g (Saturated Fat 17g, Trans Fat 0g); Cholesterol 40mg; Sodium 190mg; Total Carbohydrate 40g (Dietary Fiber 0g); Protein 9g **Exchanges:** 2 Other Carbohydrate, 1 Low-Fat Milk, 4 Fat **Carbohydrate Choices:** 2½

**Festive Touch** **Add a bit of elfish fun—garnish each steaming mug of hot chocolate with a candy cane for stirring, or sprinkle with crushed hard peppermint candies.**

**Festive Touch** **To make a delicious adult drink, substitute ⅓ cup peppermint schnapps for the ½ teaspoon peppermint extract in the hot chocolate.**

# Chai Hot Chocolate with Cinnamon Cream

**PREP TIME:** 15 Minutes    **START TO FINISH:** 25 Minutes    *4 servings*

1 cup water

3 tea bags chai black tea

¼ cup unsweetened baking cocoa

¼ cup caramel topping

3 tablespoons sugar

3 cups milk or coconut milk

½ teaspoon vanilla

1 cup whipping cream

1 teaspoon ground cinnamon

Candy sprinkles, if desired

1 In 2-quart saucepan, heat water just to boiling. Add tea bags. Remove from heat; let stand 10 minutes to steep. Remove tea bags; discard.

2 Add cocoa, caramel topping and 2 tablespoons of the sugar to tea. Heat to boiling over medium heat. Boil 1 minute, stirring constantly. Stir in milk; heat until hot (do not boil). Remove from heat; stir in vanilla. Cover to keep warm.

3 In chilled medium bowl, beat whipping cream, cinnamon and remaining 1 tablespoon sugar with electric mixer on high speed until stiff peaks form.

4 Pour hot chocolate into mugs; top with dollops of whipped cream. Decorate with sprinkles. (Store remaining whipped cream for another use: Follow Make-Ahead Magic tip below, spooning remaining whipped cream into 8 dollops. Continue as directed.)

**1 Serving:** Calories 390; Total Fat 23g (Saturated Fat 14g, Trans Fat 1g); Cholesterol 80mg; Sodium 180mg; Total Carbohydrate 37g (Dietary Fiber 2g); Protein 8g **Exchanges:** 1½ Other Carbohydrate, 1 Milk, 3½ Fat **Carbohydrate Choices:** 2½

## Make-Ahead Magic
To make whipped cream dollops ahead, line a cookie sheet with waxed paper. Spoon the whipped cream into 12 mounds on the cookie sheet. Top with candy sprinkles, if desired. Freeze about 15 minutes or until firm. Store leftover dollops in a resealable freezer plastic bag.

## Festive Touch
Instead of plain dollops, you can make whipped cream decorations. On a waxed paper–lined cookie sheet, spread the whipped cream into a 4-inch square about 1 inch thick. Top with candy sprinkles, if desired. Freeze about 1 hour 30 minutes or until firm. Use 1½- to 2-inch cookie cutters to cut out shapes. Save scraps from the cutouts to add to hot chocolate or coffee.

## Kitchen Secrets
If you want to use all of the whipped cream, triple the hot chocolate ingredients to make 12 servings.

# Spiced Tea Punch

**PREP TIME:** 20 Minutes     **START TO FINISH:** 3 Hours 20 Minutes     *18 servings*

### ICE WREATH

- 1 orange, cut into small chunks
- 16 whole cranberries
- 8 cinnamon sticks (3 inch)
  Fresh mint leaves
- 1½ quarts water

### FRAGRANT SIMPLE SYRUP

- 1½ cups packed brown sugar
- 1½ cups water
- ¼ cup honey
- ¼ cup chopped gingerroot
- 4 whole cloves
- ½ teaspoon vanilla
  Grated peel of 1 orange

### PUNCH

- 3 cups water
- 14 tea bags orange pekoe or white mango tea
- 4 cups cranberry or cranberry-pomegranate juice, chilled
- 4 cups pineapple or orange juice, chilled
- ¾ cup frozen (thawed) lemonade concentrate (from 12-oz can)
- 1 bottle (1 liter) ginger ale or club soda (4¼ cups), chilled
- 2 cups light rum (16 oz), if desired

## Make-Ahead Magic

**The flavor of the Fragrant Simple Syrup improves if it rests overnight in the refrigerator. In fact, you can keep it in the fridge up to 1 week before making the punch. The Ice Wreath can also be made ahead and kept in the freezer up to 1 month.**

1   In 12-cup fluted tube cake pan, arrange orange pieces, cranberries, cinnamon sticks and mint to look like a holiday wreath. Carefully pour enough of the 1½ quarts water along edge of pan to touch at least part of all decorations without dislodging them. Freeze about 1 hour or until firm. Add enough water to completely cover decorations. Freeze until completely frozen, about 3 hours. Keep frozen until serving time.

2   Meanwhile, in 2-quart saucepan, mix simple syrup ingredients. Cook over medium-low heat about 6 minutes, stirring frequently, until simmering, liquid is clear and spices are fragrant. Cool to room temperature. Cover; refrigerate at least 2 hours or until cold. Strain syrup; discard solids. Refrigerate until serving time.

3   In medium microwavable bowl, heat 3 cups water until very hot but not boiling. Add tea bags; let stand 5 minutes to steep. Remove tea bags; discard. Cool tea to room temperature. Cover; refrigerate at least 2 hours or until cold.

4   In large punch bowl, stir together tea, simple syrup, juices and lemonade concentrate. Stir in ginger ale and rum.

5   Briefly run outside of cake pan under warm water; invert pan to remove ice wreath. Gently slip ice wreath into punch.

**1 Serving:** Calories 200; Total Fat 0g (Saturated Fat 0g, Trans Fat 0g); Cholesterol 0mg; Sodium 15mg; Total Carbohydrate 49g (Dietary Fiber 0g); Protein 0g **Carbohydrate Choices:** 3

# Bourbon-Maple Eggnog

**PREP TIME:** 35 Minutes  **START TO FINISH:** 2 Hours 35 Minutes  *10 servings*

### CUSTARD

- 3 eggs, slightly beaten
- ½ cup real maple syrup
- Dash salt
- 2½ cups milk
- 1 teaspoon vanilla

### EGGNOG

- 1 cup whipping cream
- 2 tablespoons powdered sugar
- 2 tablespoons real maple syrup
- ½ teaspoon vanilla
- ½ cup bourbon (4 oz)
- Crisply cooked bacon, finely chopped, if desired

1  In 2-quart saucepan, stir eggs, ½ cup syrup and the salt until well mixed. Gradually stir in milk. Cook over medium heat 10 to 15 minutes, stirring constantly, until mixture just coats a metal spoon; remove from heat. Stir in 1 teaspoon vanilla. Place saucepan in cold water until custard is cool. (If custard curdles, beat vigorously with whisk or electric mixer until smooth.) Cover; refrigerate at least 2 hours but no longer than 24 hours.

2  Just before serving, in chilled medium bowl, beat whipping cream, powdered sugar, 2 tablespoons syrup and ½ teaspoon vanilla with electric mixer on high speed until stiff peaks form. Gently stir 1 cup of the whipped cream and the bourbon into custard. Store covered in refrigerator up to 2 days.

3  Pour custard mixture into small punch bowl. Drop remaining whipped cream in mounds onto custard mixture. Sprinkle each serving with bacon. Serve immediately.

**1 Serving:** Calories 220; Total Fat 12g (Saturated Fat 7g, Trans Fat 0g); Cholesterol 95mg; Sodium 90mg; Total Carbohydrate 19g (Dietary Fiber 0g); Protein 4g **Carbohydrate Choices:** 1

## Make-Ahead Magic

**Get to the sipping part more quickly by making the custard portion of this recipe up to 24 hours in advance. Cover and refrigerate until ready to top with whipped cream and serve.**

# Eggnog-Toffee Milkshakes

**PREP TIME:** 5 Minutes   **START TO FINISH:** 5 Minutes   *2 servings*

¾ cup eggnog

3 scoops vanilla ice cream (1½ cups)

2 bars (1.4 oz each) chocolate-covered English toffee candy, chopped*

Whipped cream, if desired

1 In blender, place eggnog, ice cream and half of the chopped candy. Cover; blend on medium speed 15 to 30 seconds or until blended. Pour into two 12-ounce glasses. Top with whipped cream and remaining chopped candy.

*½ cup milk chocolate–coated toffee bits can be substituted for the candy bars.

**1 Serving:** Calories 570; Total Fat 31g (Saturated Fat 18g, Trans Fat 1g); Cholesterol 95mg; Sodium 370mg; Total Carbohydrate 64g (Dietary Fiber 1g); Protein 7g **Exchanges:** 3½ Other Carbohydrate, 1 Milk, 4½ Fat **Carbohydrate Choices:** 4

**Festive Touch** For some extra glam, drizzle chocolate-flavor syrup into the glasses before adding the milkshake.

# White Chocolate–Peppermint Jelly Shots

**PREP TIME:** 20 Minutes    **START TO FINISH:** 5 Hours    *50 servings*

## PEPPERMINT LAYER

- ¼ cup sugar
- 2 envelopes unflavored gelatin
- ½ cup boiling water
- 1 cup cold water
- ¼ cup peppermint schnapps (2 oz)
- ¼ cup vodka (2 oz)
- 10 to 15 drops red food color

## WHITE CHOCOLATE LAYER

- 2 envelopes unflavored gelatin
- ¼ cup cold water
- 1 cup white chocolate liqueur (8 oz)
- 1 can (14 oz) sweetened condensed milk (not evaporated)

1  Spray 9x5-inch glass loaf dish with cooking spray; wipe out excess. In medium bowl, stir together sugar and 2 envelopes gelatin. Add boiling water; stir 1 to 2 minutes or until gelatin and sugar are dissolved. Stir in 1 cup cold water, the schnapps, vodka and enough food color to create bright red.

2  Pour gelatin mixture through fine-mesh strainer into 3- to 4-cup measuring cup. Pour ¾ cup peppermint mixture into dish; freeze about 15 minutes or until firm. (Keep remaining gelatin mixture at room temperature.)

3  Meanwhile, in 1-quart saucepan, sprinkle 2 envelopes gelatin over ¼ cup cold water. Let stand 2 to 3 minutes to soften. Heat over low heat, stirring constantly, just until gelatin is dissolved. Gradually stir in liqueur and condensed milk with whisk. Pour through fine-mesh strainer into another 3- to 4-cup measuring cup or pitcher.

4  When red gelatin is firm, pour ¾ cup white gelatin over red layer; freeze 15 minutes or until firm. (Keep remaining gelatin at room temperature.) Continue alternating layers of red and white mixtures three times, freezing until firm before adding another layer. (Gently rewarm remaining gelatin mixture if it begins to firm up before being added to the layers.) Refrigerate at least 3 hours.

5  To unmold, dip loaf dish in warm water a few seconds and gently loosen edges of gelatin with warm knife; turn out onto cutting board. Cut gelatin into ¾-inch slices. Cut each slice into five triangles or "trees" with 1-inch-wide bases. Place on serving platter. Cover; refrigerate until serving time.

**1 Serving:** Calories 50; Total Fat 0.5g (Saturated Fat 0g, Trans Fat 0g); Cholesterol 0mg; Sodium 10mg; Total Carbohydrate 8g (Dietary Fiber 0g); Protein 1g **Carbohydrate Choices:** ½

**Make-Ahead Magic** **Make these irresistible adult party bites up to 2 days in advance and store in the refrigerator.**

**Festive Touch** **Instead of cutting the gelatin into trees, use small Christmas-shaped cookie cutters to form bells, stockings or stars. "Scraps" can be stirred into whipped cream for a jelly shot mousse.**

**Festive Touch** **Add a green tree trunk by cutting green gumdrops into small rectangles. Press one into base of each "tree." For stars, roll yellow gumdrops with a rolling pin and cut stars with tiny cookie cutters or paring knife. Gently press onto top of trees.**

# Brunch

# Hot Chocolate Pancakes

**PREP TIME:** 20 Minutes   **START TO FINISH:** 20 Minutes   *16 pancakes*

## PANCAKES

- 2 cups Original Bisquick mix
- ¼ cup sugar
- 2 tablespoons unsweetened baking cocoa
- 1 cup chocolate milk
- 1 teaspoon vanilla
- 2 eggs

## TOPPINGS, IF DESIRED

- Chocolate-flavor syrup, warmed
- Sweetened whipped cream
- Miniature marshmallows
- Chocolate candy sprinkles

1 In large bowl, stir pancake ingredients with whisk until well blended.

2 Heat nonstick griddle or skillet over medium-high heat (375°F). Brush griddle with vegetable oil if necessary (or spray with cooking spray before heating).

3 For each pancake, pour slightly less than ¼ cup batter onto hot griddle. Cook until bubbles form on top and edges are dry. Turn; cook other side until golden brown.

4 Drizzle pancakes with chocolate syrup; top with whipped cream, marshmallows and sprinkles.

**1 Pancake:** Calories 100; Total Fat 3g (Saturated Fat 1g, Trans Fat 0g); Cholesterol 0mg; Sodium 200mg; Total Carbohydrate 15g (Dietary Fiber 0g); Protein 3g **Exchanges:** ½ Starch, ½ Other Carbohydrate, ½ Fat **Carbohydrate Choices:** 1

**Festive Touch** For a little seasonal "snow," dust plates or pancakes with powdered sugar. To control the amount, place a tablespoon of sugar in a small mesh strainer. Hold the strainer over the plate and tap the edge of it with a spoon.

# Cinnamon Roll Pancake Stacks

**PREP TIME:** 25 Minutes **START TO FINISH:** 25 Minutes *14 pancakes*

### ICING

- 2 cups powdered sugar
- ¼ cup whipping cream

### FILLING

- 1 cup packed brown sugar
- ½ cup butter
- 1 tablespoon ground cinnamon

### PANCAKES

- 2 cups Original Bisquick mix
- 1 cup milk
- 2 eggs
- ½ cup raisins

1 In small bowl, mix icing ingredients with whisk; set aside.

2 In 2-quart saucepan, cook filling ingredients over medium heat, stirring frequently, until butter is melted and sugar is dissolved. Remove from heat; cover to keep warm.

3 In medium bowl, stir Bisquick mix, milk and eggs with fork or whisk until blended. Stir in raisins.

4 Heat griddle or skillet over medium-high heat (375°F). Brush griddle with vegetable oil if necessary (or spray with cooking spray before heating).

5 For each pancake, pour about 3 tablespoons batter onto hot griddle. Cook until bubbles form on top and edges are dry. Turn; cook other side until golden brown.

6 Serve pancakes stacked with filling between each pair; drizzle with icing.

**1 Pancake:** Calories 310; Total Fat 12g (Saturated Fat 7g, Trans Fat 0g); Cholesterol 50mg; Sodium 280mg; Total Carbohydrate 48g (Dietary Fiber 0g); Protein 3g **Exchanges:** 1 Starch, 2 Other Carbohydrate, 2½ Fat **Carbohydrate Choices:** 3

## Make-Ahead Magic

**Cook the pancakes ahead of time so breakfast can be on the table in a snap. Let them cool in single layer on cooling rack. Place in resealable freezer plastic bag; freeze up to 1 month. To reheat, wrap frozen pancakes in foil. Bake at 350°F for 15 to 20 minutes or until heated through. Meanwhile, prepare the icing and filling.**

# Red Velvet Pancakes

**PREP TIME:** 30 Minutes **START TO FINISH:** 30 Minutes *7 servings*

### CREAM CHEESE TOPPING

4 oz (half of 8-oz package) cream cheese, softened

¼ cup butter, softened

3 tablespoons milk

2 cups powdered sugar

### PANCAKES

2 cups Original Bisquick mix

2 tablespoons granulated sugar

1 tablespoon unsweetened baking cocoa

1 cup milk

1 to 1½ teaspoons red paste food color*

2 eggs

Powdered sugar, if desired

1 In medium bowl, beat cream cheese, butter and 3 tablespoons milk with electric mixer on low speed until smooth. Gradually beat in 2 cups powdered sugar, 1 cup at a time, on low speed until topping is smooth. Cover; set aside.

2 In large bowl, stir all pancake ingredients except powdered sugar with whisk until well blended.

3 Heat griddle or skillet over medium-high heat (375°F). Brush griddle with vegetable oil if necessary (or spray with cooking spray before heating).

4 For each pancake, pour slightly less than ¼ cup batter onto hot griddle. Cook until bubbles form on top and edges are dry. Turn; cook other side until set.

5 Spoon topping into resealable food-storage plastic bag; seal bag. Cut off tiny corner of bag; squeeze bag to drizzle topping over pancakes. Sprinkle with powdered sugar.

*For the best results, liquid food color is not recommended for this recipe.

**1 Serving (3 Pancakes):** Calories 450; Total Fat 20g (Saturated Fat 10g, Trans Fat 1.5g); Cholesterol 90mg; Sodium 570mg; Total Carbohydrate 62g (Dietary Fiber 1g); Protein 7g **Exchanges:** 2 Starch, 2 Other Carbohydrate, 4 Fat **Carbohydrate Choices:** 4

## Make-Ahead Magic

**To get a jump on breakfast, make the Cream Cheese Topping the night before. Spoon it into a resealable food-storage plastic bag; refrigerate. Let it stand at room temperature while preparing the pancakes. If the mixture is too stiff to drizzle, knead the bag.**

## Make-Ahead Magic

**You can also prep the pancakes ahead. Measure the dry ingredients into a mixing bowl; cover. Add the food color and eggs to the milk in the measuring cup; cover and refrigerate until you're ready to mix the batter.**

# Gingerbread Boy Pancakes

**PREP TIME:** 20 Minutes    **START TO FINISH:** 20 Minutes    *18 pancakes*

## PANCAKES

- 2½ cups Original Bisquick mix
- 1 cup milk
- ¾ cup apple butter
- 2 tablespoons vegetable oil
- ¼ teaspoon ground cinnamon
- ¼ teaspoon ground ginger
- ¼ teaspoon ground nutmeg
- 2 eggs

## TOPPINGS, IF DESIRED

- 1 can (6.4 oz) white decorating icing
- Small candies and candy sprinkles

1 In large bowl, stir pancake ingredients with whisk until well blended.

2 Heat griddle or skillet over medium-high heat (375°F). Brush griddle with vegetable oil if necessary (or spray with cooking spray before heating).

3 For each pancake, pour ¼ cup batter onto hot griddle. Cook 2 to 3 minutes or until bubbles form on top and edges are dry. Turn; cook other side until golden brown.

4 Using 3½- to 4-inch gingerbread boy or girl cookie cutter, cut one shape from each warm pancake. Decorate as desired using icing, candies and sprinkles.

**1 Pancake:** Calories 120; Total Fat 5g (Saturated Fat 1g, Trans Fat 0g); Cholesterol 20mg; Sodium 220mg; Total Carbohydrate 17g (Dietary Fiber 0g); Protein 2g **Exchanges:** 1 Starch, 1 Fat **Carbohydrate Choices:** 1

## Make-Ahead Magic

**Get these cuties cooking in seconds when you prep everything the night before. Spoon the measured Bisquick mix and spices into a bowl. Measure the milk in a 2-cup measuring cup; stir in the apple butter and eggs until well blended. In the morning, simply dump the wet ingredients into the bowl and mix.**

# Apple Crisp Pancakes

**PREP TIME:** 25 Minutes   **START TO FINISH:** 25 Minutes   *13 pancakes*

### STREUSEL TOPPING

¼ cup plus 2 tablespoons packed brown sugar

¼ cup all-purpose flour

¼ cup old-fashioned or quick-cooking oats

½ teaspoon ground cinnamon

¼ teaspoon ground nutmeg

2 tablespoons plus 2 teaspoons cold butter

### PANCAKES

2 cups Original Bisquick mix

1 cup diced peeled Granny Smith apple

1 cup milk

2 eggs

### TOPPINGS, IF DESIRED

Real maple syrup

Sweetened whipped cream

Powdered sugar

1 In medium bowl, mix brown sugar, flour, oats and spices. Cut in butter, using pastry blender or fork, until mixture is crumbly. Set aside.

2 In large bowl, stir pancake ingredients with whisk until well blended. Heat nonstick griddle or skillet over medium-high heat (375°F). Brush lightly with vegetable oil to help prevent streusel from sticking to griddle.

3 For each pancake, pour ¼ cup batter onto hot griddle. Sprinkle each pancake evenly with slightly less than 2 tablespoons streusel mixture. Cook 2 to 3 minutes or until bubbles form on top and edges are dry. Turn; cook other side until light golden brown around edges. Scrape off griddle between batches if necessary.

4 Serve pancakes streusel side up. Top with syrup, whipped cream or powdered sugar.

**1 Pancake:** Calories 160; Total Fat 6g (Saturated Fat 3.5g, Trans Fat 0g); Cholesterol 35mg; Sodium 260mg; Total Carbohydrate 23g (Dietary Fiber 0g); Protein 3g **Exchanges:** 1 Starch, ½ Other Carbohydrate, 1 Fat **Carbohydrate Choices:** 1½

**Festive Touch** **Wake up sleepyheads with an indulgent breakfast, and serve these dessert-inspired pancakes with a scoop of vanilla ice cream on top!**

# Eggnog Pancakes with Maple-Butter-Rum Drizzle

**PREP TIME:** 10 Minutes   **START TO FINISH:** 20 Minutes   *14 pancakes*

### DRIZZLE

- ¼ cup butter
- ½ cup real maple syrup
- ⅓ cup whipping cream
- 2 tablespoons rum or ½ teaspoon rum extract

### PANCAKES

- 2 cups Original Bisquick mix
- 2 tablespoons sugar
- ¼ teaspoon ground nutmeg
- 1 cup eggnog
- 2 eggs

### TOPPINGS, IF DESIRED

- Sweetened whipped cream
- Ground nutmeg

**1** In 2-quart saucepan, melt butter over medium heat. Stir in remaining drizzle ingredients. Heat to boiling, stirring occasionally. Reduce heat; simmer 2 minutes, stirring frequently. Remove from heat. Cover; keep warm.

**2** In large bowl, stir pancake ingredients with whisk until well blended.

**3** Heat griddle or skillet over medium-high heat (375°F). Brush griddle with vegetable oil if necessary (or spray with cooking spray before heating).

**4** For each pancake, pour slightly less than ¼ cup batter onto hot griddle. Cook 2 to 3 minutes or until bubbles form on top and edges are dry. Turn; cook other side until light golden brown around edges.

**5** Serve pancakes with drizzle. Top with whipped cream; sprinkle with nutmeg.

**1 Pancake:** Calories 200; Total Fat 10g (Saturated Fat 5g, Trans Fat 0.5g); Cholesterol 55mg; Sodium 280mg; Total Carbohydrate 24g (Dietary Fiber 0g); Protein 3g **Exchanges:** 1 Starch, ½ Other Carbohydrate, 2 Fat **Carbohydrate Choices:** 1½

## Make-Ahead Magic

**You can prepare the Drizzle up to 3 days in advance. Allow to cool to room temperature before covering with plastic wrap and refrigerating. Uncover and reheat when ready to serve.**

# Stuffed French Toast with Raspberry Sauce

**PREP TIME:** 25 Minutes    **START TO FINISH:** 9 Hours 5 Minutes    *6 servings*

## FRENCH TOAST

- 12 slices (1½ inches thick) French bread
- 6 oz (from 8-oz package) cream cheese, softened
- 2 tablespoons sugar
- 2 tablespoons orange marmalade
- ½ cup dried cranberries
- 8 eggs
- 2 cups milk
- ¼ cup sugar
- ¼ teaspoon salt
- 3 tablespoons butter, melted

## RASPBERRY SAUCE

- 1 box (10 oz) frozen sweetened raspberries, thawed
- 2 teaspoons cornstarch
- 2 tablespoons sugar
- 2 tablespoons orange marmalade

1. Spray 13x9-inch (3-quart) glass baking dish with cooking spray. Cut each bread slice from top crust to bottom, cutting almost but not completely through, to create a pocket.

2. In small bowl, stir together cream cheese, 2 tablespoons sugar, 2 tablespoons marmalade and the cranberries. Open bread slices enough to spread 1 heaping tablespoon cheese mixture evenly on one cut surface of each slice; press bread slices together. Place snugly in one layer in baking dish.

3. In medium bowl, beat eggs, milk, ¼ cup sugar and the salt with whisk until well blended. Pour over bread; turn slices carefully to coat. Cover; refrigerate 8 hours or overnight.

4. Heat oven to 425°F. Uncover baking dish. Drizzle melted butter over French toast. Bake 20 to 25 minutes or until golden brown.

5. Meanwhile, drain juice from raspberries into 1-cup glass measuring cup; add enough water to measure ¾ cup. In 1-quart saucepan, stir together juice mixture, cornstarch, 2 tablespoons sugar and 2 tablespoons marmalade. Heat to boiling, stirring occasionally; remove from heat. Cool 15 minutes. Stir in raspberries. Serve sauce with French toast.

**1 Serving (2 Pieces):** Calories 760; Total Fat 26g (Saturated Fat 13g, Trans Fat 1g); Cholesterol 300mg; Sodium 870mg; Total Carbohydrate 107g (Dietary Fiber 5g); Protein 24g **Exchanges:** 3 Starch, 1 Fruit, 2½ Other Carbohydrate, ½ Low-Fat Milk, 1½ Medium-Fat Meat, 3 Fat **Carbohydrate Choices:** 7

## Make-Ahead Magic

**When preparing the French toast the night before, you can also prep the sauce; place it in a microwavable serving dish; cover and refrigerate. Warm the sauce by microwaving on High 1 to 2 minutes.**

## Festive Touch
Complete your brunch menu by serving the French toast with bacon or sausage links and a platter of colorful fresh fruit.

# Baked Caramel-Pecan French Toast

**PREP TIME:** 20 Minutes   **START TO FINISH:** 8 Hours 50 Minutes   *4 servings*

### TOPPING

- 1 cup packed brown sugar
- 6 tablespoons butter
- ⅓ cup whipping cream
- 1 tablespoon real maple syrup or light corn syrup
- 1 cup pecan halves

### FRENCH TOAST

- 3 eggs
- ½ cup half-and-half
- 1 teaspoon ground cinnamon
- 1 teaspoon vanilla
- 8 diagonally cut slices (¾ inch thick) French bread

**1** Spray 13x9-inch (3-quart) glass baking dish with cooking spray. In 2-quart saucepan, mix brown sugar, butter, whipping cream and syrup. Cook over medium heat, stirring constantly, just until smooth (do not boil). Spread topping in baking dish; sprinkle with pecans.

**2** In shallow bowl, beat eggs with fork. Add half-and-half, cinnamon and vanilla; beat until well blended. Dip bread slices into egg mixture, making sure all egg mixture is absorbed; arrange bread slices over topping in dish. Cover; refrigerate 8 hours or overnight.

**3** Heat oven to 400°F. Uncover baking dish; bake 20 to 25 minutes or until bubbly and toast is golden brown. Cool 3 minutes. Place large heatproof serving platter upside down over baking dish; turn platter and dish over. Remove baking dish, scraping any extra caramel topping onto French toast. Serve immediately.

**1 Serving (6 Pieces):** Calories 920; Total Fat 50g (Saturated Fat 20g, Trans Fat 1g); Cholesterol 240mg; Sodium 620mg; Total Carbohydrate 100g (Dietary Fiber 4g); Protein 16g **Exchanges:** 3 Starch, 3½ Other Carbohydrate, 1 High-Fat Meat, 8 Fat **Carbohydrate Choices:** 6½

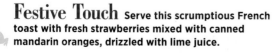

**Festive Touch** Serve this scrumptious French toast with fresh strawberries mixed with canned mandarin oranges, drizzled with lime juice.

# Snowflake French Toast Bites

**PREP TIME:** 25 Minutes   **START TO FINISH:** 25 Minutes *4 servings*

- ⅓ cup white sparkling sugar
- ½ cup sweetened condensed milk (not evaporated)
- 1 teaspoon grated orange peel
- ½ teaspoon grated lemon peel
- ½ teaspoon vanilla
  - Dash salt
- 3 eggs
- 24 (1-inch) cubes challah or French bread (4 cups)
- 2 tablespoons butter
  - Maple syrup and raspberry preserves, if desired

**1** In small bowl, place sparkling sugar; set aside. In medium bowl, beat condensed milk, orange peel, lemon peel, vanilla, salt and eggs with whisk or fork until well blended.

**2** In 12-inch nonstick skillet, melt 1 tablespoon of the butter over medium heat. Dip 12 of the bread cubes into egg mixture, using a fork to turn and coat all sides; let excess drip back into bowl. Cook cubes in butter 2 to 3 minutes, turning frequently with tongs, until golden brown.

**3** Place French toast bites in bowl with sugar; toss gently. Remove to serving platter; cover loosely with foil to keep warm. Repeat with remaining 1 tablespoon butter and 12 bread cubes. Serve with syrup and preserves.

**1 Serving (6 Bites):** Calories 460; Total Fat 16g (Saturated Fat 8g, Trans Fat 0g); Cholesterol 190mg; Sodium 270mg; Total Carbohydrate 67g (Dietary Fiber 1g); Protein 12g **Exchanges:** 2½ Starch, 2 Other Carbohydrate, ½ Medium-Fat Meat, 2½ Fat **Carbohydrate Choices:** 4½

**Festive Touch** For a more holiday feel, serve the French toast bites with raspberry, boysenberry or lingonberry syrup.

# Berry French Toast Roll-Ups

**PREP TIME:** 35 Minutes   **START TO FINISH:** 35 Minutes   *4 servings*

½ cup mascarpone cheese (from 8-oz container)

¼ cup sugar

1 teaspoon ground cinnamon

2 eggs

¼ cup milk

8 slices soft multigrain bread, crusts removed

1 to 1½ cups fresh raspberries

3 tablespoons butter

Additional raspberries, mint leaves and maple syrup, if desired

1   In small bowl, beat cheese and 1 tablespoon of the sugar with electric mixer on high speed until well blended. In small bowl, mix remaining 3 tablespoons sugar and the cinnamon; set aside.

2   In glass loaf pan or shallow dish, beat eggs and milk with whisk until well blended.

3   On work surface, roll each bread slice with rolling pin to about ¼ inch thick. Spread each slice with 1 tablespoon of the cheese mixture. Place 4 to 6 raspberries on one long side of each slice; starting with berry side, roll up tightly. Dip roll-ups, one at a time, into egg mixture.

4   In 12-inch nonstick skillet, melt 2 tablespoons of the butter over medium heat. Place 4 roll-ups, seam side down, in skillet. Cook 2 to 4 minutes, turning once, until golden brown on all sides. Immediately roll in cinnamon-sugar. Repeat with remaining 1 tablespoon butter and 4 roll-ups. Garnish with raspberries and mint leaves. Serve with syrup.

**1 Serving (2 Roll-Ups):** Calories 450; Total Fat 27g (Saturated Fat 15g, Trans Fat 1g); Cholesterol 155mg; Sodium 360mg; Total Carbohydrate 41g (Dietary Fiber 5g); Protein 11g **Exchanges:** 2 Starch, ½ Fruit, 1 Medium-Fat Meat, 4 Fat **Carbohydrate Choices:** 3

## Make-Ahead Magic
**Save time by preparing the roll-ups 2 hours in advance. Place on a plate; cover with plastic wrap and refrigerate until ready to cook.**

## Festive Touch
**Sprinkle the roll-ups with powdered sugar before serving.**

# Apple-Cinnamon French Toast Strata

**PREP TIME:** 20 Minutes    **START TO FINISH:** 7 Hours 30 Minutes    *8 servings*

⅓ cup butter, melted

½ cup plus 2 tablespoons packed brown sugar

1 loaf (16 oz) cinnamon swirl bread

8 oz Brie cheese, rind removed, cut into ¼-inch slices

1 large baking apple, coarsely chopped (about 2 cups)

8 eggs

1½ cups milk

1 teaspoon vanilla

½ teaspoon ground cinnamon

Maple syrup, if desired

1   Spray 13x9-inch (3-quart) glass baking dish with cooking spray. In small bowl, stir butter and ½ cup of the brown sugar until well blended. Spread evenly in bottom of baking dish. Top with 7 of the bread slices (cutting to fit, if necessary), the cheese, apple and remaining bread slices.

2   In large bowl, beat eggs, milk, vanilla, the remaining 2 tablespoons brown sugar and the cinnamon with whisk until well blended. Pour evenly over bread mixture. Press bread down into egg mixture to coat. Cover tightly with foil; refrigerate 6 hours or overnight.

3   Heat oven to 350°F. Bake strata covered 25 minutes. Uncover; bake 30 to 35 minutes longer or until golden brown and knife inserted in center comes out clean. Let stand 10 minutes. Invert onto serving platter. Serve with syrup.

**1 Serving:** Calories 520; Total Fat 24g (Saturated Fat 12g, Trans Fat 0.5g); Cholesterol 240mg; Sodium 610mg; Total Carbohydrate 59g (Dietary Fiber 2g); Protein 19g **Exchanges:** 1½ Starch, 2½ Other Carbohydrate, 1 Medium-Fat Meat, 1 High-Fat Meat, 2 Fat **Carbohydrate Choices:** 4

## Festive Touch
Garnish this decadent breakfast bake with a dollop of whipped cream, apple slices and a sprinkling of cinnamon.

## Kitchen Secrets
Baking apples such as Braeburn and Honeycrisp work best for the success of this recipe. Leave the peel on or peel it—it's up to you.

# Stuffed Churro French Toast

**PREP TIME:** 25 Minutes   **START TO FINISH:** 25 Minutes   *8 servings*

### GLAZE
- 3 oz (from 8-oz package) cream cheese, softened
- 3 tablespoons milk
- About 1 cup powdered sugar

### TOPPING
- ½ cup granulated sugar
- 1 teaspoon ground cinnamon

### FRENCH TOAST
- 5 oz (from 8-oz package) cream cheese, softened
- 2 tablespoons granulated sugar
- ½ teaspoon vanilla
- 16 slices white sandwich bread
- ½ cup milk
- 3 eggs

**1** In small bowl, mix 3 oz cream cheese, 3 tablespoons milk and enough powdered sugar until mixture is thin enough to drizzle. Cover; set aside.

**2** In shallow bowl or pie plate, stir together ½ cup granulated sugar and the cinnamon; set aside.

**3** In medium bowl, mix 5 oz cream cheese, 2 tablespoons granulated sugar and the vanilla until smooth.

**4** With rolling pin, gently flatten each slice of bread to ¼ inch thick. Spread 1 heaping tablespoon cream cheese mixture onto 8 slices of the bread; top with remaining 8 slices bread.

**5** Spray griddle or 12-inch skillet with cooking spray; heat to medium heat (350°F). In medium bowl, beat ½ cup milk and the eggs with whisk until well blended. Dip bread into egg mixture. Cook on hot griddle 3 to 4 minutes, turning once, until golden brown.

**6** Place French toast, one slice at a time, in bowl of cinnamon-sugar; coat both sides and shake off excess. Cut diagonally in half; drizzle with glaze.

**1 Serving:** Calories 390; Total Fat 14g (Saturated Fat 7g, Trans Fat 0g); Cholesterol 105mg; Sodium 380mg; Total Carbohydrate 58g (Dietary Fiber 1g); Protein 9g **Exchanges:** 2 Starch, 2 Other Carbohydrate, ½ Medium-Fat Meat, 2 Fat **Carbohydrate Choices:** 4

### Make-Ahead Magic
**Save time in the morning by assembling part of this recipe the night before. Make the glaze, cover tightly and refrigerate until ready to serve. Stir in an extra teaspoon of milk, if needed, until drizzling consistency.**

# Creative French Toast and Omelets

**Whether you're expecting overnight guests, hosting a holiday brunch or just wanting to raise your sleepyheads with a fun breakfast treat, French toast and omelets are great options.**

## New French Toast Trimmings

Look for the delicious new takes on French toast in this chapter, or try these delicious ideas to change up regular French toast:

**Bacon and Jam:** Top French toast with a slice or two of crisply cooked bacon and a spoonful of raspberry or apricot preserves. Sprinkle with powdered sugar, if desired.

**Blueberry-Lemon Cream Cheese:** Mix 3 ounces of softened cream cheese with 1 tablespoon of powdered sugar and ½ teaspoon of grated lemon peel. Add a teaspoon of milk at a time until drizzling consistency. Drizzle over French toast; top with blueberries.

**Caramel-Apple:** Top French toast with slices of apple and a drizzle of warm caramel sauce.

**Chocolate-Banana:** Spread a tablespoonful of chocolate-hazelnut spread on one piece of French toast. Top with banana slices and another piece of French toast.

## Omelet Feasts

Omelets are a fun, interactive way to entertain guests! When serving a crowd, the trick is being prepared. Have all the ingredients prepped ahead of time and the utensils ready to go.

**Basic Omelet:** For each omelet, beat 2 eggs in the bowl until fluffy. Add salt and pepper to taste. Heat 2 teaspoons of butter in an 8-inch pan over medium-high heat until melted and sizzling. Quickly pour eggs into pan, swirling pan to allow uncooked egg to get underneath and for eggs to thicken. Fill with desired fillings. Fold edges of eggs over filling. Flip omelet over as you place it on a dinner plate.

## Omelet Fillings:

Customize your omelets with these filling ideas.

### HERBS

Add 1 to 2 tablespoons fresh or ¼ to ½ teaspoon dried when beating the eggs.

Basil

Cilantro

Oregano

Parsley

### VEGGIES AND SAVORY TOPPINGS

Sautéed fresh veggies such as chopped onions, bell peppers, broccoli, or greens or sliced mushrooms

Chopped fresh avocados, tomatoes or green onions

Sliced olives, chopped roasted red bell peppers, drained tapenade or capers, or pesto

### MEATS AND CHEESES

Chopped pancetta, salami or luncheon meat or crisply cooked, crumbled bacon

Cooked chicken, pork or smoked ham; or cooked breakfast, Italian or chorizo sausage

Shredded cheese or crumbled cheese (such as blue cheese, feta or cotija)

### SAUCES (TOSS WITH FILLING INGREDIENTS OR DRIZZLE OVER FINISHED OMELET)

Pico de gallo, salsa or salsa verde

Bottled sauces: Thai peanut, sweet chili, coconut curry, orange-ginger or Teriyaki

Tzatziki, marinara, pizza sauce

# Impossibly Easy Maple Sausage Pie

**PREP TIME:** 15 Minutes   **START TO FINISH:** 55 Minutes

*6 servings*

- 12 oz (from 16-oz package) bulk maple pork sausage or 1 package (12 oz) maple breakfast sausage links, casings removed
- 3 green onions, thinly sliced (white and green portions separated)
- 1 cup Original Bisquick mix
- 1 cup milk
- 3 eggs
- ½ teaspoon salt
- 1 cup shredded mozzarella or Cheddar cheese (4 oz)
- 1 tablespoon real maple syrup

1 Heat oven to 375°F. Spray 9-inch glass pie plate with cooking spray.

2 In 10-inch skillet, cook sausage and white portions of onions over medium heat 7 to 8 minutes, stirring occasionally, until sausage is no longer pink; drain. Spread in pie plate.

3 In medium bowl, stir Bisquick mix, milk, eggs and salt until blended. Stir in cheese. Pour into pie plate.

4 Bake 30 to 35 minutes or until knife inserted in center comes out clean. Let stand 5 minutes. Drizzle with syrup; top with green portions of onions.

**1 Serving:** Calories 340; Total Fat 20g (Saturated Fat 7g, Trans Fat 0g); Cholesterol 140mg; Sodium 870mg; Total Carbohydrate 21g (Dietary Fiber 0g); Protein 18g **Exchanges:** 1½ Other Carbohydrate, ½ Medium-Fat Meat, 2 High-Fat Meat, ½ Fat **Carbohydrate Choices:** 1½

**Festive Touch** Cut the pie into small squares for a fun appetizer-size brunch option.

# Smoked Gouda Grits and Egg Bake

**PREP TIME:** 35 Minutes   **START TO FINISH:** 1 Hour 35 Minutes

*8 servings*

- 4 cups milk
- 1½ teaspoons salt
- 1 cup uncooked stone-ground grits
- ½ cup unsalted butter, cut into pieces
- 6 oz smoked Gouda cheese, shredded (1½ cups)
- 1 lb bulk sage pork sausage
- 10 eggs
- 1 cup whipping cream
- 2 tablespoons chopped fresh parsley
- 6 oz white Cheddar cheese, shredded (1½ cups)
  Additional chopped fresh parsley, if desired

1 In 3-quart saucepan, heat milk and salt just to boiling over medium-high heat. Gradually stir in grits. Reduce heat; cook uncovered 20 minutes, stirring frequently, until thickened. Add butter and Gouda cheese; stir until melted. Remove from heat.

2 Lightly spray 3-quart casserole with cooking spray. Pour grits mixture into casserole. Cool 20 minutes.

3 Meanwhile, in 10-inch skillet, cook sausage over medium-high heat 5 to 7 minutes, stirring occasionally, until no longer pink. Drain on paper towels.

4 Heat oven to 350°F. In large bowl, slightly beat eggs with whisk; stir in whipping cream, 2 tablespoons parsley, 1 cup of the Cheddar cheese and the cooked sausage. Pour over grits mixture. Top with remaining ½ cup Cheddar cheese.

5 Bake uncovered 35 to 40 minutes or until set and edges are lightly browned. Sprinkle with additional parsley.

**1 Serving:** Calories 770; Total Fat 59g (Saturated Fat 30g, Trans Fat 0g); Cholesterol 0mg; Sodium 1260mg; Total Carbohydrate 26g (Dietary Fiber 0g); Protein 33g **Exchanges:** 1 Starch, ½ Low-Fat Milk, 1 Medium-Fat Meat, 2½ High-Fat Meat, 6 Fat **Carbohydrate Choices:** 1½

**Festive Touch** You can bake this casserole in 8 (12-oz) individual casserole dishes. Make as directed except: in Step 2, divide grits mixture evenly among casserole dishes. Cool 10 minutes. In Step 4, divide egg mixture evenly over grits in casseroles. Bake 15 to 20 minutes.

# Ham-and-Cheese Croissant Casserole

**PREP TIME:** 15 Minutes   **START TO FINISH:** 9 Hours 30 Minutes   *6 servings*

3 large croissants (5 inch)

1 package (8 oz) chopped
   cooked ham

1¼ cups shredded Swiss cheese
   (5 oz)

6 eggs

1 cup half-and-half

2 tablespoons honey

1 tablespoon ground mustard

½ teaspoon salt

½ teaspoon pepper

¼ teaspoon ground nutmeg,
   if desired

1 Spray 10-inch glass deep-dish pie plate with cooking spray. Cut croissants in half lengthwise; cut each half into 5 pieces. Place pieces in pie plate. Sprinkle with ham and cheese.

2 In large bowl, beat eggs, half-and-half, honey, mustard, salt, pepper and nutmeg with whisk.

3 Pour egg mixture over ingredients in pie plate; press croissant pieces into egg mixture to moisten completely. Cover tightly with foil; refrigerate at least 8 hours but no longer than 24 hours.

4 Heat oven to 325°F. Bake casserole covered 35 minutes. Uncover; bake 25 to 30 minutes longer or until knife inserted in center comes out clean. Let stand 10 minutes before serving.

**1 Serving:** Calories 450; Total Fat 27g (Saturated Fat 15g, Trans Fat 0g); Cholesterol 0mg; Sodium 900mg; Total Carbohydrate 26g (Dietary Fiber 1g); Protein 22g **Exchanges:** 1 Starch, 1 Other Carbohydrate, 2 Medium-Fat Meat, 1 High-Fat Meat, 2½ Fat **Carbohydrate Choices:** 2

**Festive Touch** **For a bit of holiday color and a great flavor combination, serve this savory egg dish with a spoonful of salsa on the side.**

# Ranchero Egg Bake

**PREP TIME:** 15 Minutes  **START TO FINISH:** 9 Hours
*8 servings*

- 12 eggs
- 1½ cups milk
- ½ teaspoon ground cumin
- ½ teaspoon freshly ground pepper
- 2 cups seasoned croutons
- 1 can (15 oz) black beans, drained, rinsed
- 2 cans (4.5 oz each) chopped green chiles
- 1 ring (13 to 14 oz) fully cooked turkey smoked sausage, cut into ¼-inch slices
- 1½ cups shredded sharp Cheddar cheese (6 oz)
- ¼ cup sliced green onions (4 medium)
- 1 cup sour cream
- ¼ cup chopped fresh cilantro
- ¾ cup quartered cherry tomatoes

1  Spray 13x9-inch (3-quart) glass baking dish with cooking spray. In large bowl, beat eggs, milk, cumin and pepper with whisk. Stir in croutons, beans, chiles, sausage and cheese. Pour into baking dish. Cover; refrigerate 8 hours or overnight.

2  Heat oven to 350°F. Uncover baking dish; bake 45 minutes or until set. Sprinkle onions over top. Garnish with sour cream, cilantro and tomatoes.

**1 Serving:** Calories 450; Total Fat 28g (Saturated Fat 12g, Trans Fat 1g); Cholesterol 345mg; Sodium 1030mg; Total Carbohydrate 22g (Dietary Fiber 4g); Protein 27g **Exchanges:** 1 Starch, ½ Other Carbohydrate, 1½ Lean Meat, 1½ Medium-Fat Meat, ½ High-Fat Meat, 2½ Fat **Carbohydrate Choices:** 1½

**Festive Touch** **If you like, serve salsa on the side, for an extra layer of flavor.**

**Make-Ahead Magic** **You can assemble the Mexican Breakfast Casserole, right, as directed the night before; cover and refrigerate. In the morning, simply uncover and pop it in the oven. You may need to add an extra 5 to 10 minutes to the bake time.**

# Mexican Breakfast Casserole

**PREP TIME:** 20 Minutes  **START TO FINISH:** 1 Hour 10 Minutes
*12 servings*

- 1 bag (20 oz) refrigerated shredded hash brown potatoes
- 1 package (1 oz) taco seasoning mix
- 1 lb bulk turkey or pork breakfast sausage
- 1 medium onion, chopped (½ cup)
- 12 eggs
- 2 cups shredded Cheddar cheese (8 oz)
- ¼ cup milk
- ½ teaspoon salt
- ¼ teaspoon pepper
- 1½ cups chunky-style salsa

1  Heat oven to 350°F. Spray 13x9-inch (3-quart) glass baking dish or 3-quart casserole with cooking spray.

2  In large bowl, toss potatoes and 1 tablespoon of the taco seasoning mix until evenly coated. Pat in baking dish.

3  Spray 10 inch skillet with cooking spray. Add the sausage and onion; cook over medium-high heat 5 to 7 minutes, stirring occasionally, until sausage is no longer pink. Drain.

4  In same large bowl, beat eggs, cheese, milk, salt, pepper and remaining taco seasoning mix with whisk until well blended. Stir in sausage mixture and salsa. Carefully pour over potatoes in baking dish.

5  Bake uncovered about 40 minutes or until eggs are set in center. Let stand 10 minutes before serving.

**1 Serving:** Calories 280; Total Fat 16g (Saturated Fat 7g, Trans Fat 0g); Cholesterol 240mg; Sodium 980mg; Total Carbohydrate 15g (Dietary Fiber 1g); Protein 21g **Exchanges:** ½ Starch, ½ Low-Fat Milk, 2 Lean Meat, 1½ Fat **Carbohydrate Choices:** 1

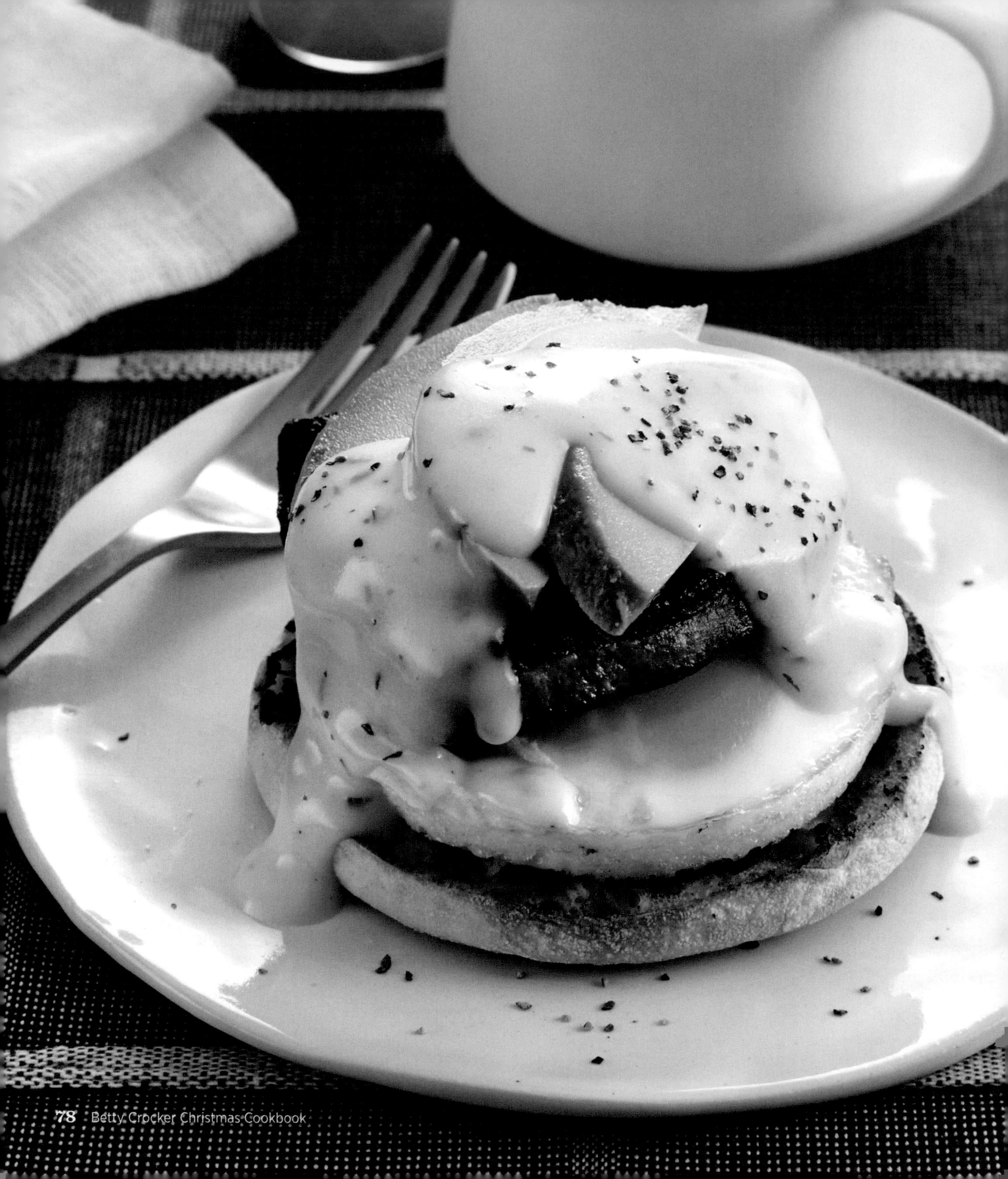

# Winter Fruit Pasta Salad

**PREP TIME:** 20 Minutes **START TO FINISH:** 50 Minutes
*8 servings*

### PASTA SALAD

- 1 cup uncooked small pasta shells (4 oz)
- 1 medium crisp red apple (such as Braeburn, Cortland or Gala), chopped (1¼ cups)
- 1 medium pear, chopped (1¼ cups)
- 4 medium green onions, chopped (¼ cup)
- ¼ cup chopped pecans
- ¼ cup dried cranberries

### DRESSING

- ⅓ cup mayonnaise or salad dressing
- 3 tablespoons orange marmalade
- ½ teaspoon dried marjoram leaves
- ¼ teaspoon salt

1 Cook and drain pasta as directed on package. Rinse with cold water; drain.

2 In large glass or plastic bowl, mix pasta, apple, pear, onions, pecans and cranberries. In small bowl, mix dressing ingredients; stir into pasta mixture.

3 Cover; refrigerate at least 30 minutes until chilled.

**1 Serving:** Calories 210; Total Fat 10g (Saturated Fat 1.5g, Trans Fat 0g); Cholesterol 0mg; Sodium 190mg; Total Carbohydrate 28g (Dietary Fiber 3g); Protein 3g **Exchanges:** 1 Starch, ½ Fruit, ½ Other Carbohydrate, 2 Fat **Carbohydrate Choices:** 2

## Make-Ahead Magic You can prep parts of this recipe up to 24 hours in advance if you like. Cook and drain the pasta as directed, and toss with a teaspoon or two of vegetable oil; cover and refrigerate. Mix the dressing ingredients; cover and refrigerate until you are ready to put the salad together.

## Festive Touch Consider the "pastabilities"! Instead of small shells, use fun holiday pasta shapes such as trees, stars, bells or ornaments.

---

# Strawberry-Marshmallow Fruit Dip

**PREP TIME:** 15 Minutes **START TO FINISH:** 1 Hour 15 Minutes
*15 servings*

- 4 oz (from 8-oz package) ⅓-less-fat cream cheese (Neufchâtel), softened
- 1 cup marshmallow creme
- 1 container (6 oz) fat-free Greek strawberry yogurt
- ½ cup chopped strawberries
- 15 whole strawberries, cut lengthwise in half
- 30 pieces cut-up melon
- 30 grapes

1 In medium bowl, beat cream cheese, marshmallow creme, yogurt and chopped strawberries with electric mixer on high speed until smooth.

2 Cover; refrigerate at least 1 hour. Serve dip with fruit.

**1 Serving (2 Tablespoons Dip and 6 Pieces Fruit):** Calories 60; Total Fat 1g (Saturated Fat 0.5g, Trans Fat 0g); Cholesterol 0mg; Sodium 50mg; Total Carbohydrate 12g (Dietary Fiber 0g); Protein 1g **Exchanges:** ½ Fruit, ½ Other Carbohydrate **Carbohydrate Choices:** 1

## Make-Ahead Magic You can make the dip up to 24 hours ahead; cover and refrigerate. Stir before serving.

# Mains & Side Dishes

# Roast Turkey with Fresh Thyme Rub and Maple Glaze

**PREP TIME:** 20 Minutes    **START TO FINISH:** 4 Hours 20 Minutes    *12 servings*

1 whole turkey (12 lb), thawed
  if frozen
2 tablespoons butter
3 tablespoons chopped fresh
  thyme leaves
1 teaspoon salt
½ teaspoon ground allspice
½ teaspoon pepper
1 tablespoon olive oil
2 tablespoons real maple
  or maple-flavored syrup

**1** Heat oven to 325°F. Discard giblets and neck, or reserve for another use. Rinse turkey inside and out with cold water; pat dry with paper towels.

**2** Fold wings across back of turkey so tips are touching. If turkey doesn't have an ovenproof plastic leg band holding legs together, tuck legs under band of skin at tail (if present); or tie legs together with kitchen string, then tie to tail if desired. Place turkey, breast side up, on rack in large roasting pan. Melt 1 tablespoon of the butter; brush over turkey.

**3** In small bowl, mix thyme, salt, allspice, pepper and oil. Rub mixture over turkey. Insert ovenproof meat thermometer into turkey so tip is in thickest part of inside thigh and does not touch bone.

**4** Roast uncovered 3 hours to 3 hours 45 minutes. After roasting about 2 hours, cut band of skin or remove tie holding legs, if desired, to allow insides of thighs to cook thoroughly and evenly. Place tent of foil loosely over turkey to prevent excessive browning.

**5** Melt remaining 1 tablespoon butter; mix with syrup. Brush half of the mixture over turkey about 20 minutes before completely cooked. Brush again about 10 minutes before completely cooked.

**6** Turkey is done when thermometer reads 165°F and legs move easily when lifted or twisted. Place turkey on warm platter; cover with foil to keep warm. Let stand 15 minutes for easiest carving.

**1 Serving:** Calories 360; Total Fat 14g (Saturated Fat 4.5g, Trans Fat 0g); Cholesterol 230mg; Sodium 430mg; Total Carbohydrate 2g (Dietary Fiber 0g); Protein 57g **Exchanges:** 8 Very Lean Meat, 2 Fat **Carbohydrate Choices:** 0

## Festive Touch
Sprigs of fresh thyme make an easy yet pretty garnish around your bird. The fresh fragrance is a beautiful bonus! Rainier cherries and apricot slices are other pretty choices.

# Doneness and Food Safety

For optimal food safety and even doneness, the USDA recommends cooking stuffing separately. However, if you choose to stuff poultry or game birds, it's necessary to use an accurate food thermometer to make sure the center of the stuffing reaches a safe minimum temperature of 165°F. Cooking home-stuffed poultry or game birds is riskier than cooking those that are not stuffed. Even if the poultry or game bird itself has reached the safe minimum internal temperature of 165°F, the stuffing may not have reached the same temperature. Bacteria can survive in stuffing that has not reached 165°F, possibly resulting in foodborne illness. Do not stuff poultry or game birds that will be grilled, smoked, fried or microwaved because the center will never get hot enough to be safe.

# Beer- and Rosemary-Roasted Turkey

**PREP TIME:** 25 Minutes  **START TO FINISH:** 3 Hours 40 Minutes  *12 servings*

**TURKEY**

1 whole turkey (12 lb), thawed
   if frozen*

¼ cup butter, melted

2 tablespoons Dijon mustard

1 tablespoon chopped fresh
   or 1 teaspoon dried
   rosemary leaves

1 teaspoon salt

½ teaspoon pepper

1 can or bottle (12 oz) dark beer

**BEER GRAVY**

½ cup cold water

¼ cup all-purpose flour

1 Heat oven to 325°F. Discard giblets and neck, or reserve for another use. Rinse turkey inside and out with cold water; pat dry with paper towels. Fasten neck skin to back of turkey with skewer. Fold wings across back of turkey so tips are touching. Place turkey, breast side up, in large roasting pan.

2 In medium microwavable bowl, stir together butter, mustard, rosemary, salt, pepper and beer. Microwave uncovered on High 1 minute to 1 minute 30 seconds, stirring after 30 seconds, until well mixed. Brush about one-third of mixture evenly over surface of turkey. If turkey doesn't have an ovenproof plastic leg band holding legs together, tuck legs under band of skin at tail (if present); or tie legs together with kitchen string, then tie to tail if desired. Insert ovenproof meat thermometer so tip is in thickest part of inside thigh and does not touch bone.

3 Roast uncovered 2 hours 30 minutes to 3 hours, brushing with additional beer mixture and pan juices every 30 minutes. Turkey is done when thermometer reads 165°F and drumsticks move easily when lifted or twisted. Place tent of foil loosely over turkey to prevent excessive browning.

4 Place turkey on warm platter; cover with foil to keep warm. Let stand 15 minutes for easiest carving.

5 Meanwhile, measure drippings and add enough water to make 2 cups. In 2-quart saucepan, heat drippings to boiling. In small bowl, mix cold water and flour until smooth. Stir flour mixture into boiling drippings. Cook 2 to 3 minutes, stirring constantly, until gravy is thickened and bubbly.

*See Doneness and Food Safety, page 86.

**1 Serving:** Calories 380; Total Fat 15g (Saturated Fat 5g, Trans Fat 0g); Cholesterol 235mg; Sodium 1190mg; Total Carbohydrate 2g (Dietary Fiber 0g); Protein 58g **Exchanges:** 8 Very Lean Meat, 2 Fat **Carbohydrate Choices:** 0

## Festive Touch  For a colorful garnish, arrange sliced onion, pattypan squash and carrots around turkey on serving platter; tuck in sprigs of fresh rosemary.

# Roasted Brined Duck with Cranberry-Chipotle Glaze

**PREP TIME:** 25 Minutes   **START TO FINISH:** 15 Hours 20 Minutes   *4 servings*

**BRINE**

- 6 cups cold water
- 2 cups cider vinegar
- 3 tablespoons dried sage leaves
- 1 tablespoon whole peppercorns
- 1 bulb garlic, cloves separated, peeled and smashed
- 1 cup boiling water
- ¾ cup coarse (kosher or sea) salt
- ¾ cup packed brown sugar

**DUCK**

- 1 whole duckling (4 to 6 lb), thawed if frozen

**GLAZE**

- 1 can (14 oz) jellied cranberry sauce
- ¼ cup cider vinegar
- 3 to 4 chipotle chiles in adobo sauce (from 7-oz can), finely chopped

1   Place 2-gallon resealable food-storage plastic bag in stockpot or very large bowl. Add cold water, 2 cups vinegar, the sage, peppercorns and garlic to the bag.

2   In medium bowl, stir together 1 cup boiling water, the salt and brown sugar until dissolved. Pour into vinegar mixture.

3   Remove excess fat from body cavity and neck of duck. Rinse inside and out under cool running water. With large sharp fork, prick the skin all over at an angle, being careful not to pierce meat. Carefully place duck in brine, making sure entire duck is submerged (weigh it down with a plate, if necessary). Cover; refrigerate at least 12 hours but no longer than 24 hours.

4   Heat oven to 350°F. Remove duck from brine; discard brine. Rinse duck inside and out and pat dry. Place duck, breast side up, on rack in large roasting pan. Tie legs with kitchen string. Insert ovenproof meat thermometer so tip is in thickest part of inside thigh and does not touch bone.

5   Roast 1 hour 40 minutes. Carefully remove duck from pan; pour drippings and cooking juices from pan into large heatproof bowl or container. Discard or save for another use. Return duck to rack in roasting pan.

6   In medium bowl, stir together cranberry sauce, ¼ cup vinegar and the chiles; reserve half of the glaze for serving. Brush about ¼ cup of the remaining glaze over duck.

7   Roast 45 minutes to 1 hour longer, brushing with glaze every 10 minutes, until meat thermometer reads 165°F. Place duck on warm serving platter. Cover; let stand 15 minutes for easiest carving. Heat reserved glaze until warm; serve with duck.

**1 Serving:** Calories 350; Total Fat 5g (Saturated Fat 1.5g, Trans Fat 0g); Cholesterol 125mg; Sodium 2530mg; Total Carbohydrate 45g (Dietary Fiber 2g); Protein 31g **Exchanges:** 3 Other Carbohydrate, 4½ Very Lean Meat, ½ Fat **Carbohydrate Choices:** 3

## Festive Touch
For simple, jolly garnishes, arrange fresh sage leaves and whole crab apples around the duck on the platter.

## Kitchen Secrets
Keep the flavorful duck-fat drippings for adding flavor to other dishes. Freeze small amounts in ice cube trays; transfer to a resealable freezer plastic bag, and keep frozen 2 to 3 months. Try stirring a small amount into steamed vegetables, or add it to mashed potatoes instead of butter. Rub it on poultry before roasting to make the skin crisp, or use a little to sear meat with a secret depth of flavor.

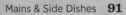

# Turkey Breast with Cranberry-Orange Glaze

**PREP TIME:** 20 Minutes  **START TO FINISH:** 3 Hours
20 Minutes  *6 servings*

    1  cup cranberry juice cocktail
    ⅓  to ½ cup orange marmalade
    2  tablespoons honey
    ⅓  cup butter
    1  teaspoon salt
    1  whole turkey breast (4½ to 5 lb)

1  Heat oven to 325°F. Line roasting pan with foil;
   spray rack with cooking spray.

2  In 1-quart saucepan, heat cranberry juice to boiling.
   Cook 10 minutes or until reduced by half. Stir in
   marmalade, honey, butter and salt. Cook over
   medium heat 2 minutes or until butter is melted,
   stirring occasionally.

3  Place turkey, skin side up, on rack in pan. Brush
   turkey with half of the glaze. Insert ovenproof meat
   thermometer so tip is in thickest part of breast and
   does not touch bone.

4  Bake 1 hour. Uncover; brush with glaze. Bake 1 hour
   45 minutes longer, brushing with remaining glaze
   every 30 minutes, until thermometer reads 165°F.
   Place tent of foil loosely over turkey to prevent
   excessive browning. Let stand 15 minutes for
   easiest carving.

**1 Serving:** Calories 500; Total Fat 12g (Saturated Fat 7g, Trans Fat 0mg);
Cholesterol 0mg; Sodium 630mg; Total Carbohydrate 29g (Dietary Fiber 0g);
Protein 66g **Exchanges:** 2 Other Carbohydrate, 9½ Very Lean Meat, 2 Fat
**Carbohydrate Choices:** 2

### Festive Touch  For a beautiful presentation,
adorn the serving platter with an assortment of
mandarin oranges, cranberries and fresh bay leaves.

### Festive Touch  Looking for a fresh take on a
holiday meal? Pair this savory pork roast with Creamy
Italian Oven Polenta (page 121) and Holiday Aloo Gobi
(page 118). Or keep it simple with mashed potatoes
and steamed carrots.

# Roast Pork Loin with Crumb Crust

**PREP TIME:** 10 Minutes  **START TO FINISH:** 1 Hour
30 Minutes  *16 servings*

    1  boneless pork loin roast (4 lb)
    2  teaspoons salt
    1  teaspoon pepper
    1  cup unseasoned dry bread crumbs
    ¼  cup olive oil
    2  tablespoons finely chopped fresh parsley
    2  tablespoons finely chopped garlic
    2  tablespoons coarse-grained mustard

1  Heat oven to 425°F. Line roasting pan with foil.
   Sprinkle pork with salt and pepper. Place pork,
   fat side up, in pan.

2  In small bowl, stir together bread crumbs, oil,
   parsley, garlic and mustard; press mixture onto top
   of pork.

3  Roast uncovered 15 minutes; cover loosely with
   foil. Roast 1 hour longer or until meat thermometer
   inserted into center of pork reads 145°F. Let stand
   3 minutes before slicing.

**1 Serving:** Calories 240; Total Fat 13g (Saturated Fat 3.5g, Trans Fat 0g);
Cholesterol 70mg; Sodium 430mg; Total Carbohydrate 5g (Dietary Fiber 0g);
Protein 26g **Exchanges:** ½ Other Carbohydrate, 4 Very Lean Meat, 2 Fat
**Carbohydrate Choices:** ½

# Cider-Brined Pork Loin Roast

**PREP TIME:** 30 Minutes  **START TO FINISH:** 13 Hours 25 Minutes  *12 servings*

2 quarts water
1 cup packed brown sugar
½ cup coarse (kosher) salt
4 cloves garlic, crushed
2 sprigs fresh rosemary
2 quarts apple cider
1 boneless pork loin roast (3 lb)
1 tablespoon vegetable oil
2¼ teaspoons coarse ground black pepper
2 teaspoons finely chopped fresh rosemary leaves
2 cups applesauce
½ cup dry white wine or chicken broth
⅓ cup golden raisins
1 clove garlic, finely chopped
1 tablespoon packed brown sugar
⅛ teaspoon kosher (coarse) salt

1  In nonreactive 6- to 8-quart stockpot, stir together 1 quart of the water, 1 cup brown sugar, ½ cup salt, the crushed garlic and rosemary sprigs. Heat to boiling, stirring until brown sugar and salt are dissolved. Stir in cider and remaining 1 quart water; cool to room temperature. Add pork. Cover; refrigerate at least 12 hours but no longer than 48 hours.

2  Heat oven to 375°F. Spray broiler pan with cooking spray. Remove pork from brine; discard brine. Pat pork dry with paper towels. Place pork on broiler pan; brush pork with oil. Sprinkle with 2 teaspoons of the pepper and 1 teaspoon of the chopped rosemary.

3  Bake uncovered 40 to 50 minutes or until thermometer inserted into center of pork reads 145°F.* Cover loosely with foil; let stand at least 3 minutes.

4  Meanwhile, in 2-quart saucepan, mix applesauce, wine, raisins, the chopped garlic, 1 tablespoon brown sugar, ⅛ teaspoon salt, the remaining ¼ teaspoon pepper and remaining 1 teaspoon chopped rosemary. Cook over medium heat 20 minutes, stirring occasionally, until raisins are plump and sauce is thickened. Serve sauce with pork.

*Pork only needs to roast to 145°F. If you prefer it more done, you can roast it to 160°F. Just allow for a few extra minutes per pound of roasting time in your overall meal game plan.

**1 Serving:** Calories 280; Total Fat 10g (Saturated Fat 3.5g, Trans Fat 0g); Cholesterol 70mg; Sodium 1240mg; Total Carbohydrate 22g (Dietary Fiber 0g); Protein 25g **Exchanges:** 1½ Other Carbohydrate, 3½ Lean Meat **Carbohydrate Choices:** 1½

### Festive Touch All you need to dress up this pork roast for your holiday table are sprigs of fresh rosemary and some fresh cranberries.

# Spicy Cherries Jubilee Ham

**PREP TIME:** 20 Minutes **START TO FINISH:** 5 Hours 5 Minutes *16 to 20 servings*

> 1 fully cooked smoked bone-in ham (10 to 12 lb)
> 1¾ cups reduced-sodium chicken broth
> 2 jars (12 oz each) cherry preserves (2¼ cups)
> ¾ cup brandy
> ¼ cup cider vinegar
> 3 tablespoons coarse-grained mustard
> 3 tablespoons honey
> 1 tablespoon freshly ground pepper
> Additional coarse-grained mustard
> Fresh cherries and fresh sage sprigs, if desired

1 Heat oven to 275°F. Line roasting pan with foil. Remove skin from ham; trim fat to ¼-inch thickness. Make shallow cuts in fat 1 inch apart in diamond pattern. Place ham in roasting pan. Insert ovenproof meat thermometer so tip is in center of thickest part of ham and does not touch bone or rest in fat. Add broth to pan.

2 In 2-quart saucepan, stir together preserves, brandy, vinegar, 3 tablespoons mustard, the honey and pepper; heat to boiling over medium-high heat, stirring constantly. Reduce heat to medium-low; simmer 5 minutes, stirring constantly, until mixture is slightly reduced. Cover and refrigerate half of cherry mixture until serving time. Brush ham with half of the remaining cherry mixture.

3 Place pan on lowest oven rack. Bake 4 hours to 4 hours 30 minutes or until thermometer reads 140°F, brushing with remaining cherry mixture every 30 minutes. Let stand 15 minutes before slicing.

4 Serve ham with mustard and reserved cherry mixture. Garnish with cherries and sage.

**1 Serving:** Calories 390; Total Fat 10g (Saturated Fat 3g, Trans Fat 0g); Cholesterol 90mg; Sodium 2220mg; Total Carbohydrate 36g (Dietary Fiber 0g); Protein 37g **Exchanges:** 2½ Other Carbohydrate, 5 Very Lean Meat, 1½ Fat **Carbohydrate Choices:** 2½

---

**QUICK FIX**

# Baked Ham with Balsamic–Brown Sugar Glaze

**PREP TIME:** 10 Minutes **START TO FINISH:** 1 Hour 55 Minutes *10 servings*

> 1 fully cooked smoked bone-in ham (6 lb)
> 1 cup packed brown sugar
> 2 tablespoons balsamic or cider vinegar
> ½ teaspoon ground mustard

1 Heat oven to 325°F. Place ham on rack in shallow roasting pan. Insert ovenproof meat thermometer so tip is in center of thickest part of ham and does not touch bone or rest in fat.

2 Bake uncovered 1 hour 30 minutes or until thermometer reads 140°F. In small bowl, mix brown sugar, vinegar and mustard. Brush mixture over ham during last 45 minutes of baking. Cover loosely with foil; let stand 10 to 15 minutes before slicing.

**1 Serving:** Calories 320; Total Fat 9g (Saturated Fat 3g, Trans Fat 0g); Cholesterol 90mg; Sodium 2000mg; Total Carbohydrate 25g (Dietary Fiber 0g); Protein 34g **Exchanges:** 1½ Other Carbohydrate, 5 Very Lean Meat, 1½ Fat **Carbohydrate Choices:** 1½

## Festive Touch
Try a different glaze instead of the Balsamic–Brown Sugar Glaze. For *Apricot-Bourbon Glaze*, mix ½ cup apricot preserves, 2 teaspoons ground ginger and ¼ cup bourbon or pineapple juice. For a *Sweet-Spicy Glaze*, mix ½ cup honey, 2 tablespoons packed brown sugar, 1 tablespoon Sriracha sauce and 1 clove garlic, finely chopped.

## Festive Touch
For a unique and beautiful garnish, arrange fresh kumquats, figs and fresh sprigs of sage and rosemary around the ham on the serving platter.

## Kitchen Secrets
If you like, score the fat side of the ham diagonally at 1-inch intervals, cutting ¼ inch deep; score in the opposite direction to form diamond shapes.

## Kitchen Secrets
Here's how to carve a bone-in ham beautifully. Place ham, fat side up with bone facing you, on carving board or platter. Cut ham in half next to bone. Turn boneless half of ham fat side up; cut slices. Cut slices from bone-in half, cutting away from bone.

# Gorgonzola- and Mushroom-Stuffed Beef Tenderloin with Merlot Sauce

**PREP TIME:** 30 Minutes   **START TO FINISH:** 1 Hour 30 Minutes   *8 servings*

### STUFFED TENDERLOIN

- 1 beef tenderloin (2½ lb)
- 1 tablespoon butter
- 1 cup sliced fresh mushrooms (3 oz)
- 1 cup soft bread crumbs (about 1½ slices bread)
- ½ cup crumbled Gorgonzola or Roquefort cheese (2 oz)
- ¼ cup chopped fresh parsley
- 1 tablespoon olive or vegetable oil
- ¼ teaspoon coarse (kosher or sea) salt

### MERLOT SAUCE

- ½ cup currant jelly
- ½ cup Merlot, Zinfandel or nonalcoholic red wine
- ¼ cup beef broth
- 1 tablespoon butter

## Make-Ahead Magic

**Take the stress out of last-minute prep by making the sauce up to 24 hours in advance. Cover and refrigerate in a microwavable serving bowl until serving time. When ready to serve, microwave on High 30 seconds to 1 minute, stirring occasionally, until hot. (Sauce may have thickened. To thin sauce, stir in an additional 1 to 2 tablespoons of wine or beef broth if desired.)**

## Festive Touch **For an easy and seasonal garnish, arrange fresh sprigs of rosemary on the platter with the meat.**

1  Heat oven to 425°F. Place tenderloin on cutting board. With long knife, cut horizontally through long side of tenderloin, halfway up side of meat, stopping approximately ½ inch from other side. Open beef as if opening a book. Cover with plastic wrap or waxed paper. Pound beef with flat side of meat mallet or rolling pin until uniformly ¼ inch thick.

2  In 10-inch skillet, melt 1 tablespoon butter over medium-high heat. Cook mushrooms in butter, stirring occasionally, until tender and liquid has evaporated. Cool 5 minutes. Add bread crumbs, cheese and parsley; toss to combine.

3  Sprinkle bread crumb mixture over beef to within 1 inch of edges. Tightly roll up, beginning with long side. Turn small end of beef under about 6 inches so it cooks evenly. Tie with kitchen string at 1½-inch intervals. Place beef, seam side down, on rack in shallow roasting pan. Brush with oil; sprinkle with salt. Insert ovenproof meat thermometer so tip is in center of thickest part of beef.

4  Bake uncovered 30 to 40 minutes or until thermometer reads at least 140°F. Cover loosely with foil; let stand about 15 minutes or until thermometer reads 145°F.

5  Meanwhile, in 1-quart saucepan, heat sauce ingredients to boiling, stirring occasionally; reduce heat to low. Simmer uncovered 35 to 40 minutes, stirring occasionally, until sauce is slightly reduced and syrupy. Remove string from beef before slicing. Serve with sauce.

**1 Serving:** Calories 390; Total Fat 17g (Saturated Fat 7g, Trans Fat 0.5g); Cholesterol 105mg; Sodium 330mg; Total Carbohydrate 24g (Dietary Fiber 1g); Protein 34g **Exchanges:** 1½ Other Carbohydrate, 5 Lean Meat, ½ Fat **Carbohydrate Choices:** 1½

# Rosemary Prime Rib Roast

**PREP TIME:** 10 Minutes　　**START TO FINISH:** 2 Hours 30 Minutes　　*8 servings*

1　beef prime rib roast (7 to 9 lb), trimmed of fat

6　cloves garlic, finely chopped

2　teaspoons salt

2　teaspoons pepper

1　teaspoon dried rosemary leaves, crushed

2　tablespoons olive oil

1　cup sour cream

2　tablespoons lemon juice

2　tablespoons prepared horseradish

**1** Place beef on rack in shallow roasting pan. In small bowl, mix garlic, salt, pepper, rosemary and oil; rub mixture over beef. Let stand at room temperature 30 minutes.

**2** Place pan on lowest oven rack. Heat oven to 450°F. Insert ovenproof meat thermometer so tip is in thickest part of beef and does not touch bone. Roast uncovered 45 minutes. Reduce oven temperature to 350°F; roast 45 to 50 minutes longer or until desired doneness (140°F for medium-rare, 155°F for medium). Cover loosely with foil; let stand 15 minutes.

**3** In small bowl, mix sour cream, lemon juice and horseradish. Carve beef; serve with horseradish sauce.

**1 Serving:** Calories 630; Total Fat 27g (Saturated Fat 11g, Trans Fat 0g); Cholesterol 0mg; Sodium 730mg; Total Carbohydrate 3g (Dietary Fiber 0g); Protein 91g **Exchanges:** 13 Very Lean Meat, 1½ Fat **Carbohydrate Choices:** 0

## Festive Touch
The specialness of prime rib calls for equally special side dishes! Try Bacon-Thyme Duchess Potatoes (page 111) and Holiday Romaine Salad (page 132).

## Kitchen Secrets
How do you accommodate guests with a range of preferences for doneness? Poll your guests, roasting the prime rib until the center is cooked to the preference for the least-done beef (such as rare or medium-rare). Serve the ends of the roast to those who like their beef the most done and the next slices (working in toward the center of the roast) to those who like their roast a little less done. Save the center for those who like their beef the least done.

# Onion- and Pepper-Braised Brisket

**PREP TIME:** 20 Minutes  **START TO FINISH:** 3 Hours  *8 servings*

2 tablespoons olive oil

2 medium onions, cut in half, sliced

2 red or orange bell peppers, sliced

¼ cup packed brown sugar

1 package (1.1 oz) onion recipe and dip soup mix

1 bottle (12 oz) chili sauce

½ teaspoon salt

½ teaspoon pepper

1 fresh beef brisket (not corned beef) (3 lb)

Fresh rosemary sprigs, if desired

**1** Heat oven to 325°F. In 4-quart ovenproof Dutch oven, heat oil over medium heat. Cook onions and bell peppers in oil 10 minutes, stirring occasionally, until tender and beginning to brown.

**2** In medium bowl, mix brown sugar, soup mix, chili sauce, salt and pepper. Move vegetables to side of Dutch oven. Place beef, fat side up, in Dutch oven; pour sauce over beef. Spoon vegetables over beef.

**3** Cover; bake 1 hour 30 minutes. Uncover; bake 1 hour longer or until beef is tender. Cover; let stand 10 minutes. Cut beef across grain into thin slices. Serve with vegetables and any remaining pan juices. Garnish with rosemary sprigs.

**1 Serving:** Calories 400; Total Fat 16g (Saturated Fat 5g, Trans Fat 0g); Cholesterol 0mg; Sodium 1590mg; Total Carbohydrate 25g (Dietary Fiber 1g); Protein 36g **Exchanges:** 1 Other Carbohydrate, 1 Vegetable, 5 Lean Meat, ½ Fat **Carbohydrate Choices:** 1

**Festive Touch** **This savory beef dish would be delicious with Garlic-Herb Roadhouse Rolls (page 160) on the side.**

# Host a Fondue Party

Is it fondue or fun-do? You and your guests will love this unique way of enjoying a meal together. Everything is prepared ahead of time, making it easy for you to relax and enjoy the gathering with your guests. With everyone sitting together and cooking their own food, it sets a relaxed pace and atmosphere for the evening, where great conversations can happen. It might just become a holiday tradition!

## Setting the Stage

- Plan what you are going to serve, and enlist the help of guests to provide something for the meal if you wish. For an appetizer/dessert fondue party, choose Cheese Fondue (page 16) and Spiced Rum–White Chocolate Fondue (page 251), or turn it into an entire meal by adding Herbed IPA Fondue (page 102) and a green salad.

- Gather fondue pots from friends and neighbors. Have one fondue pot for every four to six guests for each type of fondue served. Electric fondue pots are the easiest for controlling the heat. As cold food is added and then gets cooking, you can quickly adjust the controls to maintain the correct cooking temperature.

- Set the table using both regular silverware and two fondue forks (of the same color) per person. Fondue forks generally have colored areas on the handles so that each guest can tell which forks are theirs when in the pots.

- Use fondue plates that have compartments to keep uncooked and cooked foods separate, or provide small bowls or plates near each place setting for uncooked meat, leaving the dinner plate for cooked food.

- Cut up all foods for the fondue in advance. Prep all the ingredients for the fondue mixture or serve-with sauces.

- Have the fondue pots in place and ready to fill when guests arrive. Take care to avoid burns by securing cords so that guests won't accidentally trip over them on the way to the table or pull on them when seated.

## As Guests Arrive

- Offer your guests a beverage and then put them to work! They'll quickly get into the interactive nature of the evening when you have them fill water glasses, open wine or carry food to the table.

- Have a few competitive guests? If you're making cheese fondue for eight to twelve guests, have two guests each make a pot of it at the table and vote during the evening on which is better!

- When it's time for dessert, clear the other dishes and fondue from the table and start fresh with clean plates, silverware and fondue forks.

## Fun-Do Time

- As guests are seated, explain how each fondue works, which foods to cook in each fondue and what sauces go well with the cooked foods. For example, veggies can be cooked in the Herbed IPA Fondue (page 102) and then dunked in the Cheese Fondue (page 16) before eating!

- Have everyone designate one fondue fork for each type of fondue.

- Share joy not germs: once food is cooked, use regular forks to eat the food.

- Fondue folklore says that if you lose a piece of food in a fondue, then you have to kiss the person next to you!

# Herbed IPA Fondue

**PREP TIME:** 25 Minutes    **START TO FINISH:** 2 Hours 35 Minutes    *4 servings*

### ZESTY SOUR CREAM SAUCE

- ½ cup sour cream
- ¼ cup mayonnaise
- 1 tablespoon chopped fresh chives
- 1 tablespoon Dijon mustard
- 1½ teaspoons prepared horseradish

### DIPPERS AND SEASONING

- ¾ lb boneless beef sirloin steak, cut into 1-inch cubes
- ¾ lb boneless skinless chicken breasts, cut into 1-inch cubes
- 2 teaspoons dried parsley leaves
- 1½ teaspoons onion powder
- 1½ teaspoons garlic-pepper blend
- 1 teaspoon packed brown sugar
- ½ teaspoon salt
- ½ teaspoon dried thyme leaves
- ¼ to ½ teaspoon crushed red pepper flakes
- 4 cups bite-size fresh vegetables (such as bell peppers, mushrooms, onions, and zucchini)

### FONDUE

- 1 carton (32 oz) chicken broth (4 cups)
- 1 bottle (12 oz) IPA beer

**1** In small bowl, stir together sauce ingredients. Cover; refrigerate at least 2 hours to blend flavors.

**2** Place beef and chicken in separate 1-quart resealable food-storage plastic bags. In small bowl, mix parsley, onion powder, garlic-pepper blend, brown sugar, salt, thyme and pepper flakes. Sprinkle 2 tablespoons of the mixture over beef; sprinkle remaining mixture over chicken. Seal bags; shake to coat meat with seasoning. Let stand 10 minutes.

**3** In fondue pot, heat broth and beer to simmering. Using fondue forks, dip meat and vegetables into simmering broth to cook, adjusting temperature as necessary. Cook 2 to 3 minutes or until beef is desired doneness, chicken is no longer pink in center and vegetables are crisp-tender. Serve with sauce.

**1 Serving:** Calories 420; Total Fat 23g (Saturated Fat 7g, Trans Fat 0g); Cholesterol 125mg; Sodium 1530mg; Total Carbohydrate 11g (Dietary Fiber 3g); Protein 42g **Carbohydrate Choices:** 1

## Make-Ahead Magic
Get a jumpstart on this fondue. The Zesty Sour Cream Sauce can be made a day ahead. And the beef and chicken can be coated with the seasoning and refrigerated up to 24 hours before cooking.

## Festive Touch
For a special treat and melt-in-your-mouth tenderness, use beef tenderloin—the choicest, most tender cut of beef.

# Root Vegetable Pot Roast

**PREP TIME:** 25 Minutes   **START TO FINISH:** 8 Hours 25 Minutes   *8 servings*

1 lb parsnips, peeled, cut into 2-inch pieces

1 lb turnips, peeled, cut into wedges

1 lb carrots, cut into 2-inch pieces

1 medium red onion, cut into wedges

3 cloves garlic, finely chopped

1 tablespoon olive oil

1 boneless beef chuck roast (3 to 4 lb)

1½ teaspoons salt

½ teaspoon freshly ground pepper

1 cup beef broth

½ cup dry red wine or additional beef broth

¼ cup tomato paste

Chopped fresh parsley, if desired

1 Spray 5- to 6-quart slow cooker with cooking spray. In slow cooker, stir together parsnips, turnips, carrots, onion and garlic.

2 In 12-inch skillet, heat oil over medium-high heat. Sprinkle beef with salt and pepper; add to skillet. Cook until browned on all sides. Place beef on vegetables in slow cooker.

3 In medium bowl, stir together broth, wine and tomato paste with whisk. Pour over beef.

4 Cover; cook on Low heat setting 8 to 10 hours or until beef is very tender. Serve beef with vegetables and cooking liquid. Garnish with parsley.

**1 Serving:** Calories 500; Total Fat 27g (Saturated Fat 10g, Trans Fat 0g); Cholesterol 0mg; Sodium 720mg; Total Carbohydrate 23g (Dietary Fiber 6g); Protein 40g **Exchanges:** 1 Starch, 2 Vegetable, 5 Medium-Fat Meat, ½ Fat **Carbohydrate Choices:** 1

## Festive Touch
Cheesy Herb–Hash Brown Cups (page 113) would make a great match for this satisfying beef dish.

## Kitchen Secrets
This fix-it-and-forget-it main dish is a great choice if you need oven space for other dishes or if you need some time to focus on other dishes for your holiday meal.

# Salmon with Cranberry-Pistachio Sauce

PREP TIME: 40 Minutes   START TO FINISH: 40 Minutes   *8 servings*

## CRANBERRY-PISTACHIO SAUCE

1 lb fresh cranberries

1 cup sugar

1 cup orange juice

1 jar (10 oz) red currant jelly

½ cup chopped pistachio nuts

## SALMON

1 salmon fillet (2 lb)

2 tablespoons fresh lime juice

2 tablespoons butter, melted

½ teaspoon coarse sea salt

Additional chopped pistachio nuts and lime peel, if desired

1 In 2-quart saucepan, mix cranberries, sugar, orange juice and jelly. Heat to boiling; reduce heat. Simmer uncovered 20 minutes, skimming off any foam that collects on surface. Remove from heat. Stir in ½ cup nuts; keep warm.

2 Set oven control to broil. Spray broiler pan rack with cooking spray. Place fish, skin side down, on rack. In small bowl, mix lime juice, butter and salt; pour over fish.

3 Broil with top 4 inches from heat 8 to 10 minutes or until fish flakes easily with fork. Sprinkle with nuts and lime peel. Cut into 8 serving pieces. Serve with sauce.

**1 Serving:** Calories 470; Total Fat 13g (Saturated Fat 4g, Trans Fat 0g); Cholesterol 80mg; Sodium 250mg; Total Carbohydrate 62g (Dietary Fiber 4g); Protein 26g **Exchanges:** ½ Starch, ½ Fruit, 3 Other Carbohydrate, 3½ Lean Meat, ½ Fat **Carbohydrate Choices:** 4

## Festive Touch For an impressive holiday meal, and a nice contrast in flavors and textures, pair the salmon with Artichoke-Stuffed Portabellas (page 122).

# Shrimp and Grits Bake

**PREP TIME:** 25 Minutes   **START TO FINISH:** 50 Minutes   *6 servings*

1 tablespoon olive oil

1 container (8 oz) refrigerated prechopped onion, celery and bell pepper mix

1¾ cups milk

1 cup chicken broth

1 cup uncooked quick-cooking grits

½ teaspoon salt

¼ teaspoon freshly ground pepper

1 container (5.2 oz) Boursin cheese with garlic and herbs

1 lb uncooked medium shrimp, peeled, deveined and coarsely chopped

2 eggs, slightly beaten

1 tablespoon chopped fresh Italian (flat-leaf) parsley

2 teaspoons chopped fresh thyme leaves

**1** Heat oven to 375°F. Spray 11x7-inch (2-quart) glass baking dish or 2-quart casserole with cooking spray.

**2** In 10-inch skillet, heat oil over medium-high heat. Cook vegetable mix in oil 5 minutes, stirring occasionally, until tender.

**3** In 4-quart saucepan, heat milk and broth to boiling. Gradually add grits and salt, stirring constantly with whisk. Cook 5 minutes, stirring constantly, until thickened. Remove from heat. Stir in pepper and cheese. Stir in vegetable mixture, shrimp, eggs, parsley and thyme. Spoon mixture into baking dish.

**4** Bake uncovered 25 minutes or until set.

**1 Serving:** Calories 350; Total Fat 18g (Saturated Fat 9g, Trans Fat 0g); Cholesterol 0mg; Sodium 670mg; Total Carbohydrate 28g (Dietary Fiber 2g); Protein 19g **Exchanges:** 1½ Starch, ½ Vegetable, 1½ Very Lean Meat, ½ Medium-Fat Meat, 3 Fat **Carbohydrate Choices:** 1½

 **Festive Touch** **Make a meal your guests won't soon forget by serving this elegant dish with Green Bean and Leek Casserole (page 125).**

# Focaccia Stuffing with Apples and Pancetta

**PREP TIME:** 50 Minutes   **START TO FINISH:** 1 Hour 45 Minutes   *18 servings*

### STUFFING

- 8 cups cubed (½ inch) focaccia bread (about 1 lb)
- 8 oz pancetta, diced
- 6 tablespoons butter
- 1 cup diced onion
- 1 cup diced celery
- ¼ teaspoon salt
- ¼ teaspoon pepper
- 2 Gala apples, cut into ½-inch cubes (2 cups)
- 2 cups chicken broth
- 2 eggs, slightly beaten
- 2 tablespoons chopped fresh sage leaves
- 2 tablespoons chopped fresh thyme leaves

### WALNUT TOPPING

- ½ cup chopped walnuts, toasted
- ¼ cup chopped fresh parsley
- 1 teaspoon grated orange peel

## Kitchen Secrets

**To toast walnuts, sprinkle in ungreased skillet. Cook over medium heat 5 to 7 minutes, stirring frequently until nuts begin to brown, then stirring constantly until nuts are light brown.**

## Kitchen Secrets

**To make dicing the pancetta easier, place it in the freezer 10 minutes before cutting.**

1  Heat oven to 325°F. Place bread cubes on ungreased cookie sheet. Bake 10 to 15 minutes or until dry and crispy. Cool completely.

2  Meanwhile, spray 4-quart Dutch oven with cooking spray. Add pancetta; cook over medium-low heat 10 to 13 minutes, stirring frequently, until crisp. Using slotted spoon, transfer pancetta to large bowl; set aside. Reserve 2 tablespoons drippings in Dutch oven.

3  Add butter to drippings in Dutch oven; heat until melted. Increase heat to medium-high. Add onion, celery, salt and pepper; cook 6 to 8 minutes, stirring occasionally, until tender. Add apples; cook 2 minutes longer.

4  Add broth. Heat to boiling; reduce heat. Simmer uncovered 2 to 3 minutes, stirring frequently, using spoon to release browned bits from bottom. Remove from heat; cool 5 minutes.

5  Add eggs, sage and thyme to pancetta in bowl. Stir in bread cubes. Add broth mixture; stir to combine. Spray 13x9-inch (3-quart) glass baking dish or 3-quart casserole with cooking spray. Spoon stuffing into baking dish.

6  Bake uncovered 40 to 45 minutes or until center is hot and top is browned and crispy. Cool 5 minutes. In small bowl, stir together topping ingredients. Sprinkle over stuffing.

**1 Serving (½ Cup):** Calories 193; Total Fat 12g (Saturated Fat 5g, Trans Fat 0g); Cholesterol 40mg; Sodium 360mg; Total Carbohydrate 15g (Dietary Fiber 2g); Protein 7g **Exchanges:** 2 Starch, 2½ Fat **Carbohydrate Choices:** 2

# Vegetarian Ciabatta Stuffing with Mushrooms and Chestnuts

**PREP TIME:** 50 Minutes  **START TO FINISH:** 1 Hour 45 Minutes  *16 servings*

8 cups cubed (½ inch) ciabatta bread (about 1 lb)

½ cup butter

1 cup diced shallots

½ cup diced celery

½ teaspoon salt

¼ teaspoon pepper

1 lb cremini mushrooms, thinly sliced

1 package (5.2 oz) peeled roasted chestnuts, coarsely chopped (1 cup)

2 cups vegetable broth

2 eggs, slightly beaten

¼ cup chopped fresh Italian (flat-leaf) parsley

2 tablespoons chopped fresh thyme leaves

¼ teaspoon grated nutmeg

1 cup shredded Gruyère cheese (4 oz)

1  Heat oven to 325°F. Place bread cubes on ungreased cookie sheet. Bake 10 to 15 minutes or until dry and crispy. Cool completely.

2  Meanwhile, in 4-quart Dutch oven, melt butter over medium heat. Cook shallots, celery, salt and pepper in butter 6 to 8 minutes, stirring occasionally, until tender. Increase heat to medium-high. Add mushrooms; cook 6 to 8 minutes or until mushrooms release juices and begin to brown. Stir in chestnuts and broth; heat to simmering. Cook 2 to 3 minutes, stirring frequently, using spoon to release browned bits from bottom. Remove from heat; cool 5 minutes.

3  In large bowl, mix eggs, parsley, thyme and nutmeg. Stir in bread cubes. Add mushroom mixture; stir to combine. Spray 13x9-inch (3-quart) glass baking dish or 3-quart casserole with cooking spray. Spoon stuffing into baking dish.

4  Cover with foil; bake 30 minutes. Uncover; bake 12 to 15 minutes longer or until hot in center and top is browned and crispy. Top with cheese. Let stand 5 minutes before serving.

**1 Serving:** Calories 201; Total Fat 9g (Saturated Fat 5g, Trans Fat 0g); Cholesterol 46mg; Sodium 317mg; Total Carbohydrate 21g (Dietary Fiber 2g); Protein 6g **Exchanges:** 1 Starch, ½ Vegetable, 2 Fat **Carbohydrate Choices:** 1

## Kitchen Secrets

**Your favorite wild mushrooms, like morels, chanterelles or shiitakes, can be substituted for the creminis. If those varieties aren't available, use regular white (button) mushrooms instead.**

# Cheesy Potatoes and Leeks

**PREP TIME:** 25 Minutes   **START TO FINISH:** 1 Hour 25 Minutes   *12 servings*

2 tablespoons butter, softened

3 tablespoons all-purpose flour

2 teaspoons chopped fresh thyme leaves

1 teaspoon salt

½ teaspoon freshly ground pepper

3 cups whipping cream

6 large russet or Idaho baking potatoes (about 3 lb)

3 cloves garlic, finely chopped

1 medium leek, cut lengthwise in half, thinly sliced (2 cups)

1½ cups shredded sharp Cheddar cheese (6 oz)

1   Heat oven to 400°F. Grease 13x9-inch (3-quart) glass baking dish or 3-quart casserole with the butter.

2   In large bowl, mix flour, thyme, salt and pepper. Gradually add whipping cream, stirring with whisk until smooth.

3   Peel potatoes; cut into ¼-inch slices, then cut slices into quarters. Add potatoes, garlic and leek to cream mixture, stirring to coat. Spoon potato mixture into baking dish.

4   Cover with foil; bake 30 minutes. Uncover; bake 25 minutes longer or until top is lightly browned and potatoes are tender. Sprinkle with cheese; bake 5 minutes longer or until cheese is melted. Serve immediately.

**1 Serving:** Calories 440; Total Fat 27g (Saturated Fat 16g, Trans Fat 0g); Cholesterol 0mg; Sodium 310mg; Total Carbohydrate 42g (Dietary Fiber 3g); Protein 8g **Exchanges:** 2 Starch, ½ Vegetable, ½ High-Fat Meat, 4½ Fat **Carbohydrate Choices:** 2

## Festive Touch

**Make some green "firecracker" garnishes! Cut off tops of green onions, leaving about 4 inches of green. With a paring knife, cut several slits in each loose green end, starting as close to the white base as possible, cutting all the way to the loose end. Plunge onions, green side down, into a bowl of ice water. Refrigerate up to 2 hours in advance. (The ice water will make the green ends curl.) When ready to serve, shake off water and place on top of casserole.**

## Kitchen Secrets

**Leeks are grown in sandy soil and require thorough rinsing to remove any soil that could be trapped in the layers. After cutting the leek lengthwise in half, rinse under water or swish in a shallow bowl of water. Slice as directed, using the white and light green portions.**

# Four-Cheese Potato Bake

**PREP TIME:** 25 Minutes   **START TO FINISH:** 50 Minutes   *6 servings*

1 bag (28 oz) frozen potatoes O'Brien with onions and peppers

⅓ cup vegetable oil

1 cup shredded Cheddar cheese (4 oz)

1 cup shredded Gruyère cheese (4 oz)

⅔ cup crumbled blue cheese

1 container (8 oz) chives-and-onion cream cheese spread

5 slices bacon, crisply cooked, crumbled

½ teaspoon pepper

¼ teaspoon salt

2 medium green onions, sliced

1 Heat oven to 375°F. Spray 11x7-inch (2-quart) glass baking dish or 2-quart casserole with cooking spray.

2 Cook potatoes as directed on package, using oil. Meanwhile, in medium bowl, mix shredded cheeses, blue cheese, cream cheese spread, bacon, pepper and salt.

3 Spread cooked potatoes in baking dish. Spoon cheese mixture in dollops over potatoes (potatoes do not have to be completely covered).

4 Bake uncovered 20 to 25 minutes or until cheeses are melted and bubbly. Top with onions.

**1 Serving:** Calories 380; Total Fat 27g (Saturated Fat 12g, Trans Fat 0g); Cholesterol 0mg; Sodium 610mg; Total Carbohydrate 20g (Dietary Fiber 2g); Protein 16g **Exchanges:** 1½ Starch, 2 High-Fat Meat, 2 Fat **Carbohydrate Choices:** 1½

**Kitchen Secrets** To add some heat to these potatoes, substitute spicy jalapeño or smoky chipotle cream cheese spread for the chives-and-onion flavor.

# Bacon-Thyme Duchess Potatoes

**PREP TIME:** 25 Minutes   **START TO FINISH:** 1 Hour   *12 servings*

3 lb russet or Yukon Gold
   potatoes, peeled, cut into
   2-inch pieces
5 egg yolks
½ cup butter, melted
¼ cup half-and-half
1½ teaspoons chopped fresh or
   ½ teaspoon dried thyme leaves
¾ teaspoon salt
¼ teaspoon pepper
   Pinch ground nutmeg
4 slices bacon, crisply cooked,
   crumbled

1 Heat oven to 425°F. Line large cookie sheet with cooking parchment paper.

2 In 3-quart saucepan, place potatoes and enough water just to cover potatoes. Heat to boiling; reduce heat. Cover; simmer 12 to 15 minutes or until potatoes are very tender when pierced with fork. Drain. Shake pan with potatoes over low heat to dry (this will help make mashed potatoes fluffier).

3 Mash potatoes with potato masher until no lumps remain. Using spatula or wooden spoon, gently mix in egg yolks, one at a time (do not overmix). Fold in 6 tablespoons of the melted butter, the half-and-half, thyme, salt, pepper, nutmeg and three-fourths of the crumbled bacon.

4 Spoon mixture into large decorating bag fitted with large star tip. Pipe 12 rosettes (about 2½ inches wide and 2½ inches tall) onto cookie sheet. Drizzle with remaining 2 tablespoons melted butter; sprinkle with remaining bacon.

5 Bake 17 to 20 minutes or until ridges begin to brown. Serve immediately.

**1 Serving:** Calories 200; Total Fat 11g (Saturated Fat 6g, Trans Fat 0g); Cholesterol 100mg; Sodium 260mg; Total Carbohydrate 20g (Dietary Fiber 1g); Protein 4g **Exchanges:** 1 Starch, ½ Other Carbohydrate, 2 Fat **Carbohydrate Choices:** 1

## Make-Ahead Magic

**You can make the potatoes up to 24 hours in advance, piping them onto the cookie sheet, but do not top with butter or bacon. Cover rosettes loosely with plastic wrap and refrigerate. Just before baking, drizzle with remaining butter and sprinkle with remaining bacon.**

# Cheesy Herb–Hash Brown Cups

**PREP TIME:** 15 Minutes   **START TO FINISH:** 1 Hour 25 Minutes   *12 servings*

1 bag (20 oz) refrigerated cooked shredded hash brown potatoes

1 cup shredded Gruyére or Swiss cheese (4 oz)

½ cup shredded Parmesan cheese (2 oz)

¼ cup chopped green onions (4 medium)

1 tablespoon chopped fresh Italian (flat-leaf) parsley

2 teaspoons chopped fresh thyme leaves

1 teaspoon chopped fresh rosemary leaves

½ teaspoon freshly ground pepper

¼ teaspoon garlic powder

1 egg white, beaten

2 tablespoons olive oil

Sour cream, chopped red bell pepper and thyme sprigs, if desired

1 Heat oven to 350°F. Generously spray 12 regular-size nonstick muffin cups with cooking spray.

2 In large bowl, stir together all ingredients except the sour cream, bell pepper and thyme sprigs until well blended. Spoon mixture evenly into muffin cups, about ½ cup in each; press firmly into cups.

3 Bake 50 to 60 minutes or until golden brown and crisp around edges. Cool 10 minutes. Remove from cups to serving platter or individual plates. Garnish with sour cream, red bell pepper and fresh thyme sprigs.

**1 Serving:** Calories 120; Total Fat 6g (Saturated Fat 3g, Trans Fat 0g); Cholesterol 15mg; Sodium 170mg; Total Carbohydrate 10g (Dietary Fiber 0g); Protein 5g **Exchanges:** ½ Starch, ½ Medium-Fat Meat, ½ Fat **Carbohydrate Choices:** ½

## Make-Ahead Magic
These hash brown cups can be assembled up to 24 hours in advance. Cover with plastic wrap and refrigerate. Uncover and bake as directed.

# Polenta-Crusted Thyme-Roasted Potatoes

**PREP TIME:** 15 Minutes    **START TO FINISH:** 45 Minutes    *6 servings*

8 cups water

3 lb unpeeled russet or Idaho potatoes, cut into 1-inch cubes

¼ cup olive oil

1 tablespoon Dijon mustard

2 tablespoons chopped fresh or 2 teaspoons dried thyme leaves

3 cloves garlic, finely chopped

¾ teaspoon salt

¼ teaspoon pepper

3 tablespoons cornmeal

1 Heat oven to 450°F. Spray 15x10x1-inch pan with cooking spray.

2 In 4-quart Dutch oven or stockpot, heat water and potatoes to boiling. Simmer 5 minutes; drain.

3 In 2-gallon resealable food-storage plastic bag, mix oil, mustard, thyme, garlic, salt and pepper. Add potatoes; seal bag and shake gently to coat. Add cornmeal; shake again to coat potatoes. Arrange potatoes in single layer in pan.

4 Roast 25 to 30 minutes, stirring every 10 minutes, until potatoes are tender and golden brown.

**1 Serving:** Calories 280; Total Fat 10g (Saturated Fat 1.5g, Trans Fat 0g); Cholesterol 0mg; Sodium 370mg; Total Carbohydrate 45g (Dietary Fiber 6g); Protein 4g **Exchanges:** 1½ Starch, 1½ Other Carbohydrate, 2 Fat **Carbohydrate Choices:** 3

## Make-Ahead Magic The potatoes can be prepared up to 24 hours in advance—except do not toss with cornmeal. Refrigerate bag with potato mixture until ready to bake, then coat with cornmeal and bake as directed.

## Festive Touch If you're using fresh thyme, save a few sprigs to use as a pretty and festive garnish for the roasted potatoes.

## Festive Touch Serve these flavorful potatoes with Rosemary Prime Rib Roast (page 97) or your favorite steak or pork chop recipe.

# Curried Mashed Cauliflower Bake

**PREP TIME:** 15 Minutes   **START TO FINISH:** 1 Hour 5 Minutes   *10 servings*

2½ quarts water

2 large heads cauliflower (about 2½ lb each), cut into ½- to 1-inch florets

3 tablespoons coconut oil or olive oil

2 tablespoons chopped fresh cilantro

2 teaspoons salt

1½ to 2 teaspoons curry powder

½ teaspoon ground cumin

¼ teaspoon ground red pepper (cayenne)

4 cloves garlic, finely chopped

Additional chopped fresh cilantro, if desired

1  Heat oven to 350°F. Spray 11x7-inch (2-quart) glass baking dish or 2-quart casserole with cooking spray.

2  In 5- to 6-quart Dutch oven, heat water to boiling over high heat. Add cauliflower; return to boiling. Cook 15 to 20 minutes or until cauliflower is very tender; drain well.

3  In food processor, place half of the cauliflower and 1½ tablespoons of the oil. Cover; process until smooth, scraping bowl as needed. Return to Dutch oven. Repeat with remaining cauliflower and oil. Add 2 tablespoons cilantro, the salt, curry powder, cumin, red pepper and garlic to cauliflower mixture; mix well. Spoon into baking dish.

4  Bake uncovered 25 to 30 minutes or until hot. Garnish with cilantro.

**1 Serving:** Calories 80; Total Fat 4.5g (Saturated Fat 3.5g, Trans Fat 0g); Cholesterol 0mg; Sodium 520mg; Total Carbohydrate 6g (Dietary Fiber 2g); Protein 2g **Exchanges:** 1 Vegetable, 1 Fat **Carbohydrate Choices:** ½

## Make-Ahead Magic
**Prepare casserole as directed through Step 3. Cover and refrigerate up to 24 hours. Uncover and bake 45 to 50 minutes, stirring halfway through baking time, until hot.**

# Holiday Aloo Gobi

**PREP TIME:** 20 Minutes    **START TO FINISH:** 55 Minutes    *8 servings*

1 lb sweet potatoes, peeled, cut into 1-inch cubes

1 bag (10 oz) cauliflower florets (about 3 cups)

1 large onion, cut into ½-inch wedges (about 1½ cups)

2 cloves garlic, sliced

1 tablespoon finely chopped gingerroot

¼ cup water

3 tablespoons vegetable oil

1 teaspoon garam masala

1 teaspoon ground turmeric

½ teaspoon ground coriander

½ teaspoon ground cumin

¼ teaspoon salt

⅛ teaspoon ground red pepper (cayenne)

½ cup dried cranberries

Chopped fresh cilantro, if desired

**1** Heat oven to 400°F. Line 15x10x1-inch pan with cooking parchment paper.

**2** In large bowl, stir together all ingredients except cranberries and cilantro. Spoon mixture into pan.

**3** Bake uncovered 30 to 35 minutes, stirring once, until vegetables are crisp-tender. Add cranberries during the last 5 minutes of bake time. Sprinkle with cilantro before serving.

**1 Serving (½ Cup):** Calories 150; Total Fat 5g (Saturated Fat 1g, Trans Fat 0g); Cholesterol 0mg; Sodium 115mg; Total Carbohydrate 22g (Dietary Fiber 3g); Protein 2g **Exchanges:** 1 Starch, ½ Other Carbohydrate, 1 Fat **Carbohydrate Choices:** 1½

**Kitchen Secrets** Aloo Gobi is an Indian-style potato and cauliflower side dish. The bright colors and flavors make it a great side to any plain meat dish.

**Kitchen Secrets** Many varieties of sweet potatoes are available. Those with a dark orange skin work well for this dish because they not only make the color richer, but also make the flavor sweeter.

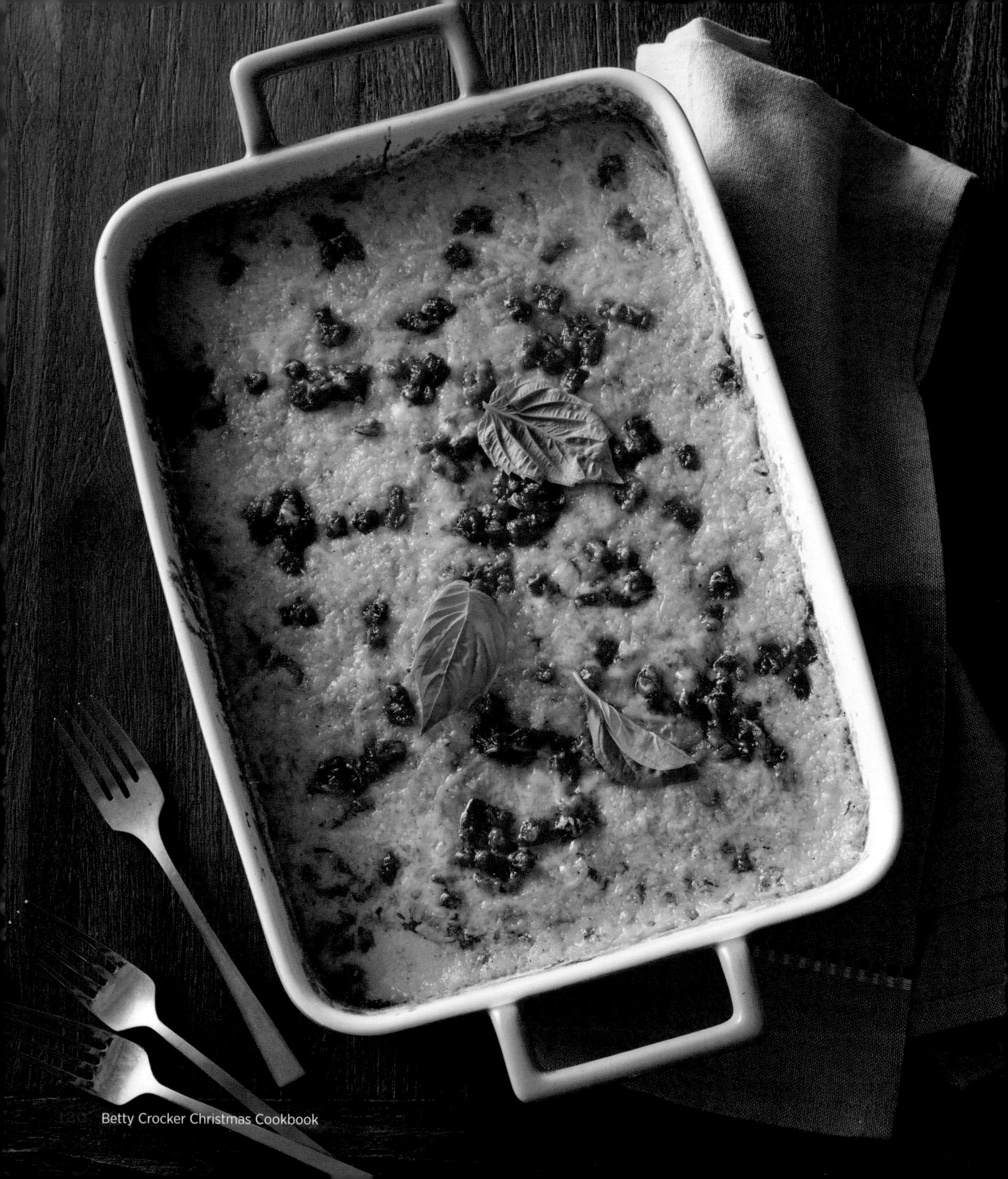

# Creamy Italian Oven Polenta

**PREP TIME:** 20 Minutes **START TO FINISH:** 1 Hour 35 Minutes *14 servings*

2 cans (14¾ oz each) cream-style corn

1¼ cups reduced-sodium chicken broth

1 cup whipping cream

1 cup milk

¼ cup butter, melted

1 teaspoon pepper

¾ teaspoon salt

½ teaspoon garlic powder

1 cup cornmeal

⅓ cup chopped fresh basil leaves, if desired

¼ cup roasted red bell peppers (from a jar), drained, chopped

½ cup shredded Parmesan cheese (2 oz)

Fresh basil leaves, if desired

1 Heat oven to 350°F. Spray 11x7-inch (2-quart) glass baking dish or 2-quart casserole with cooking spray.

2 In large bowl, stir together corn, broth, whipping cream, milk, butter, pepper, salt and garlic powder with whisk. Slowly stir in cornmeal until no lumps remain. Stir in basil. Pour into baking dish.

3 Bake uncovered 40 minutes. Stir well; bake 10 minutes longer. Stir again; top with roasted peppers and cheese. Bake an additional 10 to 15 minutes or until mixture is bubbly and the consistency of thick oatmeal.

4 Let stand 10 minutes before serving. Garnish with additional fresh basil.

**1 Serving:** Calories 200; Total Fat 10g (Saturated Fat 6g, Trans Fat 0g); Cholesterol 30mg; Sodium 450mg; Total Carbohydrate 22g (Dietary Fiber 1g); Protein 4g **Exchanges:** 1½ Starch, 2 Fat **Carbohydrate Choices:** 1½

## Make-Ahead Magic
The polenta can be assembled up to a day ahead, covered and refrigerated. When ready to serve, uncover and bake as directed.

## Festive Touch
Since the polenta has a pudding-like consistency, it's pretty to serve in individual ramekins or custard cups. After baking, spoon into cups. Garnish with additional basil, roasted red pepper or Parmesan cheese.

# Artichoke-Stuffed Portabellas

**PREP TIME:** 15 Minutes  **START TO FINISH:** 45 Minutes  *6 servings*

6 portabella mushroom caps

2 tablespoons Italian dressing

1½ cups coarsely chopped arugula

1 cup shredded Asiago cheese (4 oz)

½ cup chopped drained roasted red peppers (from a jar)

1 jar (6 to 7.5 oz) marinated artichoke hearts, drained, chopped

1 package (3 oz) thinly sliced prosciutto, chopped

1 egg, slightly beaten

½ cup unseasoned dry bread crumbs

2 teaspoons butter, melted

**1** Heat oven to 400°F. Line cookie sheet with foil.

**2** Remove stems from mushrooms. Place caps, gill side down, on cookie sheet. Brush with Italian dressing. Bake about 15 minutes or until mushrooms begin to soften.

**3** Meanwhile, in medium bowl, stir together arugula, cheese, roasted peppers, artichokes, prosciutto, egg and 6 tablespoons of the bread crumbs. Turn mushroom caps over; spoon filling evenly into caps.

**4** Toss remaining 2 tablespoons bread crumbs and the melted butter. Sprinkle over filling. Bake 10 to 15 minutes or until thoroughly heated and crumbs begin to brown.

**1 Serving:** Calories 230; Total Fat 15g (Saturated Fat 7g, Trans Fat 0g); Cholesterol 60mg; Sodium 740mg; Total Carbohydrate 13g (Dietary Fiber 3g); Protein 11g **Exchanges:** 2 Vegetable, 1 Medium-Fat Meat, 2 Fat **Carbohydrate Choices:** 1

## Make-Ahead Magic
Mushrooms can be made ahead through Step 3 up to 4 hours before baking. Cover and refrigerate. Continue as directed—except increase bake time to 20 minutes.

## Festive Touch
These flavorful stuffed mushrooms pair perfectly with roast beef, pork loin or grilled steaks and are great on a buffet as they are easy for guests to pick up.

## Kitchen Secrets
Portabella mushroom caps can vary widely in size. Look for ones that are about 4 inches in diameter. If you find yourself with extra filling, use it as an omelet filling or stir it into scrambled eggs.

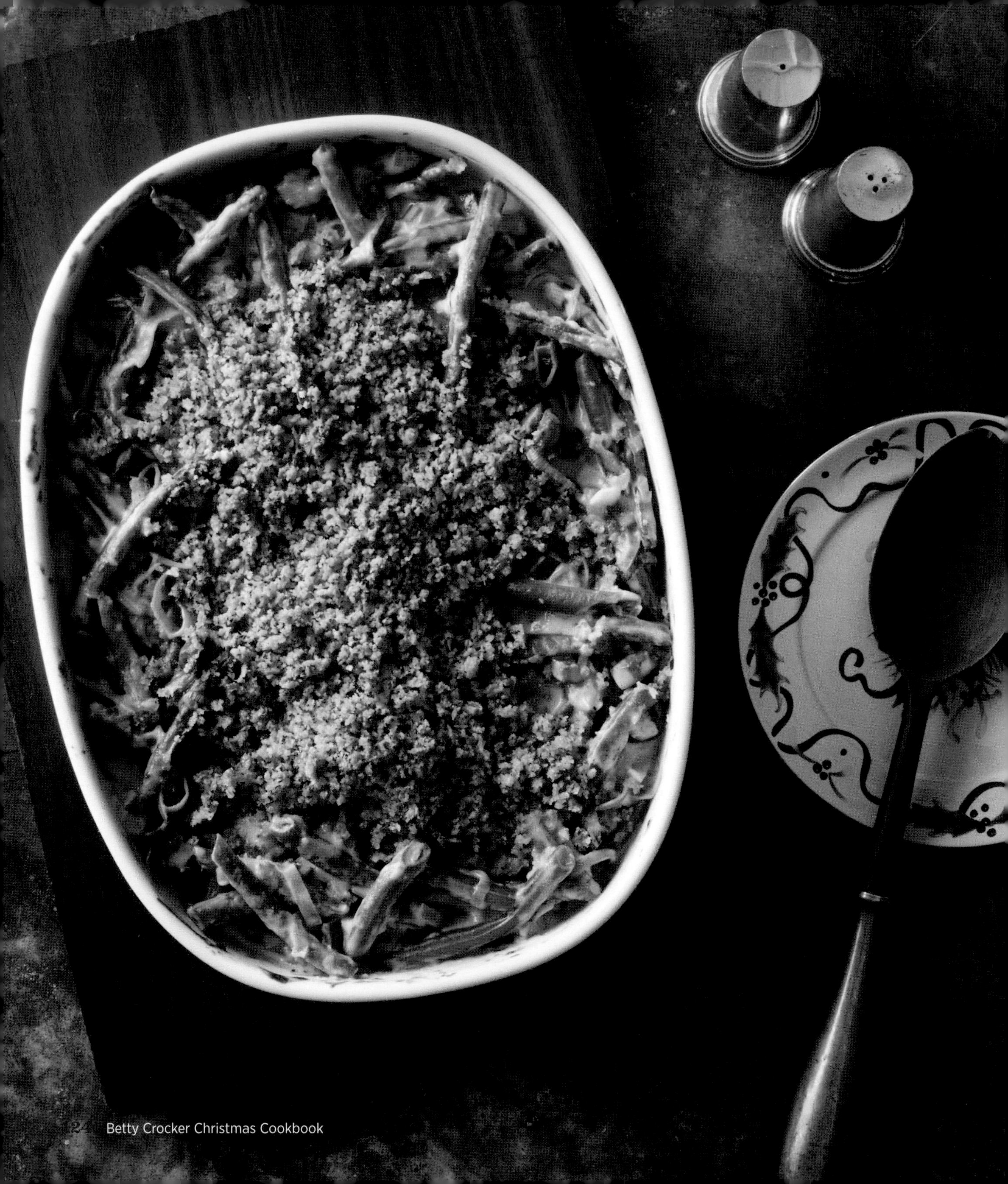

# Green Bean and Leek Casserole

**PREP TIME:** 25 Minutes    **START TO FINISH:** 1 Hour    *12 servings*

2 bags (12 oz each) steam-in-the-bag fresh green beans

¼ cup butter

1 large leek (1 lb), cut lengthwise in half, thinly sliced (about 2½ cups)

¼ cup all-purpose flour

¼ teaspoon salt

¼ teaspoon pepper

½ cup milk

½ cup chicken broth

1½ cups shredded fontina cheese (6 oz)

½ cup shredded Parmesan cheese (2 oz)

½ cup diced red bell pepper

¾ cup Italian-style panko crispy bread crumbs

2 tablespoons butter, melted

1 Heat oven to 350°F. Microwave bags of beans on High 3 minutes 30 seconds. Remove beans from bags to large bowl; set aside.

2 Meanwhile, in 12-inch skillet, melt ¼ cup butter over medium heat. Cook leeks in butter 6 to 8 minutes, stirring occasionally, until tender.

3 Sprinkle flour, salt and pepper over leeks; cook and stir until well blended. Gradually stir in milk and broth. Heat to boiling, stirring constantly; boil 1 minute. Stir in cheeses; cook about 1 minute, stirring constantly, until melted. Pour over green beans in bowl; stir to combine. Stir in bell pepper.

4 Spoon into ungreased 2-quart casserole. In small bowl, mix bread crumbs and 2 tablespoons melted butter. Sprinkle over casserole.

5 Bake uncovered 30 to 35 minutes or until bubbly and topping is golden brown.

**1 Serving (½ Cup):** Calories 210; Total Fat 12g (Saturated Fat 7g, Trans Fat 0g); Cholesterol 35mg; Sodium 430mg; Total Carbohydrate 17g (Dietary Fiber 2g); Protein 7g **Exchanges:** ½ Other Carbohydrate, 1½ Vegetable, ½ High-Fat Meat, 1½ Fat **Carbohydrate Choices:** 1

## Make-Ahead Magic
You can prep this casserole through Step 4 up to 4 hours before baking. Cover and refrigerate. Uncover and continue as directed—except increase bake time to 45 to 50 minutes.

## Kitchen Secrets
Leeks are grown in sandy soil and require thorough rinsing to remove any soil that could be trapped in the layers. After cutting the leek lengthwise in half, rinse under water or swish in a shallow bowl of water. Slice as directed, using the white and light green portions.

# Sweet Potato and Pear Gratin

**PREP TIME:** 45 Minutes   **START TO FINISH:** 2 Hours 15 Minutes   *12 servings*

**CREAMY LEEKS**

- ¼ cup butter
- 3 tablespoons all-purpose flour
- 5 cups thinly sliced leeks (about 1½ lb)
- 3 cloves garlic, finely chopped
- ¾ teaspoon ground nutmeg
- ½ teaspoon salt
- ½ teaspoon pepper
- ¼ cup dry white wine or cognac
- 1¼ cups whipping cream
- ½ cup chicken broth
- 2 tablespoons chopped fresh or ¾ tablespoon dried thyme leaves
- 1½ cups shredded Gruyère or fontina cheese (6 oz)

**SWEET POTATOES AND PEARS**

- 2 lb dark-orange sweet potatoes, peeled, cut into ¼-inch slices (6 cups)
- 1 lb ripe pears, cut into ¼-inch slices (4 cups)

**TOPPING**

- ½ cup panko crispy bread crumbs
- 1 tablespoon butter, melted
- 1 tablespoon chopped fresh or 1 teaspoon dried thyme leaves

1 Heat oven to 350°F. Butter bottom and sides of 3-quart casserole.

2 In 12-inch skillet, melt ¼ cup butter over medium heat. Stir in flour until smooth. Stir in leeks, garlic, nutmeg, salt and pepper. Cook 4 to 6 minutes, stirring occasionally, until leeks are softened. Add wine; heat to boiling. Reduce heat; simmer 3 minutes. Stir in whipping cream, broth and 2 tablespoons thyme. Heat just to simmering. Cook 7 to 8 minutes, stirring occasionally, until thickened. Remove from heat; let stand 10 minutes. Stir in cheese.

3 Arrange half of the sweet potatoes in casserole. Pour half of the leek mixture over sweet potatoes. Arrange pears over leek mixture. Top with remaining sweet potatoes. Pour remaining leek mixture over potatoes; press gently to submerge potatoes. Cover with foil; bake 40 minutes.

4 In small bowl, mix bread crumbs and melted butter. Add 1 tablespoon thyme; toss to mix. Sprinkle topping over casserole.

5 Increase oven temperature to 375°F. Bake uncovered 25 to 30 minutes longer or until potatoes are tender when pierced with knife and topping is golden brown. Let stand 10 minutes before serving.

**1 Serving:** Calories 310; Total Fat 17g (Saturated Fat 10g, Trans Fat 0.5g); Cholesterol 55mg; Sodium 340mg; Total Carbohydrate 32g (Dietary Fiber 4g); Protein 7g **Exchanges:** 2 Starch, 3 Fat **Carbohydrate Choices:** 2

## Kitchen Secrets
Leeks are grown in sandy soil and require thorough rinsing to remove any soil that could be trapped in the layers. After cutting the leek lengthwise in half, rinse under water or swish in a shallow bowl of water. Slice as directed, using the white and light green portions.

## Kitchen Secrets
Leeks are grown in sandy soil and require thorough rinsing to remove any soil that could be trapped in the layers. After cutting the leek lengthwise in half, rinse under water or swish in a shallow bowl of water. Slice as directed, using the white and light green portions.

# Mixed Greens Salad with Dijon Vinaigrette

**PREP TIME:** 15 Minutes   **START TO FINISH:** 15 Minutes   *6 servings*

**VINAIGRETTE**

- 1 tablespoon Dijon mustard
- 1 tablespoon red wine vinegar
- ½ teaspoon sugar
- 3 tablespoons olive oil
- Dash salt and pepper

**SALAD**

- 1 bag (5 oz) mixed spring greens
- 1 cup grape tomatoes, cut lengthwise in half
- 1 cup sliced seeded peeled cucumber
- 1 cup sliced halved red onion

1  In small bowl, mix mustard, vinegar and sugar with whisk. Gradually add oil, beating constantly until well blended. Season to taste with salt and pepper.

2  In large bowl, gently toss greens, tomatoes, cucumber and onion. Pour vinaigrette over salad; toss gently to mix. Serve immediately.

**1 Serving:** Calories 90; Total Fat 7g (Saturated Fat 1g, Trans Fat 0g); Cholesterol 0mg; Sodium 95mg; Total Carbohydrate 5g (Dietary Fiber 1g); Protein 1g **Exchanges:** 1 Vegetable, 1½ Fat **Carbohydrate Choices:** ½

## Make-Ahead Magic
You can make the dressing up to 24 hours in advance; cover and refrigerate. Stir before using. You also can slice the cucumber and onion and refrigerate in resealable food-storage plastic bags, making it even quicker to get the salad on the table when you're ready!

## Kitchen Secrets
Do you stay away from red onions because the flavor is too strong? After cutting the onions, place them in a small bowl of cold water to help mellow the flavor. Let stand at room temperature 30 minutes, or cover and refrigerate up to 24 hours. Drain and pat dry before using.

# Clementine, Date and Stilton Salad

**PREP TIME:** 15 Minutes   **START TO FINISH:** 15 Minutes   *8 servings*

6 clementines

2 tablespoons white balsamic vinegar

2 teaspoons honey

¼ cup olive oil

¼ teaspoon salt

¼ teaspoon freshly ground pepper

8 cups mixed spring greens

¾ cup chopped dried Medjool dates

¾ cup crumbled Stilton cheese (3 oz)

½ cup coarsely chopped candied walnuts

1 Grate peel from 2 clementines to equal 1 teaspoon. Cut 2 clementines in half; squeeze enough juice to equal 2 tablespoons. Peel and slice remaining 4 clementines.

2 In small bowl, stir clementine juice and peel, vinegar, honey, oil, salt and pepper with whisk until blended.

3 On serving platter or individual plates, arrange salad greens. Top with sliced clementines, dates, cheese and walnuts. Drizzle with vinaigrette, or serve on the side.

**1 Serving:** Calories 240; Total Fat 15g (Saturated Fat 3g, Trans Fat 0g); Cholesterol 0mg; Sodium 290mg; Total Carbohydrate 25g (Dietary Fiber 4g); Protein 6g **Exchanges:** 1½ Fruit, ½ High-Fat Meat, 2½ Fat **Carbohydrate Choices:** 1½

## Festive Touch This special salad would be a great side for Rosemary Prime Rib Roast (page 97).

# Arugula-Pear Salad

**PREP TIME:** 10 Minutes   **START TO FINISH:** 10 Minutes   *8 servings*

**DRESSING**
- ⅓ cup fig preserves
- ¼ cup olive oil
- 3 tablespoons white balsamic vinegar
- ¼ teaspoon salt
- ⅛ teaspoon pepper

**SALAD**
- 6 cups torn arugula
- 2 medium pears, thinly sliced
- ½ cup crumbled blue cheese (2 oz)
- ½ cup chopped walnuts or pecans, toasted

**1** In food processor, place all dressing ingredients. Cover; process until smooth.

**2** On serving platter or individual plates, arrange arugula and pears. Sprinkle with cheese and nuts. Drizzle with dressing. Serve immediately.

**1 Serving:** Calories 200; Total Fat 14g (Saturated Fat 3g, Trans Fat 0g); Cholesterol 0mg; Sodium 180mg; Total Carbohydrate 18g (Dietary Fiber 2g); Protein 3g **Exchanges:** ½ Fruit, ½ Other Carbohydrate, 3 Fat **Carbohydrate Choices:** 1

## Kitchen Secrets To toast nuts, sprinkle in ungreased skillet. Cook over medium heat 5 to 7 minutes, stirring frequently until nuts begin to brown, then stirring constantly until nuts are light brown.

## Kitchen Secrets This assertive-flavored salad is great paired with mildly seasoned meat or poultry.

# Balsamic Kale-and-Strawberry Salad

**PREP TIME:** 20 Minutes    **START TO FINISH:** 20 Minutes    *4 servings*

2 slices whole-grain bread, cut into ½-inch cubes

Cooking spray

¼ cup balsamic vinegar

2 tablespoons Dijon mustard

2 tablespoons honey

¼ teaspoon pepper

1 tablespoon olive oil

1 bunch (8 oz) fresh kale, ribs removed, cut into bite-size pieces (6 cups)

½ shallot, thinly sliced

2 cups sliced fresh strawberries

¼ cup shredded Parmesan cheese (1 oz)

1 Heat oven to 400°F. Line cookie sheet with cooking parchment paper. Place bread cubes on cookie sheet; spray bread with cooking spray. Bake 8 to 12 minutes, turning halfway through, until toasted. Cool.

2 In large bowl, beat vinegar, mustard, honey and pepper with whisk. Add oil; beat until smooth.

3 Add kale and shallot to the bowl; toss until kale is thoroughly coated. Gently mix in strawberries. Divide salad among 4 serving plates; top with croutons and cheese. Serve immediately.

**1 Serving:** Calories 210; Total Fat 7g (Saturated Fat 2g, Trans Fat 0g); Cholesterol 0mg; Sodium 390mg; Total Carbohydrate 31g (Dietary Fiber 4g); Protein 7g **Exchanges:** 1 Starch, ½ Fruit, 1 Vegetable, 1½ Fat **Carbohydrate Choices:** 2

## Make-Ahead Magic
**Bake the croutons the night before; store in an airtight container. Prepare the dressing up to 3 days in advance; cover and refrigerate. Just before serving, pour dressing into a large bowl and continue as directed in Step 3.**

# Holiday Romaine Salad

**PREP TIME:** 30 Minutes    **START TO FINISH:** 2 Hours 40 Minutes    *12 servings*

### ALMOND-PISTACHIO DRESSING

- 3 tablespoons blanched almonds
- 1 tablespoon chopped pistachio nuts
- ⅓ cup water
- 2 teaspoons honey
- ¼ teaspoon coarse (kosher or sea) salt
- ⅛ teaspoon cracked black pepper
- ½ teaspoon grated lemon peel
- 5 tablespoons fresh lemon juice
- ½ cup vegetable oil

### CANDIED PISTACHIOS

- 1 tablespoon butter
- 3 tablespoons packed brown sugar
- ¼ teaspoon ground red pepper (cayenne)
- 1 cup roasted salted pistachio nuts
- 1 teaspoon coarse (kosher or sea) salt

### SALAD

- 12 cups torn romaine lettuce
- ½ cup thinly sliced red onion
- 1¼ cups thinly sliced fennel bulb (½ lb)
- 2 ripe avocados, pitted, peeled and thinly sliced

1 In blender, place almonds, 1 tablespoon pistachios and the water. Cover; blend on high speed 10 to 20 seconds or until smooth. Add honey, ¼ teaspoon salt, the pepper, lemon peel and lemon juice. Cover; blend until smooth. With blender running on medium-low speed, slowly add oil through center opening in cap until dressing is thick and creamy. Transfer to bowl or jar. Cover; refrigerate at least 2 hours to blend flavors.

2 Heat oven to 350°F. Line cookie sheet with foil; spray foil with cooking spray.

3 In 1-quart saucepan, cook butter, brown sugar and red pepper over medium heat 2 to 3 minutes, stirring frequently, until butter is melted and sugar is completely dissolved. Add 1 cup pistachios; stir to coat. Spread in single layer on cookie sheet.

4 Bake about 10 minutes, stirring once, until golden brown. Immediately sprinkle with 1 teaspoon salt. Cool on cookie sheet.

5 In large bowl, toss lettuce, onion and fennel; arrange on serving platter. Top with avocados; sprinkle with candied pistachios. Serve with dressing.

**1 Serving:** Calories 250; Total Fat 20g (Saturated Fat 3g, Trans Fat 0g); Cholesterol 0mg; Sodium 310mg; Total Carbohydrate 13g (Dietary Fiber 4g); Protein 4g **Exchanges:** ½ Other Carbohydrate, ½ Vegetable, ½ Very Lean Meat, 4 Fat **Carbohydrate Choices:** 1

## Make-Ahead Magic
The Almond-Pistachio Dressing can be made up to 3 days before serving. It's a creamy dressing that would be a big hit with anyone avoiding dairy products. The Candied Pistachios can be made the day before, and you can prep the lettuce, onion and fennel ahead, too. Then all you'll have to do is peel and slice the avocados and assemble the salad.

# Wine-Roasted Winter Fruit

**PREP TIME:** 15 Minutes   **START TO FINISH:** 55 Minutes   *12 servings*

1 cup dry white wine

¼ cup butter

2 tablespoons packed brown sugar

2 teaspoons grated gingerroot

1 teaspoon cardamom seed

½ teaspoon whole ground cloves

3 cinnamon sticks (3 inch)

2 cups seedless red grapes

1 cup fresh or frozen cranberries

3 medium apples, cut into ¼-inch slices (6 cups)

2 ripe red pears, cut into ¼-inch slices (3 cups)

2 teaspoons fresh lime juice

1 teaspoon grated lime peel

**1** Heat oven to 400°F. Spray 15x10x1-inch pan with cooking spray.

**2** In 1-quart saucepan, heat wine, butter, brown sugar, gingerroot, cardamom, cloves and cinnamon sticks over medium-high heat to boiling. Reduce heat; simmer 15 minutes. Strain mixture to remove spices; discard spices.

**3** Place grapes, cranberries, apples and pears in single layer in pan. Pour wine mixture evenly over fruit.

**4** Bake uncovered 20 to 25 minutes, stirring twice, until fruit is tender when pierced with knife. Stir in lime juice; spoon fruit into serving dish. Just before serving, sprinkle with lime peel. Serve warm or at room temperature; let stand up to 2 hours before serving.

**1 Serving (½ Cup):** Calories 120; Total Fat 4g (Saturated Fat 2.5g, Trans Fat 0g); Cholesterol 10mg; Sodium 35mg; Total Carbohydrate 19g (Dietary Fiber 3g); Protein 0g **Exchanges:** 1 Fruit, 1 Fat **Carbohydrate Choices:** 1

 **Festive Touch** This not-too-sweet fresh fruit compote makes a lovely addition to a brunch buffet, or serve it as a side dish with a casserole or pork roast.

# Holiday
# Breads

# Raspberry-Apple Stocking Coffee Cake

**PREP TIME:** 45 Minutes    **START TO FINISH:** 3 Hours 25 Minutes    *12 servings*

## PASTRY

- 3½ to 4½ cups all-purpose flour
- ⅓ cup granulated sugar
- 1 teaspoon salt
- 2 packages regular active or fast-acting dry yeast (4½ teaspoons)
- 1 cup milk
- ¼ cup butter
- 1 whole egg
- 1 teaspoon vanilla
- 1 egg yolk, beaten
- 1 tablespoon water

## FILLING

- 1 cup raspberry pie filling (from 21-oz can)
- 1 large apple, peeled, chopped
- 2 teaspoons lemon juice

## GLAZE

- 1¾ cups powdered sugar
- 2 to 3 tablespoons half-and-half or milk

**1** In large bowl, mix 2 cups of the flour, the granulated sugar, salt and yeast. In 1-quart saucepan, heat 1 cup milk and the butter over medium heat until very warm (120°F to 130°F). Add warm liquid, whole egg and vanilla to flour mixture. Beat with electric mixer on low speed until moistened; beat 1 minute on medium speed. By hand, stir in enough of the remaining 1½ to 2½ cups flour, ½ cup at a time, until dough pulls away from side of bowl.

**2** On floured surface, knead dough until smooth and elastic, 3 to 5 minutes. Grease large bowl with shortening or cooking spray. Place dough in bowl, turning dough to grease all sides. Cover loosely with plastic wrap and cloth towel; let rise in warm place 50 to 60 minutes or until doubled in size.

**3** Meanwhile, in medium bowl, stir together filling ingredients.

**4** Line large cookie sheet with cooking parchment paper; sprinkle lightly with flour. Gently push fist into dough to deflate. Turn dough onto cookie sheet; roll into 12x15-inch rectangle. On both long sides of rectangle, cut 1-inch-wide slits about 4 inches deep. Spread filling down center of dough. Bring strips up over filling, overlapping and pressing in center. Tuck ends in if necessary. Carefully shape into a stocking.

**5** Cover with plastic wrap sprayed with cooking spray; cover with cloth towel. Let rise in warm place 30 to 45 minutes or until almost doubled in size.

**6** Heat oven to 350°F. In small bowl, mix egg yolk and water; brush over coffee cake. Bake 20 to 25 minutes or until deep golden brown. Remove coffee cake from cookie sheet to cooling rack; cool 30 minutes.

**7** In small bowl, mix powdered sugar and 2 tablespoons half-and-half. Gradually stir in remaining half-and-half, 1 teaspoon at a time, until glaze is of spreading consistency. Spread glaze over coffee cake to create top, heel and toe of stocking.

**1 Serving:** Calories 320; Total Fat 6g (Saturated Fat 3g, Trans Fat 0g); Cholesterol 45mg; Sodium 250mg; Total Carbohydrate 61g (Dietary Fiber 2g); Protein 6g **Exchanges:** 2 Starch, 2 Other Carbohydrate, 1 Fat **Carbohydrate Choices:** 4

## Festive Touch
Customize your stocking however you wish! Flaked coconut sprinkled over the glaze before it's dry will look like fur . . . write your last name on the top of the stocking using a tube of decorator icing or gel . . . sprinkle small candies or candy sprinkles over the glaze.

## Kitchen Secrets
If your family and friends might "fight" over the iced portions of this coffee cake, reserve a little of the glaze and drizzle it lightly over the entire stocking.

# Fig-Pear Sweet Rolls

**PREP TIME:** 45 Minutes    **START TO FINISH:** 3 Hours 55 Minutes    *12 rolls*

## DOUGH

4 to 4½ cups all-purpose flour
½ cup granulated sugar
1 package regular active or fast-acting dry yeast (2¼ teaspoons)
1 teaspoon salt
¾ cup butter
¾ cup milk
¾ cup water

## FILLING

2 bags (9 oz each) dried Mission figs, chopped (about 2 cups)
½ cup granulated sugar
1 cup water
1 tablespoon grated orange peel
1 teaspoon ground cinnamon
1 ripe pear, peeled, finely chopped

## GLAZE

1 cup powdered sugar
1 teaspoon grated orange peel
4 to 5 teaspoons orange juice

**1** In large bowl, mix 2½ cups of the flour, ½ cup granulated sugar, the yeast and salt. In 1-quart saucepan, heat butter, milk and ¾ cup water over medium-low heat until very warm (120°F to 130°F). Add to flour mixture; beat with electric mixer on medium speed, scraping bowl occasionally, until smooth. Stir in enough of the remaining 1½ to 2 cups flour to make the dough easy to handle.

**2** On lightly floured surface, knead dough about 5 minutes or until smooth and elastic. Grease large bowl with shortening or cooking spray. Place dough in bowl, turning dough to grease all sides. Cover loosely with plastic wrap and cloth towel; let rise in warm place 1 hour to 1 hour 30 minutes or until doubled in size and indentation remains when dough is touched.

**3** Meanwhile, in 2-quart saucepan, stir together figs, ½ cup granulated sugar, 1 cup water, 1 tablespoon orange peel and the cinnamon. Cook over medium-high heat 5 to 10 minutes, stirring frequently, until figs are tender and liquid is absorbed. Cool 30 minutes.

**4** Spray 13x9-inch pan with cooking spray. Gently push fist into dough to deflate. On lightly floured surface, roll dough into 18x14-inch rectangle. Spread fig mixture over dough to within ½ inch of edge. Sprinkle pear evenly over fig mixture. Starting from long side, roll up tightly; pinch edge to seal. Cut into 12 (1½-inch) slices. Place slices, cut side down, in pan. Cover with plastic wrap; let rise in warm place 30 to 45 minutes or until doubled in size.

**5** Heat oven to 375°F. Uncover rolls; bake 30 to 35 minutes or until golden brown. Cool 20 minutes.

**6** In small bowl, stir glaze ingredients until smooth; drizzle over rolls. Serve warm.

**1 Roll:** Calories 500; Total Fat 13g (Saturated Fat 8g, Trans Fat 0g); Cholesterol 30mg; Sodium 300mg; Total Carbohydrate 89g (Dietary Fiber 6g); Protein 6g **Exchanges:** 2 Starch, 1 Fruit, 3 Other Carbohydrate, 2½ Fat **Carbohydrate Choices:** 6

## Make-Ahead Magic
After placing slices in pan, cover tightly with foil and refrigerate overnight. About 2 hours before serving, remove from refrigerator; remove foil and cover loosely with plastic wrap. Let rise in warm place 30 to 60 minutes or until dough has doubled in size. If some rising has occurred in refrigerator, rising time may be less. Bake as directed.

## Kitchen Secrets
Use dental floss to easily cut dough into slices. Place floss under the roll, bring ends up and cross over at the top of the roll, then pull in opposite directions.

# Mini Sweet Potato–Cinnamon Rolls

**PREP TIME:** 40 Minutes    **START TO FINISH:** 2 Hours 40 Minutes    *24 mini rolls*

**CINNAMON ROLLS**

1½ to 1¾ cups all-purpose or
    bread flour

2 tablespoons granulated sugar

½ teaspoon salt

¼ teaspoon ground cinnamon

1¼ teaspoons fast-acting dry yeast

¼ cup very warm milk
    (120°F to 130°F)

⅓ cup mashed cooked sweet
    potato, cooled

3 tablespoons butter, softened

1 egg yolk

**FILLING**

2 tablespoons butter, softened

2 tablespoons packed
    brown sugar

2 teaspoons ground cinnamon

½ teaspoon ground ginger

½ teaspoon ground nutmeg

¼ teaspoon ground cardamom

⅛ teaspoon ground cloves

**ICING**

2 tablespoons butter, melted

1 tablespoon plus 1 to 2
    teaspoons milk

1 cup powdered sugar

**1** In large bowl, mix 1 cup of the flour, 2 tablespoons granulated sugar, the salt, ¼ teaspoon cinnamon and the yeast. Add warm milk, sweet potato, 3 tablespoons butter and the egg yolk. Beat with electric mixer on low speed 1 minute, scraping bowl frequently. Beat on medium speed 1 minute, scraping bowl frequently. Stir in enough of the remaining ½ to ¾ cup flour, ¼ cup at a time, to make dough easy to handle.

**2** On lightly floured surface, knead dough 3 to 5 minutes or until smooth and elastic. Grease medium bowl with shortening. Place dough in bowl, turning dough to grease all sides. Cover bowl loosely with plastic wrap sprayed with cooking spray; let rise in warm place about 1 hour 15 minutes or until dough has doubled in size and indentation remains when dough is touched.

**3** In small bowl, mix 1 tablespoon of the butter and remaining filling ingredients; set aside.

**4** Grease bottoms and sides of 24 mini muffin cups with shortening or cooking spray. Gently push fist into dough to deflate. On lightly floured surface, flatten dough with hands or rolling pin into 12x9-inch rectangle. Cut dough in half, forming 2 (9x6-inch) rectangles. Spread rectangles with remaining 1 tablespoon butter; sprinkle with filling, covering entire surface. Starting with 9-inch side, roll up tightly. Pinch edge to seal. Stretch and shape until even. Using serrated knife or dental floss, cut each roll into 12 (¾-inch) slices.

**5** Place slices, cut side up, in muffin cups. Cover loosely with plastic wrap sprayed with cooking spray; let rise in warm place 30 minutes.

**6** Heat oven to 350°F. Uncover rolls; bake 10 to 12 minutes or until light golden brown. Immediately remove from pans to cooling racks.

**7** In small bowl, stir together melted butter, 1 tablespoon milk and the powdered sugar. Stir in additional milk, 1 teaspoon at a time, until icing is smooth and consistency of thick syrup. Drizzle over rolls. Serve warm.

**1 Mini Roll:** Calories 100; Total Fat 3.5g (Saturated Fat 2.5g, Trans Fat 0g); Cholesterol 20mg; Sodium 75mg; Total Carbohydrate 14g (Dietary Fiber 0g); Protein 1g **Exchanges:** ½ Starch, ½ Other Carbohydrate, ½ Fat **Carbohydrate Choices:** 1

 **Kitchen Secrets** **To easily cook the sweet potato, pierce with a fork and place on microwavable paper towel. Microwave on High 5 to 7 minutes or until tender. When cooled enough to handle, slit potato skin and peel away from flesh; mash flesh with fork. Cool to room temperature.**

# Bread Machine Potato-Rosemary Bread

**PREP TIME:** 10 Minutes   **START TO FINISH:** 3 Hours 40 Minutes   *12 or 16 slices*

## 1½-POUND LOAF (12 SLICES)

- 1¼ cups water
- 2 tablespoons butter, softened
- 3 cups bread flour
- ½ cup plain mashed potato mix (dry)
- 1 tablespoon dried rosemary leaves, crushed
- 1 tablespoon sugar
- 1½ teaspoons salt
- 2 teaspoons bread machine yeast

## 2-POUND LOAF (16 SLICES)

- 1⅔ cups water
- 2 tablespoons butter, softened
- 4 cups bread flour
- ⅔ cup plain mashed potato mix (dry)
- 1 tablespoon sugar
- 1½ teaspoons salt
- 1½ teaspoons bread machine yeast*

**1** Make 1½-pound recipe with bread machines that use 3 cups flour, or make 2-pound recipe with bread machines that use 4 cups flour.

**2** Measure carefully, placing all ingredients in bread machine pan in order recommended by manufacturer.

**3** Select Basic/White cycle. Use Medium or Light crust color. Remove baked bread from pan; cool on cooling rack.

*Yeast amount for 2-pound recipe is correct although proportionately less than that called for in the 1½-pound recipe.

**1 Slice:** Calories 150; Total Fat 2.5g (Saturated Fat 1.5g, Trans Fat 0g); Cholesterol 5mg; Sodium 310mg; Total Carbohydrate 28g (Dietary Fiber 1g); Protein 4g **Exchanges:** 1 Starch, 1 Other Carbohydrate, ½ Fat **Carbohydrate Choices:** 2

## Make-Ahead Magic
You can assemble this bread earlier in the day, using the Delay cycle, then bake it when you're ready. If using the Delay cycle, the butter does not need to be softened before being added to the pan.

# Cherry-Eggnog Cream Pastries

**PREP TIME:** 50 Minutes     **START TO FINISH:** 10 Hours 55 Minutes     *12 pastries*

### PASTRY

- 4 to 5 cups all-purpose flour
- ⅓ cup granulated sugar
- 1 teaspoon salt
- 1 package fast-acting dry yeast (2¼ teaspoons)
- 1 cup milk
- ⅔ cup butter, cut into pieces
- 1 whole egg

### FILLING

- 3 oz (from 8-oz package) cream cheese, softened
- 1 tablespoon granulated sugar
- 1 egg yolk
- ⅛ to ¼ teaspoon rum extract
  Dash ground nutmeg
- 1 egg yolk beaten with 1 tablespoon water
- 36 to 48 cherries with pie filling (from 21-oz can)

### ICING

- ¾ cup powdered sugar
- ¼ teaspoon rum extract
- 3 to 4 teaspoons milk

**1** In large bowl, stir 2 cups of the flour, ⅓ cup granulated sugar, the salt and yeast. In 1-quart saucepan, heat 1 cup milk and the butter until very warm (120°F to 130°F). Add milk mixture and whole egg to flour mixture. Beat with electric mixer on low speed 1 minute. Beat on medium speed 1 minute, scraping bowl occasionally. Stir in enough of the remaining 2 to 3 cups flour to make dough easy to handle.

**2** On lightly floured surface, knead dough until smooth, about 5 minutes. Cover with large bowl; let rest 10 minutes.

**3** Line 2 large cookie sheets with cooking parchment paper. Divide dough into 24 equal pieces. Roll each piece into 12-inch rope. Twist 2 ropes together; coil into circle with edge built up higher than center. On cookie sheets, place pastries 3 inches apart. Cover loosely with plastic wrap sprayed with cooking spray. Refrigerate at least 8 hours or overnight.

**4** About 2 hours before serving, remove pastries from refrigerator. Let stand covered in warm place 1 hour or until almost doubled in size.

**5** Heat oven to 350°F. In small bowl, stir cream cheese, 1 tablespoon granulated sugar, 1 egg yolk, ⅛ to ¼ teaspoon rum extract and the nutmeg with spoon until smooth.

**6** Gently shape each pastry with fingers to form 2-inch-wide indentation in center. Brush dough with egg yolk–water mixture. Spoon 1½ teaspoons cream cheese mixture into one side of each indentation; spoon 3 or 4 cherries into other side.

**7** Bake 20 to 25 minutes or until golden brown. Remove from cookie sheets to cooling racks; cool 30 minutes.

**8** In small bowl, stir icing ingredients until smooth and thin enough to drizzle. Drizzle icing over pastries.

**1 Pastry:** Calories 390; Total Fat 15g (Saturated Fat 9g, Trans Fat 0.5g); Cholesterol 80mg; Sodium 330mg; Total Carbohydrate 57g (Dietary Fiber 1g); Protein 6g **Exchanges:** 1½ Starch, 2½ Other Carbohydrate, 3 Fat **Carbohydrate Choices:** 4

## Festive Touch
Leftover cherry pie filling can make anything festive! Spread it on toast or atop cream cheese on your breakfast bagel, or spoon over ice cream or brownies for a special treat.

## Kitchen Secrets
If you want to make and bake these pastries the same day, make as directed through Step 3—except do not refrigerate. Let rise in warm place 45 minutes or until almost doubled in size. Heat oven and continue as directed.

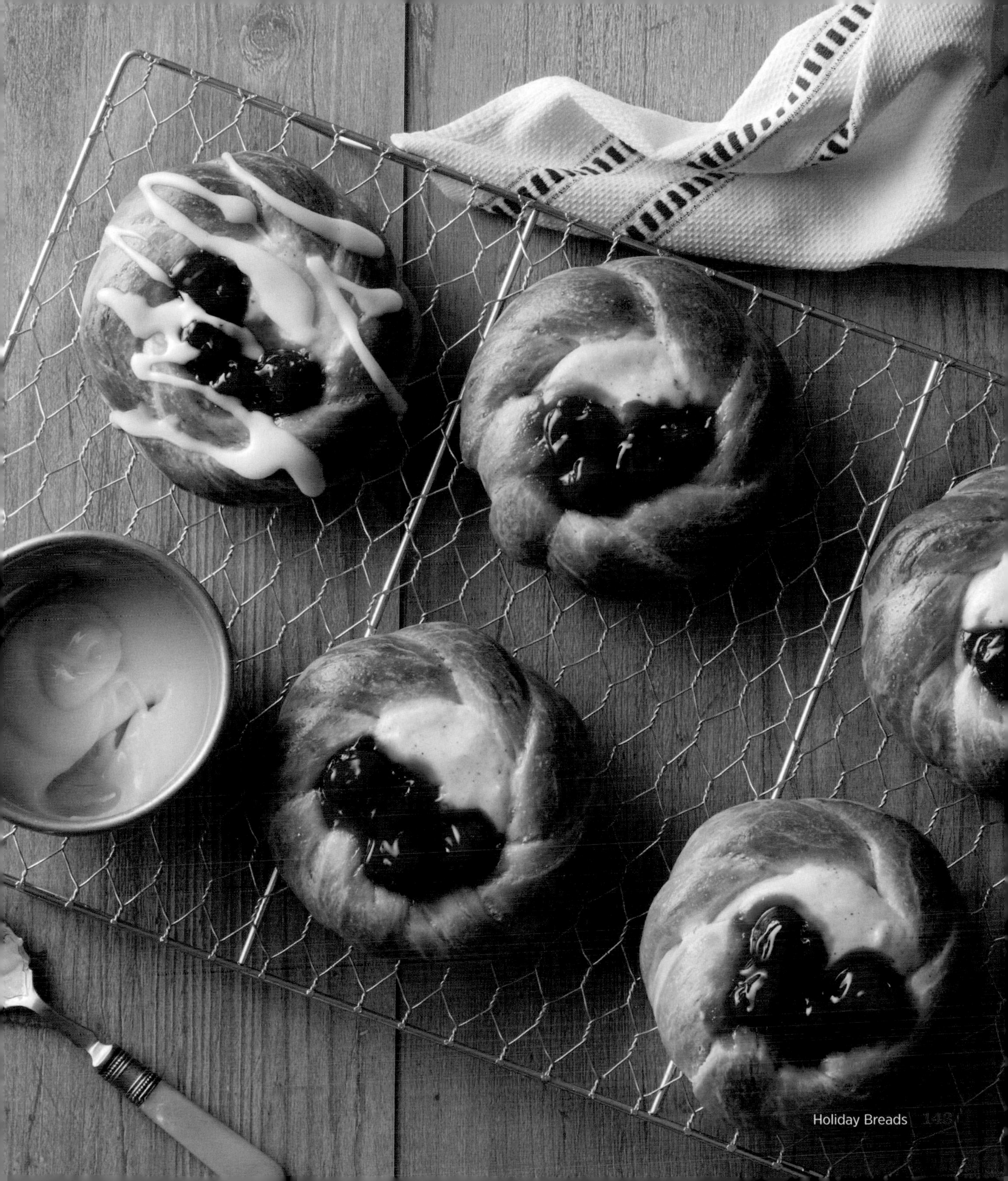

# Spiced Apple Bread

**PREP TIME:** 25 Minutes    **START TO FINISH:** 3 Hours 25 Minutes    *24 slices*

## BREAD

- 1½ cups granulated sugar
- ¾ cup vegetable oil
- 2 teaspoons vanilla
- 4 eggs
- 4 oz (from 8-oz package) cream cheese, softened
- 2 cups shredded peeled baking apples (about 2 large)
- ⅔ cup applesauce
- 3 cups all-purpose flour
- 1 tablespoon apple pie spice
- 1½ teaspoons baking soda
- 1 teaspoon baking powder
- ½ teaspoon salt
- ½ cup walnut or pecan pieces
- ½ cup raisins, if desired

## ICING

- 2 oz (from 8-oz package) cream cheese, softened
- 2 to 3 tablespoons milk
- 1 cup powdered sugar
- ¼ teaspoon ground cinnamon

1  Heat oven to 350°F. Grease bottom only of 2 (8x4- or 9x5-inch) loaf pans with shortening or cooking spray. (Do not use dark pans.)

2  In large bowl, beat granulated sugar, oil, vanilla, eggs and 4 oz cream cheese with electric mixer on medium speed until smooth. Stir in apples and applesauce. Stir in flour, apple pie spice, baking soda, baking powder and salt. Stir in nuts and raisins. Divide batter evenly between pans.

3  Bake 45 to 50 minutes or until toothpick inserted in center comes out clean. Cool 10 minutes; remove from pans to cooling racks. Cool completely, about 2 hours.

4  In microwavable bowl, microwave 2 oz cream cheese and 1 tablespoon of the milk on High about 10 seconds or just until warm. Stir in powdered sugar and cinnamon with whisk until smooth. Stir in remaining milk, 1 teaspoon at a time, as needed until desired consistency. Spread icing on bread.

**1 Slice:** Calories 250; Total Fat 12g (Saturated Fat 3g, Trans Fat 0g); Cholesterol 40mg; Sodium 190mg; Total Carbohydrate 33g (Dietary Fiber 1g); Protein 3g **Exchanges:** 1 Starch, 1 Other Carbohydrate, 2½ Fat **Carbohydrate Choices:** 2

**Make-Ahead Magic** The loaves can be baked ahead, and the flavors will only improve. Wrap tightly and store in the refrigerator up to 4 days.

**Festive Touch** For a special treat, serve slices topped with whipped cream and a sprinkling of cinnamon.

# Jumbo Cherry Doughnut Holes

**PREP TIME:** 45 Minutes   **START TO FINISH:** 45 Minutes   *30 doughnut holes*

**SNICKERDOODLE COATING**

1 cup granulated sugar

1 teaspoon ground cinnamon

**DOUGHNUT HOLES**

4 cups vegetable oil

½ cup buttermilk

2 tablespoons butter, melted

1 teaspoon vanilla

¼ teaspoon almond extract

1 egg

2½ cups all-purpose flour

½ cup granulated sugar

1 teaspoon baking powder

¼ teaspoon baking soda

½ teaspoon salt

1 jar (10 oz) maraschino cherries, drained, finely chopped

**1** In 1-quart resealable food-storage plastic bag, mix coating ingredients; set aside.

**2** In 4-quart Dutch oven or 3-quart saucepan, heat oil to 350°F. Cover cooling rack with paper towels.

**3** In large bowl, beat buttermilk, butter, vanilla, almond extract and egg with spoon until well blended. Stir in flour, ½ cup granulated sugar, the baking powder, baking soda, salt and cherries.

**4** Use #40 cookie scoop (about 1½ tablespoons) to scoop dough into hot oil; fry doughnut holes, 4 or 5 at a time, 2 to 3 minutes, turning once, until golden brown. Remove with slotted spoon to cooling rack.

**5** Immediately add 2 or 3 doughnut holes to bag with coating; seal bag and gently shake. Repeat with remaining doughnut holes.

**1 Doughnut Hole:** Calories 130; Total Fat 5g (Saturated Fat 1g, Trans Fat 0g); Cholesterol 10mg; Sodium 80mg; Total Carbohydrate 21g (Dietary Fiber 0g); Protein 1g **Exchanges:** 1½ Other Carbohydrate, 1 Fat **Carbohydrate Choices:** 1½

## Festive Touch

Try other coatings on your doughnut holes instead of Snickerdoodle. For *Cappuccino Coating*, substitute powdered sugar for the granulated sugar and 2 teaspoons espresso coffee powder for the cinnamon. Mix in resealable bag and continue as directed. For *Candy Cane Coating*, in small bowl, mix 1 cup powdered sugar, 1 tablespoon half-and-half or milk and ¼ teaspoon peppermint extract. Cool fried doughnut holes slightly, then top with icing and sprinkle with ¼ cup crushed candy canes.

# Chocolate-Hazelnut Doughnuts

**PREP TIME:** 1 Hour   **START TO FINISH:** 1 Hour   *16 doughnuts and doughnut holes*

## DOUGHNUTS

3½  cups all-purpose flour

2  teaspoons baking powder

½  teaspoon salt

1  cup sugar

2  eggs

½  cup mashed potatoes

2  oz unsweetened chocolate, melted, cooled

2  tablespoons butter, melted

⅓  cup milk

4  cups vegetable oil

## TOPPING

1  cup hazelnut spread with cocoa

¼  cup chopped hazelnuts (filberts), toasted

1. In medium bowl, mix flour, baking powder and salt; set aside. In large bowl, beat sugar, eggs, potatoes, chocolate and butter with electric mixer on medium speed until blended. On low speed, beat in flour mixture alternately with milk, beating after each addition until soft dough forms (dough will be soft).

2. On floured surface, roll dough with rolling pin until ½ inch thick. Cut with 3-inch doughnut cutter; reroll dough as necessary.

3. In 4-quart Dutch oven or 3-quart saucepan, heat oil to 375°F. Carefully place 2 or 3 doughnuts at a time in hot oil. Fry doughnuts and doughnut holes 2 to 3 minutes, turning once, until golden brown. Using slotted spoon, remove doughnuts to cooling racks. Cool 5 minutes.

4. In small microwavable bowl, microwave hazelnut spread on High 20 to 30 seconds or until dipping consistency. Dip one side of each doughnut and doughnut hole in hazelnut spread; sprinkle with nuts.

**1 Doughnut:** Calories 400; Total Fat 20g (Saturated Fat 4g, Trans Fat 0g); Cholesterol 30mg; Sodium 170mg; Total Carbohydrate 49g (Dietary Fiber 2g); Protein 5g **Exchanges:** 1 Starch, 2 Other Carbohydrate, ½ Very Lean Meat, 4 Fat **Carbohydrate Choices:** 3

## Kitchen Secrets

The key to perfect doughnuts is maintaining an oil temperature of 375°F. Use a deep-fat thermometer for best results. Frying for too long can make the doughnuts dry.

## Kitchen Secrets

To toast hazelnuts, sprinkle in ungreased skillet. Cook over medium heat 5 to 7 minutes, stirring frequently until nuts begin to brown, then stirring constantly until nuts are light brown.

# Mocha Streusel Coffee Cake

**PREP TIME:** 25 Minutes    **START TO FINISH:** 2 Hours 30 Minutes    *12 servings*

## STREUSEL

- ⅔ cup miniature semisweet chocolate chips
- ½ cup chopped pecans
- ⅓ cup packed brown sugar
- 2 tablespoons all-purpose flour
- 1 tablespoon instant coffee granules or crystals

## COFFEE CAKE

- 2¾ cups all-purpose flour
- 2 teaspoons baking powder
- 1 teaspoon ground cinnamon
- ¼ teaspoon baking soda
- ¼ teaspoon salt
- 1 cup granulated sugar
- 1 cup butter, softened
- ½ teaspoon almond extract
- 3 eggs
- 1 container (8 oz) sour cream

1 Heat oven to 350°F. Spray bottom and side of 10-inch angel food (tube) cake pan with cooking spray. In small bowl, mix streusel ingredients; set aside.

2 In medium bowl, mix 2¾ cups flour, the baking powder, cinnamon, baking soda and salt. In large bowl, beat granulated sugar and butter with electric mixer on medium speed until light and fluffy. Beat in almond extract. Add eggs, one at a time, beating well after each addition. Add half of the flour mixture; beat on low speed just until combined. Beat in sour cream until well blended. Beat in remaining flour mixture.

3 Spoon half of the batter into pan; spread evenly. Sprinkle with half of the streusel. Repeat with remaining batter and streusel.

4 Bake 55 to 65 minutes or until toothpick inserted in center comes out clean. Cool upright in pan on cooling rack 1 hour. Remove cake from pan.

**1 Serving:** Calories 480; Total Fat 27g (Saturated Fat 14g, Trans Fat 0.5g); Cholesterol 95mg; Sodium 310mg; Total Carbohydrate 54g (Dietary Fiber 2g); Protein 6g **Exchanges:** 2 Starch, 1½ Other Carbohydrate, 5 Fat **Carbohydrate Choices:** 3½

## Make-Ahead Magic

**Bake as directed and cool completely. Wrap the cake tightly and freeze up to 2 months.**

# Chocolate–Cream Cheese Coffee Cake

**PREP TIME:** 20 Minutes   **START TO FINISH:** 2 Hours 5 Minutes   *12 servings*

### PECAN MIXTURE
- 1⅓ cups all-purpose flour
- ½ cup cold butter
- ½ cup packed brown sugar
- 1 cup chopped pecans

### CREAM CHEESE MIXTURE
- 1 package (8 oz) cream cheese, softened
- ¼ cup granulated sugar
- 1 tablespoon all-purpose flour
- 1 egg
- 1 teaspoon vanilla

### CAKE
- 1 box dark chocolate cake mix with pudding
- 1¼ cups water
- ½ cup vegetable oil
- 2 eggs

### ICING
- 1 cup powdered sugar
- 2 tablespoons milk

1  Heat oven to 350°F. Spray 13x9-inch pan with cooking spray. In medium bowl, mix 1⅓ cups flour and brown sugar. Cut in butter until crumbly. Stir in pecans; set aside. In separate medium bowl, beat cream cheese with electric mixer on medium speed until smooth. Add granulated sugar and 1 tablespoon flour; beat until blended. Add 1 egg and ½ teaspoon of the vanilla; beat until blended.

2  Make cake mix as directed on box, using water, oil and 2 eggs. Spoon batter into pan. Dollop cream cheese mixture over batter and swirl with knife. Sprinkle reserved pecan mixture over top. Bake 45 minutes or until set. Cool completely on cooling rack, about 1 hour.

3  In small bowl, mix powdered sugar, milk and remaining ½ teaspoon vanilla with whisk. Drizzle over coffee cake.

**1 Serving:** Calories 530; Total Fat 25g (Saturated Fat 10g, Trans Fat 0g); Cholesterol 0mg; Sodium 540mg; Total Carbohydrate 75g (Dietary Fiber 2g); Protein 6g **Exchanges:** 2 Starch, 3 Other Carbohydrate, 5 Fat **Carbohydrate Choices:** 5

## Make-Ahead Magic
**Bake and cool as directed. Wrap coffee cake tightly in heavy-duty foil; freeze up to 1 month. Thaw partially at room temperature; continue as directed in Step 3.**

# Danish Cherry-Orange Cake

**PREP TIME:** 15 Minutes   **START TO FINISH:** 1 Hour 15 Minutes   *8 servings*

## CAKE

- ½ cup butter, softened
- ½ cup granulated sugar
- 3 eggs
- 1 teaspoon vanilla
- 1½ cups Original Bisquick mix
- 1 can (11 oz) mandarin oranges, well drained
- ½ cup dried cherries
- ½ cup chopped pecans

## ICING

- 2 oz (from 8-oz package) cream cheese, softened
- ¼ cup powdered sugar
- 1 to 2 tablespoons milk
- 1 teaspoon grated orange peel

**1** Heat oven to 325°F. Spray bottom only of 9-inch springform pan with cooking spray.

**2** In large bowl, beat butter and granulated sugar with electric mixer on high speed 1 minute or until smooth and creamy. Add eggs and vanilla; beat on medium speed about 10 seconds or until well blended. Add Bisquick mix; beat on medium speed about 30 seconds or until mixed.

**3** Spread batter evenly in bottom of pan. Arrange mandarin oranges and cherries on batter. Sprinkle with pecans.

**4** Bake 35 to 40 minutes or until golden brown and toothpick inserted in center comes out clean. Cool 20 minutes in pan on cooling rack. Remove side of pan.

**5** In small bowl, beat cream cheese, powdered sugar and 1 tablespoon milk with electric mixer on medium speed until smooth. Beat in remaining milk, 1 teaspoon at a time, if needed for desired consistency. Drizzle icing over warm cake. Sprinkle with orange peel. Store in refrigerator.

**1 Serving:** Calories 420; Total Fat 24g (Saturated Fat 11g, Trans Fat 0.5g); Cholesterol 110mg; Sodium 420mg; Total Carbohydrate 45g (Dietary Fiber 1g); Protein 5g **Exchanges:** 1 Starch, ½ Fruit, 1½ Other Carbohydrate, ½ High-Fat Meat, 4 Fat **Carbohydrate Choices:** 3

**Make-Ahead Magic** Bake and cool cake, but do not top with icing; wrap in plastic wrap and foil. Freeze up to 2 weeks. Remove plastic wrap and foil; rewrap in foil and place on ungreased cookie sheet. Bake at 350°F for 20 to 25 minutes or until heated through. Unwrap cake; drizzle with icing.

**Festive Touch** This delicious cake would be a perfect hostess gift. Wrap in plastic wrap and tie with a festive ribbon.

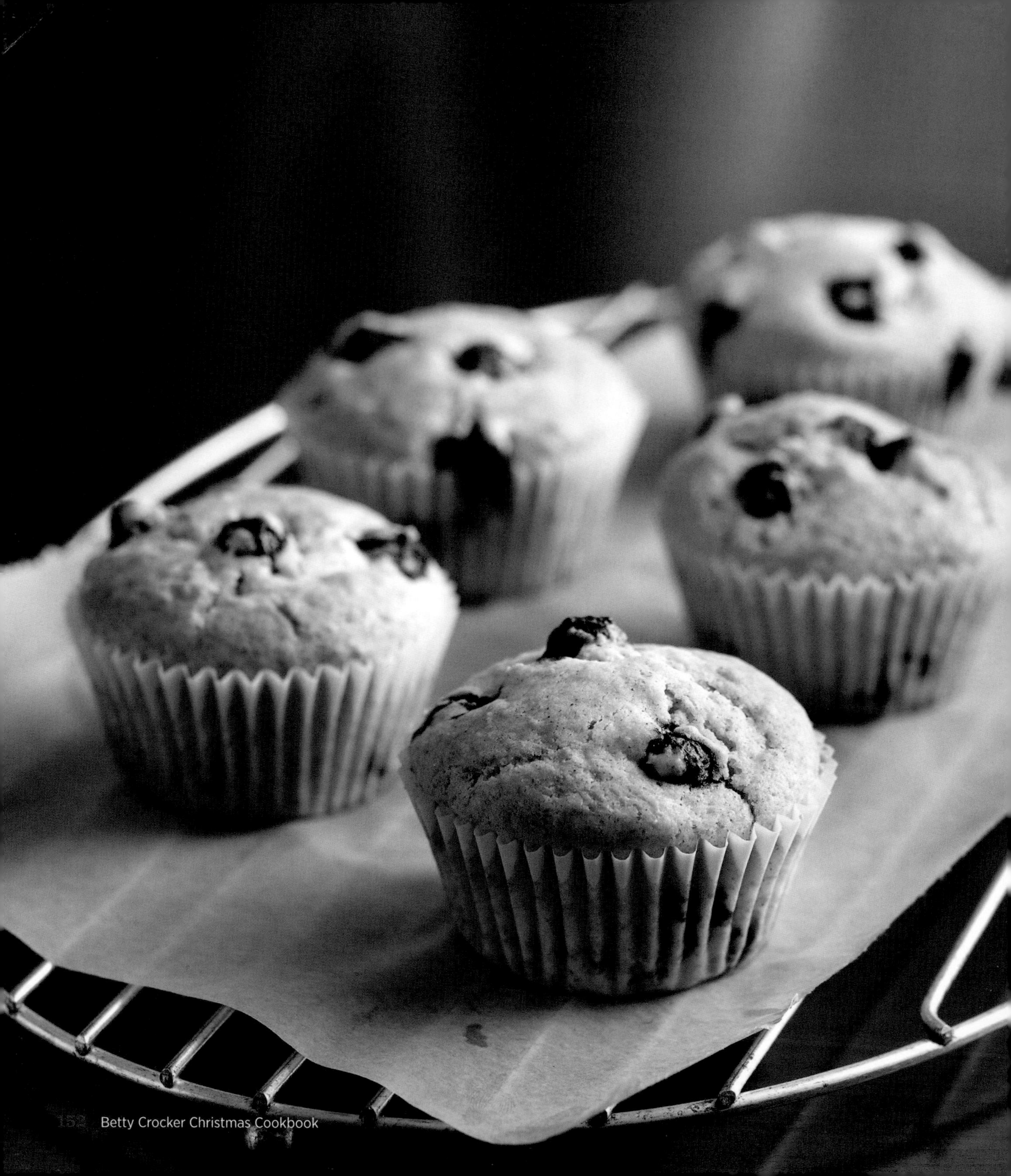

# Spiced Blueberry Muffins

**PREP TIME:** 10 Minutes    **START TO FINISH:** 30 Minutes
*12 muffins*

      2  cups Original Bisquick mix
     ⅔  cup milk
     ¼  cup butter, melted
      1  egg
     ⅓  cup sugar
     ¾  teaspoon ground cinnamon
     ½  teaspoon ground ginger
     ¼  teaspoon ground nutmeg
     ¾  cup fresh or frozen (do not thaw) blueberries

1   Heat oven to 400°F. Place paper baking cup in each of 12 regular-size muffin cups.

2   In large bowl, mix all ingredients except blueberries. Gently fold in blueberries. Divide batter evenly among muffin cups, using slightly less than ¼ cup for each.

3   Bake 17 to 20 minutes or until golden brown and toothpick inserted in center comes out clean. Immediately remove from pan to cooling rack. Serve warm or cool.

**1 Muffin:** Calories 160; Total Fat 7g (Saturated Fat 3.5g, Trans Fat 1g); Cholesterol 30mg; Sodium 280mg; Total Carbohydrate 21g (Dietary Fiber 0g); Protein 2g **Exchanges:** 1 Starch, ½ Other Carbohydrate, 1½ Fat **Carbohydrate Choices:** 1½

### Make-Ahead Magic  Muffins can be baked up to a month in advance. Freeze cooled muffins in resealable freezer plastic bags. To reheat, remove muffins from bag and wrap in foil. Bake at 350°F for 15 to 20 minutes or until warm.

# Caramel-Spice French Breakfast Muffins

**PREP TIME:** 20 Minutes    **START TO FINISH:** 50 Minutes
*18 muffins*

**MUFFINS**
     ½  cup butter, softened
     ½  cup sugar
     ½  cup caramel topping or caramel apple dip
      2  eggs
     ¾  cup milk
      2  cups all-purpose flour
    1½  teaspoons baking powder
     ½  teaspoon salt
     ½  teaspoon ground cinnamon
     ½  teaspoon ground nutmeg

**TOPPING**
     ¾  cup butter
     ¾  cup sugar
    1½  teaspoons pumpkin pie spice
        Caramel topping or caramel apple dip, if desired

1   Heat oven to 375°F. Spray 18 regular-size muffin cups with cooking spray.

2   In large bowl, beat ½ cup butter, ½ cup sugar, ½ cup caramel topping, the eggs and milk with electric mixer on low speed (mixture will appear curdled). Stir in flour, baking powder, salt, cinnamon and nutmeg just until moistened. Divide batter evenly among muffin cups, filling each two-thirds full.

3   Bake 20 to 25 minutes or until toothpick inserted in center comes out clean. Cool 5 minutes.

4   Meanwhile, in medium microwavable bowl, microwave ¾ cup butter on High until melted. In small bowl, mix ¾ cup sugar and the pumpkin pie spice. Remove muffins from pan. Roll in melted butter, then in sugar mixture. Drizzle with caramel topping. Serve warm.

**1 Muffin:** Calories 260; Total Fat 14g (Saturated Fat 8g, Trans Fat 0.5g); Cholesterol 60mg; Sodium 240mg; Total Carbohydrate 31g (Dietary Fiber 0g); Protein 2g **Exchanges:** ½ Starch, 1½ Other Carbohydrate, 2½ Fat **Carbohydrate Choices:** 2

# Mocha Muffins

**PREP TIME:** 15 Minutes    **START TO FINISH:** 35 Minutes
*12 muffins*

- 2 cups all-purpose flour
- 2 tablespoons unsweetened baking cocoa
- 2½ teaspoons baking powder
- ½ teaspoon salt
- ⅓ cup packed brown sugar
- 1 cup milk
- ⅓ cup vegetable oil
- 1 tablespoon instant coffee granules or crystals
- 1 egg
- 1 cup semisweet chocolate chunks or chips (about 6 oz)
- 2 teaspoons instant espresso coffee powder or granules
- 1 container (1 lb) chocolate creamy ready-to-spread frosting

1  Heat oven to 400°F. Grease bottoms only of 12 regular-size muffin cups with shortening or cooking spray, or place paper baking cup in each muffin cup.

2  In medium bowl, mix flour, cocoa, baking powder and salt. In large bowl, beat brown sugar, milk, oil, 1 tablespoon coffee granules and the egg with fork or whisk. Stir in flour mixture just until flour is moistened. Fold in chocolate chunks. Divide batter evenly among muffin cups.

3  Bake 18 to 20 minutes or until toothpick inserted in center comes out clean. Immediately remove from pan to cooling rack.

4  Spoon frosting into a small microwavable bowl; stir 2 teaspoons espresso powder into frosting. Heat on High 10 seconds or until frosting can be stirred to drizzling consistency. Drizzle over warm muffins. Serve warm or cool.

**1 Muffin:** Calories 410; Total Fat 18g (Saturated Fat 6g, Trans Fat 1.5g); Cholesterol 15mg; Sodium 330mg; Total Carbohydrate 59g (Dietary Fiber 2g); Protein 4g **Exchanges:** 1 Starch, 3 Other Carbohydrate, 3½ Fat **Carbohydrate Choices:** 4

# Cheddar-Chile Cornbread Scones

**PREP TIME:** 20 Minutes    **START TO FINISH:** 45 Minutes
*8 scones*

- 1¼ cups white whole wheat or all-purpose flour
- 1 cup cornmeal
- 1 tablespoon sugar
- 2 teaspoons baking powder
- ½ teaspoon salt
- ½ cup cold butter
- ¼ cup milk
- 1 egg, beaten
- ¾ cup shredded Cheddar cheese (3 oz)
- 1 can (4.5 oz) chopped green chiles, undrained
- ⅔ cup crumbled crisply cooked bacon, if desired
  Honey, if desired

1  Heat oven to 425°F. Grease cookie sheet with shortening or cooking spray.

2  In large bowl, mix flour, cornmeal, sugar, baking powder and salt. Cut in butter, using pastry blender or fork, until mixture looks like coarse crumbs. Stir in milk, egg, cheese, chiles and bacon.

3  On lightly floured surface, knead dough lightly 10 times. On cookie sheet, roll or pat dough into 8-inch round. Cut into 8 wedges, but do not separate.

4  Bake 18 to 23 minutes or until golden brown. Immediately remove from cookie sheet to cooling rack; carefully separate wedges. Serve warm with honey.

**1 Scone:** Calories 347; Total Fat 20.5g (Saturated Fat 11g, Trans Fat 0.5g); Cholesterol 72mg; Sodium 384mg; Total Carbohydrate 33g (Dietary Fiber 3g); Protein 9g **Exchanges:** 1 Starch, 1 Other Carbohydrate, ½ High-Fat Meat, 2½ Fat **Carbohydrate Choices:** 2

**Festive Touch** These south-of-the-border scones are a perfect choice when you are looking to break free from traditional rolls at your holiday table. They would also be a big hit as part of a breakfast buffet.

# Buttermilk-Herb Biscuits

**PREP TIME:** 15 Minutes  **START TO FINISH:** 35 Minutes  *12 biscuits*

2 cups all-purpose flour

2 teaspoons baking powder

1½ teaspoons dried herb leaves (rosemary, basil or thyme) or Italian seasoning

½ teaspoon salt

½ teaspoon baking soda

⅓ cup shortening

1 cup buttermilk

1 tablespoon butter, melted

1 Heat oven to 400°F. In medium bowl, mix flour, baking powder, herb, salt and baking soda. Cut in shortening, using pastry blender or fork, until mixture looks like fine crumbs. Stir in buttermilk until dough leaves side of bowl (dough will be soft and sticky).

2 On lightly floured surface, lightly knead dough 10 times. Roll or pat dough about 1 inch thick. Cut with floured 2-inch biscuit cutter. On ungreased cookie sheet, place biscuits about 1 inch apart. Brush with melted butter.

3 Bake 14 to 16 minutes or until golden brown. Immediately remove from cookie sheet. Serve warm.

**1 Biscuit:** Calories 150; Total Fat 7g (Saturated Fat 2.5g, Trans Fat 0g); Cholesterol 0mg; Sodium 260mg; Total Carbohydrate 17g (Dietary Fiber 0g); Protein 3g **Exchanges:** 1 Starch, 1½ Fat **Carbohydrate Choices:** 1

## Kitchen Secrets

Push the biscuit cutter straight down into the dough, trying not to twist as you cut, and cut biscuits as close together as possible. You can lightly press—but don't knead—leftover dough scraps together to cut out a few more biscuits. They may be slightly uneven, but they'll taste just as good!

# Butter Trio

**PREP TIME:** 15 Minutes   **START TO FINISH:** 2 Hours 15 Minutes   *About ½ cup of each butter*

### RASPBERRY-JALAPEÑO BUTTER

- ½ cup butter, softened
- 1½ teaspoons finely chopped seeded jalapeño chile (about 1 small)
- 1 teaspoon cider vinegar
- ⅛ to ½ teaspoon ground red pepper (cayenne)
- ¼ cup fresh raspberries, mashed

### APRICOT-CURRY BUTTER

- ½ cup butter, softened
- 2 tablespoons finely chopped dried apricots
- 1 teaspoon curry powder
- 1½ teaspoons honey

### CHOCOLATE-HAZELNUT BUTTER

- ½ cup butter, softened
- 2 tablespoons hazelnut spread with cocoa
- 1 tablespoon finely chopped hazelnuts (filberts), toasted
- 1 tablespoon miniature semisweet chocolate chips

**1** In small bowl, mix ½ cup butter, the chile, vinegar and red pepper until well blended. Fold in raspberries. In two separate small bowls, mix Apricot-Curry Butter ingredients and Chocolate-Hazelnut Butter ingredients until well blended.

**2** Spoon butters into serving dishes; cover with plastic wrap. Refrigerate at least 2 hours to blend flavors. Remove from refrigerator about 30 minutes before serving to soften.

**1 Tablespoon Raspberry-Jalapeño Butter:** Calories 110; Total Fat 12g (Saturated Fat 7g, Trans Fat 0g); Cholesterol 30mg; Sodium 90mg; Total Carbohydrate 1g (Dietary Fiber 0g); Protein 0g **Exchanges:** 2½ Fat **Carbohydrate Choices:** 0

## Make-Ahead Magic These elegant butters can be prepared and refrigerated up to 2 days before serving.

## Festive Touch Make logs of butter to slice and serve or to give as gifts. Form small log shape of butter on plastic wrap. Tuck plastic wrap tightly around log and roll gently to make a smooth shape. Refrigerate as directed. To serve, unwrap and slice while cold; arrange slices on serving plate.

## Festive Touch For a special added touch, roll each log in a coating before wrapping. For *Raspberry-Jalapeño Butter*, use 2 tablespoons chopped fresh cilantro. For *Apricot-Curry Butter*, use 2 tablespoons chopped fresh parsley. For *Chocolate-Hazelnut Butter*, use an additional 2 tablespoons finely chopped hazelnuts or chocolate chips.

## Kitchen Secrets

To toast hazelnuts, sprinkle in ungreased skillet. Cook over medium heat 5 to 7 minutes, stirring occasionally until nuts begin to brown, then stirring constantly until nuts are light brown.

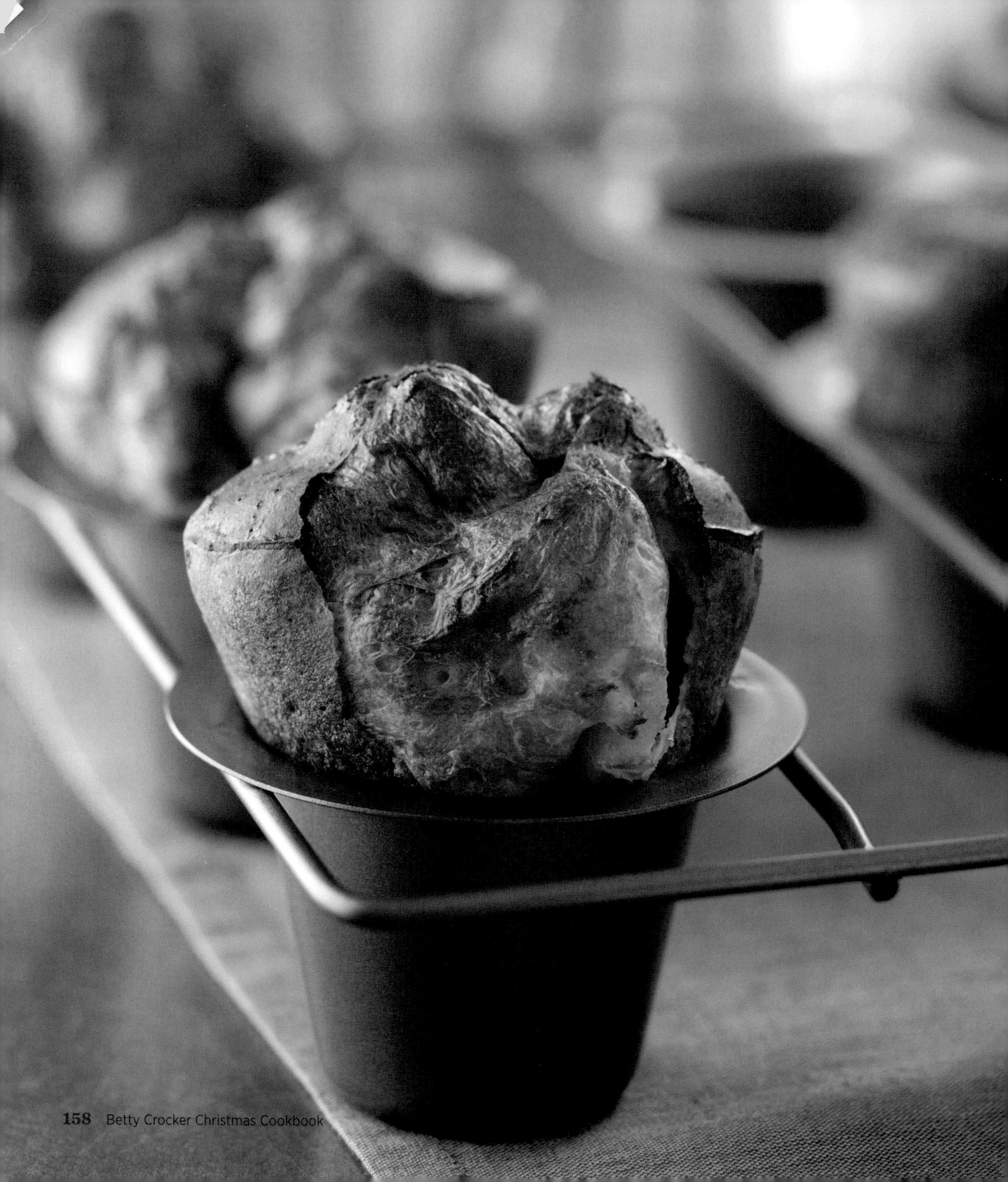

# Popovers

**PREP TIME:** 10 Minutes    **START TO FINISH:** 45 Minutes    *6 popovers*

2 eggs
1 cup all-purpose flour
1 cup milk
½ teaspoon salt

**1** Heat oven to 450°F. Generously grease 6-cup popover pan with shortening. Heat popover pan in oven 5 minutes.

**2** Meanwhile, in medium bowl, beat eggs slightly with fork or whisk. Beat in flour, milk and salt just until smooth (do not overbeat or popovers may not puff as high). Divide batter evenly among cups, filling each about half full.

**3** Bake 20 minutes. Reduce oven temperature to 325°F. Bake 10 to 15 minutes longer or until deep golden brown. Immediately remove from cups. Serve hot.

**1 Popover:** Calories 120; Total Fat 3g (Saturated Fat 1g, Trans Fat 0g); Cholesterol 65mg; Sodium 240mg; Total Carbohydrate 18g (Dietary Fiber 0g); Protein 5g **Exchanges:** 1 Starch, ½ Fat **Carbohydrate Choices:** 1

## Festive Touch
Popover batter can be used to make Yorkshire Pudding—a traditional side dish often served with roast beef. Heat oven to 350°F. Place ¼ cup vegetable oil or beef drippings in 9-inch square pan; place pan in oven, and heat until hot. Increase oven temperature to 450°F. Prepare popover batter as directed; carefully pour into hot oil. Bake 18 to 23 minutes or until puffy and golden brown (pudding will puff during baking but will deflate shortly after being removed from oven). Cut pudding into squares; serve immediately.

## Kitchen Secrets
Popovers seem fancy but are easy and quick to make. Serve them with Butter Trio (page 157) to really wow your guests.

# Garlic-Herb Roadhouse Rolls

**PREP TIME:** 30 Minutes    **START TO FINISH:** 2 Hours 30 Minutes    *12 rolls*

### ROLLS

3½ to 4 cups all-purpose flour

1 package regular active or fast-acting dry yeast (2¼ teaspoons)

¼ cup sugar

1 teaspoon salt

2 teaspoons chopped fresh basil leaves

1 teaspoon chopped fresh thyme leaves

½ teaspoon chopped fresh rosemary leaves

¼ teaspoon garlic powder

1 cup milk

¼ cup water

3 tablespoons butter

2 tablespoons honey

1 egg

1 tablespoon butter, melted

### GARLIC-HERB BUTTER

½ cup butter, softened

½ teaspoon chopped fresh basil leaves

½ teaspoon chopped fresh thyme leaves

¼ teaspoon chopped fresh rosemary leaves

¼ teaspoon garlic powder

**1** In large bowl, mix 1½ cups of the flour, the yeast, sugar, salt, 2 teaspoons basil, 1 teaspoon thyme, ½ teaspoon rosemary and ¼ teaspoon garlic powder. In 1-quart saucepan, heat milk, water, 3 tablespoons butter and the honey over medium heat until very warm (120°F to 130°F). Pour over flour mixture. Add egg; beat with electric mixer on low speed 1 minute, scraping bowl frequently. Add enough of the remaining 2 to 2½ cups flour, beating on medium speed 5 minutes, until dough is smooth. (Dough will be slightly sticky.)

**2** Grease large bowl with shortening or cooking spray. Place dough in bowl, turning dough to grease all sides. Cover loosely with plastic wrap and cloth towel; let rise in warm place 1 hour or until doubled in size.

**3** Line cookie sheets with cooking parchment paper. Gently push fist into dough to deflate. On floured surface, roll dough into 12x9-inch rectangle about ½ inch thick. Using pizza cutter, cut dough into 12 (3-inch) squares. On cookie sheets, place dough squares 2 inches apart. Cover loosely with plastic wrap; let rise in warm place 30 to 40 minutes or until doubled in size.

**4** Heat oven to 350°F. Uncover rolls; bake 15 to 20 minutes or until golden brown. Brush with melted butter. Remove from cookie sheets to cooling racks.

**5** In small bowl, beat garlic-herb butter ingredients with electric mixer until well blended. Serve warm rolls with butter.

**1 Roll:** Calories 280; Total Fat 13g (Saturated Fat 8g, Trans Fat 0g); Cholesterol 50mg; Sodium 300mg; Total Carbohydrate 36g (Dietary Fiber 1g); Protein 5g **Exchanges:** 1½ Starch, 1 Other Carbohydrate, 2½ Fat **Carbohydrate Choices:** 2½

## Make-Ahead Magic
**Make these rolls 2 to 3 months in advance. For that just-baked aroma and texture, store baked cooled rolls in the freezer in resealable freezer plastic bags. To reheat, remove rolls from bag; wrap together in foil. Bake at 350°F for 15 to 20 minutes or until warm.**

## Festive Touch
**These rolls paired with a small jar of the herb butter would be a great hostess gift. Place rolls in a basket lined with a colorful napkin, and add the jar to the basket. Wrap in cellophane or holiday-themed plastic wrap.**

# Jalapeño Hawaiian Rolls

**PREP TIME:** 35 Minutes    **START TO FINISH:** 2 Hours 25 Minutes    *24 rolls*

3½ to 4½ cups all-purpose flour

⅓ cup pineapple juice

¼ cup packed brown sugar

1 teaspoon salt

1 package regular active or fast-acting dry yeast (2¼ teaspoons)

½ cup milk

¼ cup butter

2 tablespoons water

1 egg

1 cup shredded Cheddar or pepper Jack cheese (4 oz)

½ cup chopped red bell pepper

2 tablespoons chopped seeded jalapeño chiles (about 2 medium)

1 tablespoon butter, melted

1 tablespoon pineapple juice

**1** In large bowl, stir 2 cups of the flour, ⅓ cup pineapple juice, the brown sugar, salt and yeast with wooden spoon until well mixed. In 1-quart saucepan, heat milk, ¼ cup butter and the water over medium heat, stirring frequently, until very warm (120°F to 130°F). Add milk mixture and egg to flour mixture. Beat with electric mixer on low speed 1 minute, scraping bowl frequently, until flour mixture is moistened. Beat on medium speed 1 minute. Stir in enough of the remaining 1½ to 2½ cups flour, about ½ cup at a time, then the cheese, bell pepper and chile until dough is soft, leaves side of bowl and is easy to handle (dough may be slightly sticky).

**2** On lightly floured surface, knead dough about 5 minutes or until smooth and elastic (sprinkle surface with more flour if dough starts to stick). Grease large bowl with shortening or cooking spray; place dough in bowl, turning dough to grease all sides. Cover loosely with plastic wrap and cloth towel; let rise in warm place about 1 hour or until doubled in size.

**3** Spray 24 regular-size muffin cups with cooking spray. Gently punch fist into dough to deflate. Divide dough into 24 equal pieces. Using floured fingers, shape each piece into a ball, pulling edges under to make a smooth top. Place dough ball, smooth side down, in each muffin cup. Cover loosely; let rise in warm place about 30 minutes or until doubled in size.

**4** Heat oven to 375°F. Uncover rolls; bake 15 to 18 minutes or until golden brown. Remove from pan to cooling rack.

**5** In small bowl, mix 1 tablespoon melted butter and 1 tablespoon pineapple juice. Brush over tops of rolls. Serve warm or cool.

**1 Roll:** Calories 120; Total Fat 4.5g (Saturated Fat 2.5g, Trans Fat 0g); Cholesterol 20mg; Sodium 150mg; Total Carbohydrate 17g (Dietary Fiber 0g); Protein 3g **Exchanges:** 1 Starch, 1 Fat **Carbohydrate Choices:** 1

## Make-Ahead Magic  Cool rolls after baking, and place in a resealable freezer plastic bag; seal bag and freeze up to 3 months. To reheat, remove frozen rolls from bag; wrap together in foil. Bake at 350°F for 15 to 20 minutes or until warm.

# Easy Cheesy Pesto Bread

**PREP TIME:** 10 Minutes  **START TO FINISH:** 30 Minutes  *24 Slices*

1 loaf (1 lb) unsliced French bread

⅔ cup sun-dried tomato pesto or basil pesto

2 cups shredded mozzarella cheese (8 oz)

**1** Heat oven to 400°F. Spray large sheet of heavy-duty foil with cooking spray.

**2** Cut bread diagonally into 24 slices to within ½ inch of bottom of loaf. In medium bowl, mix pesto and cheese; spoon and spread mixture between slices. Securely wrap loaf in foil.

**3** Bake 15 to 20 minutes or until hot.

**1 Slice :** Calories 120; Total Fat 6g (Saturated Fat 2g, Trans Fat 0g); Cholesterol 5mg; Sodium 220mg; Total Carbohydrate 12g (Dietary Fiber 0g); Protein 5g **Exchanges:** 1 Starch, 1 Fat **Carbohydrate Choices:** 1

**Make-Ahead Magic** You can assemble the bread and wrap it in foil up to 8 hours ahead of time. Keep it in the refrigerator until you're ready to bake it.

**Festive Touch** Rather than make just one kind of pesto-cheese mixture, why not make both and alternate it between slices of bread? Just mix ⅓ cup of each pesto with 1 cup of cheese.

**Kitchen Secrets** If you don't have heavy-duty foil, use two sheets of regular foil.

# Soft Pretzel Rolls

**PREP TIME:** 45 Minutes     **START TO FINISH:** 2 Hours 45 Minutes     *18 rolls*

## ROLLS

3½  to 4½ cups all-purpose flour

½  cup whole wheat flour

2  tablespoons packed brown sugar

¾  teaspoon table salt

1  package fast-acting dry yeast (2¼ teaspoons)

1½  cups very warm water (120°F to 130°F)

## SODA BATH

2  quarts water

¼  cup baking soda

1  tablespoon packed brown sugar

## TOPPING

1  egg yolk

1  tablespoon water

2  teaspoons coarse (kosher or sea) salt

**1** In large bowl, stir together 2 cups of the all-purpose flour, the whole wheat flour, 2 tablespoons brown sugar, the table salt and yeast. Add warm water; beat with electric mixer on low speed 1 minute, scraping bowl occasionally. Beat on medium speed 1 minute, scraping bowl frequently. With spoon, stir in enough remaining 1½ to 2½ cups all-purpose flour, ½ cup at a time, until dough is soft and leaves side of bowl.

**2** On lightly floured surface, knead dough 5 minutes or until smooth and elastic. Grease large bowl with shortening or cooking spray. Place dough in bowl, turning dough to grease all sides. Cover loosely with plastic wrap and cloth towel; let rise in warm place 1 hour or until doubled in size.

**3** Line 2 large cookie sheets with cooking parchment paper; spray paper with cooking spray. Divide dough into 18 equal pieces. Shape into rolls; place 3 inches apart on cookie sheets. Cover loosely with plastic wrap; let rise 30 to 45 minutes or until almost doubled in size.

**4** Heat oven to 425°F. In large stockpot, heal 2 quarts water to boiling. Stir in baking soda and 1 tablespoon brown sugar until dissolved (mixture will foam). Reduce heat to low. Carefully place 3 rolls in simmering water. Cook 30 seconds; turn and cook 30 seconds longer. With slotted spoon, remove rolls and return to cookie sheet. Repeat with remaining rolls.

**5** In small bowl, beat egg yolk and 1 tablespoon water. Brush egg mixture over each roll. Using scissors or serrated knife, cut ½-inch crosses in center of each roll. Sprinkle with coarse salt.

**6** Bake 10 to 15 minutes or until deep golden brown. Remove from cookie sheets to cooling racks. Serve warm or at room temperature.

**1 Roll:** Calories 110; Total Fat 0.5g (Saturated Fat 0g, Trans Fat 0g); Cholesterol 10mg; Sodium 430mg; Total Carbohydrate 23g (Dietary Fiber 1g); Protein 3g **Exchanges:** 1 Starch, 1 Other Carbohydrate **Carbohydrate Choices:** 1½

## Make-Ahead Magic
Rolls can be made and shaped a day before baking. Once they're placed on the cookie sheets, cover with plastic wrap and refrigerate overnight. Remove rolls from refrigerator and let stand at room temperate 30 minutes or until almost doubled. Continue as directed in Step 4.

## Festive Touch
Serve rolls warm with a specialty mustard or flavored butter (see Butter Trio, page 157).

# Easy Snowflake Buns

**PREP TIME:** 15 Minutes    **START TO FINISH:** 3 Hours 40 Minutes    *12 buns*

12 frozen dinner roll dough balls
   (from 3-lb bag)
 3 tablespoons all-purpose flour
 3 tablespoons butter, softened
 ¾ teaspoon hot water

**1** Grease 9-inch round pan with shortening or cooking spray. Arrange 8 balls of dough evenly around outside of pan; place 4 balls in center. Cover loosely with plastic wrap; let thaw and rise in warm place 2 to 3 hours or as directed on package.

**2** Heat oven to 350°F. In small bowl, mix flour, butter and hot water. Spoon into decorating bag fitted with #4 writing tip. Pipe mixture onto center of each ball in snowflake design, 1 to 1½ inches in diameter.

**3** Bake 20 to 25 minutes or until golden brown. Immediately lift buns from pan (do not turn upside down). Serve warm.

**1 Bun:** Calories 130; Total Fat 4.5g (Saturated Fat 2g, Trans Fat 0g); Cholesterol 10mg; Sodium 150mg; Total Carbohydrate 20g (Dietary Fiber 0g); Protein 2g **Exchanges:** ½ Starch, 1 Other Carbohydrate, 1 Fat **Carbohydrate Choices:** 1

## Make-Ahead Magic

These buns can be baked and frozen up to 3 months in advance. Freeze cooled buns in resealable freezer plastic bags. To reheat, remove rolls from bag and wrap together in foil. Bake at 350°F for 15 to 20 minutes or until warm.

# Double-Quick Dinner Rolls

**PREP TIME:** 15 Minutes    **START TO FINISH:** 1 Hour 35 Minutes    *12 rolls*

2¼  cups all-purpose flour

2  tablespoons sugar

1  teaspoon salt

1  package regular active or fast-acting dry yeast (2¼ teaspoons)

1  cup very warm water (120°F to 130°F)

2  tablespoons shortening

1  egg

**1** In large bowl, mix 1¼ cups of the flour, the sugar, salt and yeast. Add warm water, shortening and egg; beat with spoon until smooth. Stir in remaining 1 cup flour until smooth. Scrape batter from side of bowl. Cover loosely with plastic wrap and cloth towel; let rise in warm place about 30 minutes or until doubled in size.

**2** Grease 12 regular-size muffin cups with shortening or cooking spray. Stir down batter by beating about 25 strokes. Divide batter evenly among muffin cups. Let rise 20 to 30 minutes or until batter rounds over tops of cups.

**3** Heat oven to 400°F. Bake rolls 15 to 20 minutes or until golden brown. Serve warm.

**1 Roll:** Calories 120; Total Fat 3g (Saturated Fat 0.5g, Trans Fat 0g); Cholesterol 20mg; Sodium 200mg; Total Carbohydrate 20g (Dietary Fiber 1g); Protein 3g **Exchanges:** 1 Starch, ½ Other Carbohydrate, ½ Fat **Carbohydrate Choices:** 1

## Make-Ahead Magic
Get a jump on your holiday baking by making these rolls ahead. Freeze the cooled rolls in a resealable freezer plastic bag for 2 to 3 months. To reheat, remove from bag and wrap rolls in foil. Bake at 350°F for 20 minutes or until hot.

## Festive Touch
Sprinkle the rolls with sesame seed or poppy seed before baking.

# Christmas Cookies

# Easy Gingerdoodle Cookies

**PREP TIME:** 45 Minutes   **START TO FINISH:** 45 Minutes
*2½ dozen cookies*

- 1 pouch (17.9 oz) snickerdoodle cookie mix
- 1 pouch (17.5 oz) gingerbread cookie mix
- 1 cup butter, softened
- 2 tablespoons water
- 2 eggs

1. Heat oven to 375°F. Place cinnamon-sugar from snickerdoodle cookie pouch in small shallow bowl. In separate large bowls, make each cookie mix as directed on pouch, using butter, water and eggs.

2. For each cookie, shape 1 level tablespoon each of snickerdoodle dough and gingerbread dough into a single ball. Roll ball in cinnamon-sugar. On ungreased cookie sheets, place balls 2 inches apart.

3. Bake 10 to 12 minutes or until light golden brown around edges. Cool 5 minutes; remove from cookie sheets to cooling racks. Store cooled cookies tightly covered up to 3 days.

**1 Cookie:** Calories 190; Total Fat 8g (Saturated Fat 4g, Trans Fat 0g); Cholesterol 30mg; Sodium 190mg; Total Carbohydrate 27g (Dietary Fiber 0g); Protein 1g **Exchanges:** ½ Starch, 1½ Other Carbohydrate, 1½ Fat **Carbohydrate Choices:** 2

# Coconut Cream Macaroons

**PREP TIME:** 1 Hour 15 Minutes   **START TO FINISH:** 1 Hour 45 Minutes   *3½ dozen cookies*

- 3 packages (7 oz each) flaked coconut (7⅔ cups)
- 1 cup all-purpose flour
- ½ teaspoon salt
- 1 can (14 oz) sweetened condensed milk (not evaporated)
- ⅔ cup canned cream of coconut (not coconut milk)
- 1 tablespoon vanilla
- ¼ teaspoon almond extract
- 1 egg
- 1 cup semisweet chocolate chips (about 6 oz), if desired
- 1 tablespoon vegetable oil, if desired

1. Heat oven to 350°F. Line cookie sheets with foil or cooking parchment paper. Sprinkle 1 cup of the coconut on one cookie sheet. Bake 5 to 7 minutes, stirring occasionally, until golden brown; cool.

2. In large bowl, mix toasted coconut, remaining coconut, the flour and salt. In medium bowl, beat condensed milk, cream of coconut, vanilla, almond extract and egg until well mixed. Pour milk mixture over coconut mixture; stir until well mixed. Onto cookie sheets, drop mixture by heaping tablespoonfuls about 2 inches apart.

3. Bake 12 to 14 minutes or until golden brown (cookies will be soft in center and set at edges). Immediately slide foil with cookies from cookie sheets to cooling racks. Cool completely, about 30 minutes.

4. In 1-quart saucepan, heat chocolate chips and oil over low heat, stirring constantly, until chips are melted and mixture is smooth. Drizzle over cookies. Let stand about 30 minutes or until chocolate is set.

**1 Cookie:** Calories 130; Total Fat 7g (Saturated Fat 6g, Trans Fat 0g); Cholesterol 10mg; Sodium 80mg; Total Carbohydrate 17g (Dietary Fiber 0g); Protein 1g **Exchanges:** 1 Other Carbohydrate, 1½ Fat **Carbohydrate Choices:** 1

**Festive Touch** For a richer, indulgent flavor, substitute dark chocolate chips for the semisweet chips.

# Decorate-Before-You-Bake Cookies

**PREP TIME:** 50 Minutes    **START TO FINISH:** 1 Hour 50 Minutes    *6 dozen cookies*

### COOKIES

- ¾ cup butter, softened
- ½ cup sugar
- 1 egg
- 1¾ cups all-purpose flour
- ½ teaspoon baking soda
- ¼ teaspoon cream of tartar
- ¼ teaspoon salt

### DECORATING MIXTURE

- ½ cup butter, softened
- 1 tablespoon milk
- ½ cup all-purpose flour
- ¼ teaspoon liquid red food color
- 4 drops liquid green food color
- 2 tablespoons sugar

1. In large bowl, beat ¾ cup butter and ½ cup sugar with electric mixer on medium speed until light and fluffy. Add egg; beat well. Stir in 1¾ cups flour, the baking soda, cream of tartar and salt. Knead dough into smooth ball. Wrap in plastic wrap; refrigerate until firm, about 1 hour.

2. Meanwhile, in small bowl, mix ½ cup butter, the milk and ½ cup flour with fork until well mixed. Divide mixture in half. Stir red food color into one half and green food color into other half. Spoon each mixture into separate decorating bag fitted with small writing tip; set aside.

3. Heat oven to 375°F. Shape cookie dough into ¾-inch balls. On ungreased cookie sheets, place balls 2 inches apart. In small bowl, place 2 tablespoons sugar. Dip bottom of glass into sugar and flatten each ball into 1½-inch round. Pipe colored mixture from decorating bags onto each cookie in holiday designs.

4. Bake 7 to 9 minutes or until set. Immediately remove from cookie sheets to cooling racks.

**1 Cookie:** Calories 50, Total Fat 3.5g (Saturated Fat 2g, Trans Fat 0g); Cholesterol 10mg; Sodium 45mg; Total Carbohydrate 5g (Dietary Fiber 0g); Protein 0g **Exchanges:** ½ Other Carbohydrate, ½ Fat **Carbohydrate Choices:** ½

## Festive Touch

**For holiday designs, try piping a tree, star, candy cane, gift, holly, garland, snowflakes or ornaments.**

## Kitchen Secrets

**If you don't have decorating bags and tips, use small resealable food-storage plastic bags. Cut off the tip of one corner for piping.**

# Double-Sugar Cookies

**PREP TIME:** 1 Hour 20 Minutes    **START TO FINISH:** 3 Hours 20 Minutes    *10 dozen cookies*

1 cup granulated sugar
1 cup powdered sugar
1 cup butter, softened
1 cup vegetable oil
1 teaspoon vanilla
2 eggs
4¼ cups all-purpose flour
1 teaspoon baking soda
1 teaspoon cream of tartar
1 teaspoon salt
   Colored sugar

1. In large bowl, beat granulated sugar, powdered sugar and butter with electric mixer on medium speed until light and fluffy. Beat in oil, vanilla and eggs until well blended.

2. On low speed, beat in flour, baking soda, cream of tartar and salt until dough forms. Cover with plastic wrap; refrigerate at least 2 hours or overnight.

3. Heat oven to 375°F. Shape dough into 1-inch balls. On ungreased cookie sheets, place balls 2 inches apart. Flatten each with bottom of glass dipped in colored sugar.

4. Bake 5 to 8 minutes or until set but not brown. Immediately remove from cookie sheets to cooling racks.

**1 Cookie:** Calories 60; Total Fat 3.5g (Saturated Fat 1.5g, Trans Fat 0g); Cholesterol 5mg; Sodium 45mg; Total Carbohydrate 6g (Dietary Fiber 0g); Protein 0g **Exchanges:** ½ Other Carbohydrate, ½ Fat **Carbohydrate Choices:** ½

## Festive Touch
Use a "cut-glass" tumbler with a pretty design on the bottom to press the dough balls.

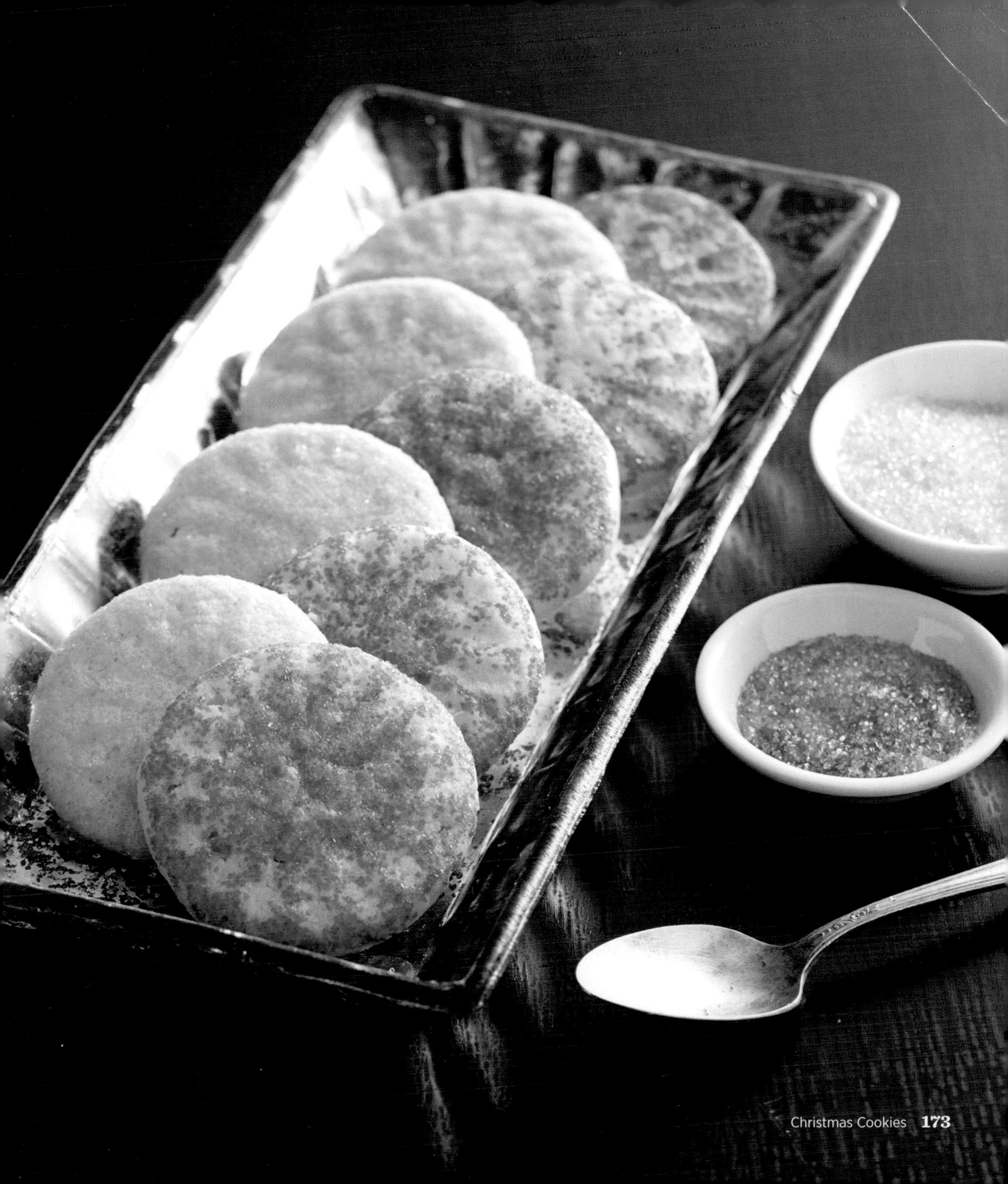

# Double Chocolate–Hazelnut Cookie Truffles

**PREP TIME:** 1 Hour 20 Minutes   **START TO FINISH:** 2 Hours   *52 truffles*

- 1 pouch (17.5 oz) double chocolate chunk cookie mix
- ¼ cup vegetable oil
- 2 tablespoons water
- 1 egg
- 4 oz (half of 8-oz package) cream cheese, cut into cubes, softened
- ½ cup hazelnut spread with cocoa
- 2 cups dark chocolate chips (about 12 oz)
- 2 tablespoons shortening
- 2 tablespoons chocolate candy sprinkles

1 Heat oven to 375°F. Make and bake cookies as directed on pouch, using oil, water and egg. Cool completely, at least 15 minutes.

2 Line cookie sheet with waxed paper. In food processor, place half of the cookies. Cover; process until fine crumbs form. Remove; set aside. Repeat with remaining cookies. Return first batch of crumbs to food processor; add cream cheese and hazelnut spread. Process until well combined and mixture can be pressed into a ball, 1 to 2 minutes. Using small cookie scoop, shape mixture into 1¼-inch balls; place on cookie sheet. Refrigerate 15 minutes.

3 In medium microwavable bowl, microwave chocolate chips and shortening uncovered on High 1 minute to 1 minute 30 seconds or until chips are softened and mixture can be stirred smooth.

4 Remove half of the cookie balls from refrigerator. Using 2 forks, dip and roll chilled cookie balls, one at a time, in melted chocolate. Return to cookie sheet; immediately decorate top with sprinkles. (If chocolate has cooled too much, reheat in microwave.) Refrigerate truffles about 10 minutes or until coating is set. Repeat with second half of cookie balls. Store covered in refrigerator.

**1 Truffle:** Calories 107; Total Fat 7g (Saturated Fat 3g, Trans Fat 0g); Cholesterol 2mg; Sodium 38mg; Total Carbohydrate 12g (Dietary Fiber 1g); Protein 1g **Exchanges:** ½ Other Carbohydrate, 1 Fat **Carbohydrate Choices:** 1

## Make-Ahead Magic
Truffles can be frozen in airtight containers with waxed paper between layers. Store up to 3 months.

## Festive Touch
Place truffles in colorful paper candy cups or miniature cupcake liners for serving.

# Raspberry Poinsettia Blossoms

**PREP TIME:** 50 Minutes    **START TO FINISH:** 1 Hour 50 Minutes    *3 dozen cookies*

¾  **cup butter, softened**
½  **cup sugar**
1  **teaspoon vanilla**
1  **box (4-serving size) raspberry-flavored gelatin**
1  **egg**
2  **cups all-purpose flour**
2  **tablespoons yellow candy sprinkles**

**1** In large bowl, beat butter, sugar, vanilla, gelatin and egg with electric mixer on medium speed, or mix with spoon until well blended. On low speed, beat in flour. Shape dough into 1¼-inch balls. Cover; refrigerate 1 hour.

**2** Heat oven to 375°F. On ungreased cookie sheets, place balls 2 inches apart. With sharp knife, make 6 cuts in top of each ball about three-fourths of the way through to make 6 wedges. Spread wedges apart slightly to form flower petals (cookies will separate and flatten as they bake). Sprinkle about ⅛ teaspoon candy sprinkles into center of each cookie.

**3** Bake 9 to 11 minutes or until set and edges begin to brown. Cool 2 to 3 minutes; remove from cookie sheets to cooling racks.

**1 Cookie:** Calories 90; Total Fat 4g (Saturated Fat 2.5g, Trans Fat 0g); Cholesterol 15mg; Sodium 45mg; Total Carbohydrate 11g (Dietary Fiber 0g); Protein 1g **Exchanges:** 1 Other Carbohydrate, 1 Fat **Carbohydrate Choices:** 1

## Kitchen Secrets For a flavor twist, use strawberry-, cranberry- or cherry-flavored gelatin instead of the raspberry.

# Lime-Coconut Shortbread

**PREP TIME:** 45 Minutes    **START TO FINISH:** 1 Hour 35 Minutes    *3 dozen cookies*

### COOKIES

    1  cup butter, softened
    1  cup powdered sugar
    2  teaspoons grated lime peel
    2  cups all-purpose flour
    1  cup shredded coconut
    ¾  cup granulated sugar

### GLAZE AND DECORATION

    2½  cups powdered sugar
    2  to 3 tablespoons lime juice
    2  to 3 tablespoons half-and-half
       or milk
    2  drops green food color
    2  drops yellow food color
    2  cups shredded coconut, toasted

1   Heat oven to 350°F. In large bowl, beat butter, 1 cup powdered sugar and the lime peel with electric mixer on medium speed until light and fluffy. On medium-low speed, beat in flour and 1 cup coconut 2 to 3 minutes or until blended.

2   Shape dough into 1-inch balls; roll in granulated sugar. Place on ungreased cookie sheet. With bottom of glass dipped in granulated sugar, flatten each ball until about ¼ inch thick.

3   Bake 10 to 12 minutes or until light golden brown. Cool 2 minutes; remove from cookie sheet to cooling rack. Cool completely.

4   In small bowl, mix 2½ cups powdered sugar, 2 tablespoons lime juice, 2 tablespoons half-and-half and the food colors until glaze is of desired consistency, stirring in remaining lime juice and half-and-half, ½ teaspoon at a time, if needed. Place toasted coconut in shallow dish.

5   Dip edge of each cookie in glaze; roll in toasted coconut. Place on cooling rack; let stand 10 to 15 minutes or until set. Store in airtight container.

**1 Cookie:** Calories 180; Total Fat 8g (Saturated Fat 6g, Trans Fat 0g); Cholesterol 15mg; Sodium 60mg; Total Carbohydrate 25g (Dietary Fiber 0g); Protein 1g **Exchanges:** ½ Starch, 1 Other Carbohydrate, 1½ Fat **Carbohydrate Choices:** 1½

## Festive Touch

**Make the cookies look extra special by adding holly and berry sprinkles to them while the glaze is still wet, or use tiny dabs of glaze as glue to adhere them to the cookies.**

## Kitchen Secrets

**To toast coconut, heat oven to 350°F. Spread coconut in ungreased shallow pan. Bake uncovered 5 to 7 minutes, stirring occasionally, until golden brown.**

# Salted Caramel–Stuffed Snickerdoodles

**PREP TIME:** 55 Minutes    **START TO FINISH:** 1 Hour 55 Minutes    *40 cookies*

1 can (13.4 oz) dulce de leche
  (caramelized sweetened
  condensed milk)
1¾ cups sugar
½ cup butter, softened
½ cup shortening
2 eggs
2¾ cups all-purpose flour
2 teaspoons cream of tartar
1 teaspoon baking soda
¾ teaspoon salt
2 teaspoons ground cinnamon

**1** Line cookie sheet with waxed paper or foil. Spoon 40 slightly-less-than-level measuring teaspoonfuls dulce de leche onto cookie sheet. Freeze about 1 hour or until slightly firm (dollops will not freeze solid).

**2** Heat oven to 400°F. In large bowl, mix 1½ cups of the sugar, the butter, shortening and eggs. Stir in flour, cream of tartar, baking soda and ¼ teaspoon of the salt.

**3** Shape dough into 40 (1¼-inch) balls. Press thumb into center of each cookie to make deep indentation, but do not press all the way to cookie sheet. Place 1 dollop dulce de leche into center of each cookie, making sure to form dough around dollop to enclose. (If necessary, work with lightly floured fingers so dough doesn't stick.) You may have to return dulce de leche dollops to freezer if they become too warm to work with.

**4** In shallow bowl, mix remaining ¼ cup sugar, remaining ½ teaspoon salt and the cinnamon. Roll balls in sugar mixture. On ungreased cookie sheet, place balls 2 inches apart.

**5** Bake 8 to 10 minutes or until set (centers will be soft). Cool 2 minutes; remove from cookie sheet to cooling rack. Store cooled cookies tightly covered up to 3 days.

**1 Cookie:** Calories 140; Total Fat 6g (Saturated Fat 2.5g, Trans Fat 0g); Cholesterol 20mg; Sodium 110mg; Total Carbohydrate 21g (Dietary Fiber 0g); Protein 2g **Exchanges:** ½ Starch, 1 Other Carbohydrate, 1 Fat **Carbohydrate Choices:** 1½

# Melting Snowman Cookies

**PREP TIME:** 55 Minutes    **START TO FINISH:** 1 Hour 55 Minutes    *20 cookies*

1 pouch (17.5 oz) sugar cookie mix
¼ cup all-purpose flour
½ cup butter, softened
1 egg
1 package (1 lb) vanilla-flavored candy coating (almond bark)
Black confetti candy sprinkles
5 orange gumdrops, cut into tiny slivers, or orange candy sprinkles
Red candy sprinkles or small candies
Chocolate decorating cookie icing

**1** Heat oven to 375°F. In medium bowl, stir together cookie mix, flour, butter and egg until soft dough forms.

**2** Divide dough in half. Using one-half of dough, shape into 20 (1⅛-inch) balls. On ungreased cookie sheets, place balls 2 inches apart; flatten slightly. Shape remaining dough into 40 (¾-inch) balls. Place 20 of the balls on cookie sheets, 2 inches apart; flatten slightly. Place remaining balls on cookie sheets 2 inches apart, but do not flatten.

**3** Bake 7 to 9 minutes or until edges are light golden brown. Cool 5 minutes or until cookies are firm enough to be transferred to cooling rack; cool completely.

**4** In large microwavable bowl, microwave candy coating at 30-second intervals until it can be stirred smooth. Cover work surface with waxed or cooking parchment paper. Place a dot of melted coating on bottom of 1 small cookie and place it toward the edge on top of 1 larger cookie. Place a dot of melted coating on bottom of larger cookie, and sandwich it between small cookie and the largest cookie. Spoon coating over entire cookie, allowing some to spill over edge of bottom cookie.

**5** On top cookie, place 2 black sprinkles for eyes and 1 piece of orange gumdrop for carrot nose. On bottom cookie, place 3 red sprinkles for buttons. Use cookie icing to draw on arms. Let dry completely. Store in airtight container.

**1 Cookie:** Calories 290; Total Fat 14g (Saturated Fat 10g, Trans Fat 0g); Cholesterol 20mg; Sodium 135mg; Total Carbohydrate 38g (Dietary Fiber 0g); Protein 1g **Exchanges:** 2½ Other Carbohydrate, 3 Fat **Carbohydrate Choices:** 2½

## Kitchen Secrets
If you can't find black confetti sprinkles, use mini chocolate chips turned upside down for snowman eyes. You can also use chips for buttons.

## Kitchen Secrets
Decorate single large cookies for a completely melted snowman appearance—or stack two cookies high for a less melted appearance.

# Chocolate-Cherry Snowballs

**PREP TIME:** 45 Minutes   **START TO FINISH:** 2 Hours   *4 dozen cookies*

1 cup butter, softened
1 cup powdered sugar
½ teaspoon almond extract
2 cups all-purpose flour
¼ teaspoon salt
1 cup candied cherries, finely chopped
½ cup dark chocolate chips

**1** Heat oven to 400°F. In large bowl, beat butter with electric mixer on medium speed until fluffy. Gradually beat in ½ cup of the powdered sugar until light and fluffy. Stir in almond extract. On low speed, beat in flour and salt until well blended. Stir in cherries.

**2** Shape dough into 1-inch balls. On ungreased cookie sheets, place balls 2 inches apart.

**3** Bake 9 to 11 minutes or until edges just begin to brown. Cool 2 to 3 minutes. In small bowl, place remaining ½ cup powdered sugar. Roll each cookie in powdered sugar. Place on cooling rack; cool completely.

**4** In small microwavable bowl, microwave chocolate chips on High 30 to 60 seconds or until chips are softened and can be stirred smooth. Use spoon to drizzle chocolate over cookies. (Or spoon melted chocolate into small resealable food-storage plastic bag, and cut off corner of bag to pipe chocolate onto cookies.) Let stand at room temperature at least 30 minutes until chocolate hardens before storing.

**1 Cookie:** Calories 90; Total Fat 4.5g (Saturated Fat 3g, Trans Fat 0g); Cholesterol 10mg; Sodium 45mg; Total Carbohydrate 11g (Dietary Fiber 0g); Protein 0g **Exchanges:** 1 Other Carbohydrate, 1 Fat **Carbohydrate Choices:** 1

**Kitchen Secrets** **To make it easier to chop the cherries, dip the knife in water, or use kitchen scissors sprayed with cooking spray.**

# Chocolate-Filled Russian Tea Cakes

**PREP TIME:** 1 Hour  **START TO FINISH:** 1 Hour 30 Minutes  *4 dozen cookies*

## COOKIES

- 1 **cup butter, softened**
- ½ **cup powdered sugar**
- 1 **teaspoon vanilla**
- 2 **cups all-purpose flour**
- ¼ **teaspoon salt**
- ¾ **cup finely chopped walnuts or pecans**
- 48 **milk chocolate stars**

## SUGAR COATING

- 1 **cup powdered sugar**
- 1 **tablespoon red sugar**
- 1 **tablespoon green sugar**

1 Heat oven to 400°F. In large bowl, beat butter, ½ cup powdered sugar and the vanilla with electric mixer on medium speed until well mixed. On low speed, beat in flour, salt and walnuts.

2 For each cookie, shape slightly less than 1 measuring tablespoon of dough around chocolate star to make 1-inch ball. On ungreased cookie sheets, place balls 2 inches apart.

3 Bake 12 to 15 minutes or until set and bottoms begin to turn golden brown. Meanwhile, in small bowl, mix sugar coating ingredients.

4 Immediately remove cookies from cookie sheets; roll in sugar coating. Place on cooling racks; cool completely, about 30 minutes. Roll in sugar coating again.

**1 Cookie:** Calories 100; Total Fat 6g (Saturated Fat 3.5g, Trans Fat 0g); Cholesterol 10mg; Sodium 45mg; Total Carbohydrate 11g (Dietary Fiber 0g); Protein 1g **Exchanges:** 1 Other Carbohydrate, 1 Fat **Carbohydrate Choices:** 1

**Festive Touch** For cookies with more dazzle, use coarse red and green sparkling sugars.

# Caramel-Fudge Turtle Cookies

**PREP TIME:** 45 Minutes   **START TO FINISH:** 1 Hour 10 Minutes   *3 dozen cookies*

 1 pouch (17.5 oz) sugar cookie mix
½ cup butter, softened
 1 egg
 2 tablespoons all-purpose flour
12 caramels, unwrapped
 1 tablespoon milk
 1 cup hot fudge topping
36 pecan halves

**1** Heat oven to 375°F. Line cookie sheets with cooking parchment paper.

**2** Make cookie mix as directed on pouch, using butter and egg, and stirring in flour. Shape dough into 36 (1-inch) balls. On cookie sheets, place balls 2 inches apart.

**3** Bake 11 to 12 minutes or until set. Cool 1 minute; remove cookies from cookie sheets to cooling racks.

**4** In small microwavable bowl, microwave caramels and milk uncovered on High 1 minute to 1 minute 30 seconds, stirring once, until caramels are melted and mixture can be stirred smooth. Dip one side of each cookie at an angle into caramel mixture to coat top half; spread if necessary. If caramel thickens, add up to 1 teaspoon additional milk and reheat.

**5** Spread about 1 teaspoon fudge topping on top of each cookie. Place pecan half on fudge topping. Let stand about 15 minutes until toppings are set.

**1 Cookie:** Calories 130; Total Fat 6g (Saturated Fat 2.5g, Trans Fat 0g); Cholesterol 10mg; Sodium 100mg; Total Carbohydrate 20g (Dietary Fiber 0g); Protein 1g **Exchanges:** ½ Other Carbohydrate, 1 Fat **Carbohydrate Choices:** 1

**Make-Ahead Magic** You can bake the cookies—but don't add the toppings or pecans—up to 2 months ahead and store tightly covered in the freezer.

# Best-Ever Chewy Gingerbread Cookies

**PREP TIME:** 1 Hour 30 Minutes    **START TO FINISH:** 3 Hours 30 Minutes    *7½ dozen cookies*

- 1 **cup plus 2 tablespoons unsalted butter, softened**
- 1 **cup packed brown sugar**
- 1 **egg**
- ¼ **cup plus 2 tablespoons molasses**
- 2½ **cups all-purpose flour**
- 2¼ **teaspoons baking soda**
- ½ **teaspoon coarse (kosher or sea) salt**
- 1 **tablespoon ground cinnamon**
- 1 **tablespoon ground ginger**
- 2 **teaspoons ground cloves**
- 1½ **teaspoons ground nutmeg**
- ½ **teaspoon ground allspice**
- ⅔ **cup granulated or coarse sugar**

1 In large bowl, beat butter and brown sugar with electric mixer on medium speed until light and fluffy, about 5 minutes. Beat in egg and molasses. Stir in remaining ingredients except granulated sugar. Cover; refrigerate at least 2 hours.

2 Heat oven to 350°F. Line cookie sheets with cooking parchment paper. In small bowl, place granulated sugar. Shape dough into 1-inch balls; roll in sugar. On cookie sheets, place balls 2 inches apart.

3 Bake 8 to 10 minutes or just until set and soft in center. Cool 2 minutes; remove from cookie sheets to cooling racks. Store cooled cookies tightly covered up to 1 week.

**1 Cookie:** Calories 50; Total Fat 2.5g (Saturated Fat 1.5g, Trans Fat 0g); Cholesterol 10mg; Sodium 45mg; Total Carbohydrate 8g (Dietary Fiber 0g); Protein 0g **Exchanges:** ½ Other Carbohydrate, ½ Fat **Carbohydrate Choices:** ½

# Coconut-Butterscotch-Fudge Cookies

**PREP TIME:** 45 Minutes   **START TO FINISH:** 45 Minutes   *2½ dozen cookies*

1  pouch (17.5 oz) sugar cookie mix
½  cup butter, melted
1  egg
1  to 1½ cups flaked coconut
½  cup butterscotch topping
¾  cup hot fudge topping

**1** Heat oven to 375°F. In large bowl, stir together cookie mix, butter and egg until soft dough forms.

**2** Shape dough into 1-inch balls; roll in coconut. On ungreased cookie sheets, place balls 2 inches apart.

**3** Bake 9 to 11 minutes or until edges are light golden brown and coconut starts to toast. Cool 3 minutes; remove from cookie sheets to waxed paper.

**4** Drizzle each warm cookie with butterscotch topping. In small microwavable bowl, microwave hot fudge topping uncovered on High 15 to 30 seconds or until spreadable. Carefully spread on top of each cookie. Serve warm or cool. Store loosely covered.

**1 Cookie:** Calories 150; Total Fat 6g (Saturated Fat 3.5g, Trans Fat 0g); Cholesterol 15mg; Sodium 130mg; Total Carbohydrate 24g (Dietary Fiber 0g); Protein 1g **Exchanges:** 1½ Other Carbohydrate, 1 Fat **Carbohydrate Choices:** 1½

# Peppermint-Fudge Thumbprints

**PREP TIME:** 45 Minutes   **START TO FINISH:** 1 Hour 15 Minutes   *3½ dozen cookies*

### COOKIES

¾ cup sugar
¾ cup butter, softened
½ teaspoon vanilla
1 egg
1¾ cups all-purpose flour
3 tablespoons unsweetened baking cocoa
¼ teaspoon salt
1 cup crushed hard peppermint candies (about 40)

### FUDGE FILLING

¼ cup whipping cream
1 cup milk chocolate chips (about 6 oz)

1 Heat oven to 350°F. In large bowl, beat sugar, butter, vanilla and egg with electric mixer on medium speed, or mix with spoon, until well blended. Stir in flour, cocoa and salt until dough forms.

2 Shape dough by rounded teaspoonfuls into 40 (1-inch) balls. On ungreased cookie sheets, place balls 2 inches apart. Press thumb or end of wooden spoon handle into center of each cookie, but do not press all the way to cookie sheet.

3 Bake 7 to 11 minutes or until edges are firm. If necessary, quickly remake indentations with spoon handle. Immediately remove from cookie sheets to cooling racks. Cool completely, about 30 minutes.

4 Meanwhile, in 1-quart saucepan, heat whipping cream over medium heat, stirring occasionally, until steaming. Remove from heat; stir in chocolate chips until melted. Cool about 10 minutes or until thickened.

5 Spoon rounded ½ teaspoon filling into indentation in each cookie. Top each with about 1 teaspoon crushed candies.

**1 Cookie:** Calories 110; Total Fat 5g (Saturated Fat 3g, Trans Fat 0g); Cholesterol 15mg; Sodium 45mg; Total Carbohydrate 15g (Dietary Fiber 0g); Protein 1g **Exchanges:** 1 Other Carbohydrate, 1 Fat **Carbohydrate Choices:** 1

# Christmas Tree Cookie Pops

**PREP TIME:** 30 Minutes   **START TO FINISH:** 1 Hour 35 Minutes   *20 cookie pops*

1 pouch (17.5 oz) sugar cookie mix
½ cup butter, softened
1 egg
3 tablespoon all-purpose flour
20 paper lollipop sticks
1 container (1 lb) vanilla creamy ready-to-spread frosting
Various shades of green gel and/or liquid food color
Assorted green and white candy sprinkles and green edible glitter

1 Heat oven to 350°F. Make cookie mix as directed on pouch for cutout cookies, using butter, egg and flour.

2 On lightly floured work surface, roll dough until ¼ inch thick. Use various sizes tree-shaped cutters to cut trees from dough, rerolling as necessary. On ungreased cookie sheet, place cookies 2 inches apart. Press lollipop stick into center of each cookie.

3 Bake 10 to 12 minutes or until edges are set and cookies are light golden brown. Cool 5 minutes; remove from cookie sheet to cooling rack. Cool completely, about 30 minutes.

4 Divide frosting among 3 or 4 bowls; color with assorted shades of green food color. Frost cookies; decorate as desired.

**1 Cookie Pop:** Calories 230; Total Fat 9g (Saturated Fat 4g, Trans Fat 1g); Cholesterol 15mg; Sodium 140mg; Total Carbohydrate 35g (Dietary Fiber 0g); Protein 1g **Exchanges:** 2½ Other Carbohydrate, 2 Fat **Carbohydrate Choices:** 2

## Festive Touch
Wrap individual pops in cellophane wrap or small cellophane bags. Tighten the cellophane around the sticks with rubber bands and cover the bands with pieces of ribbon.

## Festive Touch
Cookie pop "roses"? Treat these pops like roses, and you'll have a great way to give them as gifts! Either place them in tissue in a box (wrapping the sticks with ribbon), or arrange them in a vase.

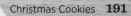

# Christmas Icebox Cookie Rounds

**PREP TIME:** 35 Minutes  **START TO FINISH:** 3 Hours 35 Minutes  *5 dozen cookies*

1 cup butter, softened

½ cup sugar

1 teaspoon vanilla

½ teaspoon almond extract

2 cups all-purpose flour

2 to 3 tablespoons candy sprinkles or colored sugars

**1** In large bowl, beat butter, sugar, vanilla and almond extract with electric mixer on medium speed, or mix with spoon until well blended. Stir in flour.

**2** Divide dough in half. Shape each half into roll, about 2 inches in diameter and 6 inches long. Roll in candy sprinkles. Wrap in plastic wrap; refrigerate at least 2 hours or until firm.

**3** Heat oven to 350°F. Unwrap rolls; cut into ⅛-inch slices. On ungreased cookie sheets, place slices 2 inches apart.

**4** Bake 10 to 12 minutes or until light brown. Immediately remove from cookie sheets to cooling racks.

**1 Cookie:** Calories 50; Total Fat 3g (Saturated Fat 2g, Trans Fat 0g); Cholesterol 10mg; Sodium 25mg; Total Carbohydrate 5g (Dietary Fiber 0g); Protein 0g **Exchanges:** ½ Other Carbohydrate, ½ Fat **Carbohydrate Choices:** ½

## Make-Ahead Magic

**The dough can be mixed, rolled and refrigerated up to 24 hours before baking.**

## Kitchen Secrets

**Start with 3 tablespoons of the candy sprinkles or colored sugar to get good coverage on the rolls. You'll end up with about 1 tablespoon leftover.**

# Holiday Cookie Ornaments

**PREP TIME:** 1 Hour 15 Minutes   **START TO FINISH:** 2 Hours 15 Minutes   *3 dozen cookies*

|   |   |
|---|---|
| 1 | pouch (17.5 oz) sugar cookie mix |
| ⅓ | cup butter, melted |
| 2 | tablespoons all-purpose flour |
| 1 | egg |
| 36 | small candy canes |
| 2 | containers (1 lb each) creamy white or vanilla creamy ready-to-spread frosting |

1. Heat oven to 375°F. Line cookie sheets with cooking parchment paper or nonstick foil.

2. In medium bowl, stir together cookie mix, butter, flour and egg until soft dough forms. On floured surface, roll dough until about ⅛ inch thick. Cut with 3- to 3½-inch cookie cutters. On cookie sheets, place cutouts 1 inch apart.

3. Bake 5 minutes. Meanwhile, break off top of each candy cane to create hanging loop. Remove cookies from oven; press 1 candy piece on top of each cookie. Bake 1 to 2 minutes longer or until edges are set. Cool 2 minutes; remove from cookie sheets to cooling racks. Cool completely, about 20 minutes.

4. Into shallow medium microwavable bowl, spoon 1 container of frosting. Microwave uncovered on High 45 to 60 seconds, stirring every 15 seconds, until melted. Dip each cookie in frosting, allowing excess to drip off. Place on parchment paper. Repeat with second container of frosting and remaining cookies. Let stand until frosting is set, about 1 hour.

**1 Cookie:** Calories 190; Total Fat 6g (Saturated Fat 2.5g, Trans Fat 1g); Cholesterol 10mg; Sodium 110mg; Total Carbohydrate 32g (Dietary Fiber 0g); Protein 0g **Exchanges:** ½ Starch, 1½ Other Carbohydrate, 1 Fat **Carbohydrate Choices:** 2

## Festive Touch

**Get creative! Decorate your cookie ornaments with colored or coarse sugar, small candies or sprinkles. Tie a piece of ribbon through each candy cane loop for hanging.**

## Kitchen Secrets

**To evenly break candy canes, cut with scissors while still in the wrapper, then unwrap and use.**

# Date-Filled Cookie Wraps

**PREP TIME:** 1 Hour    **START TO FINISH:** 2 Hours    *50 cookies*

## COOKIES

- 4 oz (half of 8-oz package) cream cheese, softened
- ½ cup butter, softened
- 1 tablespoon granulated sugar
- 1 cup all-purpose flour
- 1 egg white
- 1 tablespoon water
- 4 teaspoons coarse white sparkling sugar

## DATE FILLING

- 1 box (8 oz) chopped dates
- ½ cup water
- 2 tablespoons granulated sugar
- 1 teaspoon grated orange peel
- ½ teaspoon vanilla
- ¼ cup chopped walnuts

**1** In large bowl, beat cream cheese, butter and 1 tablespoon granulated sugar with electric mixer on medium speed until fluffy. On low speed, gradually beat in flour. On large piece of plastic wrap, form dough into 10x5-inch rectangle. Wrap in plastic wrap; refrigerate until firm, about 1 hour.

**2** Meanwhile, in 2-quart saucepan, stir together dates, ½ cup water and 2 tablespoons granulated sugar. Heat to boiling. Reduce heat to low; cook 5 to 8 minutes, stirring constantly, until thickened. Cool 5 minutes. Stir in orange peel, vanilla and walnuts; set aside.

**3** Heat oven to 325°F. Line 2 cookie sheets with cooking parchment paper.

**4** Cut dough in half into 2 squares. On floured surface, roll 1 square of dough into 10-inch square. Using fluted pastry wheel, cut into 5 rows by 5 rows to create 25 (2-inch) squares. Spoon 1 teaspoon date mixture onto center of each 2-inch square. Bring 2 opposite corners of dough together, partially overlapping and covering date mixture. Using fingers dipped in water, press dough to seal. On cookie sheets, place dough wraps 1 inch apart. Repeat with other half of dough and remaining date mixture.

**5** In small bowl, beat egg white and 1 tablespoon water; brush onto dough wraps. Sprinkle with coarse sugar.

**6** Bake 13 to 15 minutes or until edges begin to turn light golden brown. Cool 2 to 3 minutes; remove from cookie sheets to cooling racks.

**1 Cookie:** Calories 60; Total Fat 3g (Saturated Fat 1.5g, Trans Fat 0g); Cholesterol 5mg; Sodium 25mg; Total Carbohydrate 7g (Dietary Fiber 0g); Protein 0g **Exchanges:** ½ Other Carbohydrate, ½ Fat **Carbohydrate Choices:** ½

**Festive Touch** **A plate of these cookies wrapped in cellophane and a bow would make a wonderful hostess or thank-you gift. You could put them on a decorative paper plate or purchase a special plate at the store or a thrift shop.**

# Striped Peppermint Cookies

**PREP TIME:** 45 Minutes    **START TO FINISH:** 2 Hours 45 Minutes    *64 cookies*

1 cup butter, softened
1 cup sugar
1 egg
½ teaspoon peppermint extract
2¼ cups all-purpose flour
¼ teaspoon salt
1 teaspoon red paste food color

## Festive Touch

**To make checkerboard cookies, cut dough lengthwise into quarters. Stack slices to create a checkerboard pattern before cutting into ¼-inch slices.**

**1** Line 8x4-inch loaf pan with plastic wrap, leaving 1 inch of plastic wrap overhanging at 2 opposite sides of pan. In large bowl, beat butter and sugar with electric mixer on medium speed until light and fluffy. Beat in egg and peppermint extract. On low speed, beat in flour and salt until blended.

**2** Divide dough in half. Tint half of dough with food color, kneading with gloved hands until well blended. Divide red dough and plain dough in half. Press half of plain dough evenly in bottom of pan; gently press half of red dough evenly over plain dough. Repeat layers with remaining dough. Cover with plastic wrap; refrigerate 2 hours or until firm.

**3** Heat oven to 350°F. Remove dough from loaf pan; unwrap. Cut dough in half lengthwise. Cut each half crosswise into ¼-inch slices. On ungreased cookie sheets, place slices 2 inches apart. Bake 10 to 12 minutes or until set. Cool 2 minutes; remove from cookie sheets to cooling racks.

**1 Cookie:** Calories 60; Total Fat 3g (Saturated Fat 2g, Trans Fat 0g); Cholesterol 0mg; Sodium 40mg; Total Carbohydrate 7g (Dietary Fiber 0g); Protein 1g **Exchanges:** ½ Starch, ½ Fat **Carbohydrate Choices:** ½

# Storing and Gifting Cookies

Making cookies ahead is a great way to keep your holidays stress free. Knowing how to store them correctly will mean you can have irresistible sweets whenever you want them. Pull some out for a holiday party, a hostess gift or when you're wrapping presents and need a little treat.

## Storing Cookies

Store only one type of cookie in each container to keep the texture and flavor intact. Otherwise, they can transfer moisture (making crisp cookies soft) as well as flavors to one another.

To freeze cookies, place them in resealable freezer bags or airtight containers. Unfrosted cookies can be frozen up to 12 months and frosted cookies up to 3 months. Thaw most cookies in their container at room temperature 1 to 2 hours. Crisp cookies should be removed from the container to thaw.

**Crisp Cookies:** Store at room temperature in loosely covered containers.

**Chewy/Soft Cookies:** Store at room temperature in resealable food-storage plastic bags or tightly covered containers.

**Frosted or Decorated Cookies:** Let frosting set or harden before storing. Place cookies between layers of cooking parchment or waxed paper, plastic wrap or foil.

**Bars:** Typically, bars are stored tightly covered, but follow specific recipe directions as some may need to be stored loosely covered or may need refrigeration.

## Gifting Cookies

Homemade cookies are such a thoughtful gift, guaranteed to bring a smile—and will never be returned! Package them in a fun way with the endless wrapping options available from cake supply, kitchen or craft stores or online. Here are a few of our favorites you might want to try:

### INDIVIDUAL COOKIES

- Slip a cookie into a waxed paper "sleeve" or wax-lined bag, and seal with a sticker. The waxiness will prevent the fat in the cookie from leaving marks on the bag.

- Wrap a cookie in decorative waxed paper to resemble an envelope. Or use thin cardboard to create an envelope (wrap the cookie in waxed paper first). Seal the bag with raffia and add a gift tag.

### MULTIPLE COOKIES

- Place several small cutout cookies in a sturdy paper cupcake liner. Wrap with cellophane, and tie a cookie cutter with a ribbon around the cellophane to close.

- Stack cookies in a mason jar, placing decorative waxed paper between them. Add a gift tag, and write the type of cookie on the tag.

- To give an assortment of cookies, bars or fudge, arrange holiday paper cupcake liners in a box or bowl, or on a tray or plate. Stack several flat cookies of the same type (or one bar or one piece of fudge) in each of the liners, alternating types.

# Holiday Cutouts

**PREP TIME:** 1 Hour   **START TO FINISH:** 4 Hours 10 Minutes   *5 dozen 2-inch cookies*

## COOKIES

- 1½ cups powdered sugar
- 1 cup butter or margarine, softened
- 1 teaspoon vanilla
- ½ teaspoon almond extract
- 1 egg
- 2½ cups all-purpose flour
- 1 teaspoon baking soda
- 1 teaspoon cream of tartar

  Colored sugars, candy sprinkles and nonpareils, if desired

## FROSTING

- 2 cups powdered sugar
- ½ teaspoon vanilla
- 2 tablespoons milk or half-and-half

  Food colors, if desired

1   In large bowl, mix 1½ cups powdered sugar, the butter, 1 teaspoon vanilla, the almond extract and egg until well blended. Stir in flour, baking soda and cream of tartar. Cover and refrigerate at least 3 hours.

2   Heat oven to 375°F. Divide dough in half. On lightly floured, cloth-covered surface, roll each half of dough to ¼ inch thick. Cut into assorted shapes with cookie cutters, or cut around patterns traced from storybook illustrations. If cookies are to be hung as decorations, use the end of a plastic straw to make a hole in each one ¼ inch from top edge. Place 2 inches apart on ungreased cookie sheets.

3   Bake 7 to 8 minutes or until light brown. Remove from cookie sheet to cooling rack. Cool completely, about 30 minutes.

4   In medium bowl, beat frosting ingredients until smooth and spreadable. Tint with food color. Frost and decorate cookies as desired with frosting and colored sugars.

**1 Cookie:** Calories 80; Total Fat 3.5g (Saturated Fat 2g, Trans Fat 0g); Cholesterol 10mg; Sodium 45mg; Total Carbohydrate 11g (Dietary Fiber 0g); Protein 0g **Exchanges:** I Other Carbohydrate, ½ Fat **Carbohydrate Choices:** 1

## Make-Ahead Magic

**These cookies can be made ahead and frozen until you need them. Let the frosting dry before storing. Place cookies in a freezer-storage container, with waxed paper between layers. Freeze up to 3 months. Remove cookies from container to thaw.**

## Kitchen Secrets

**For melt-in-your-mouth treats, be sure to mix cookies just enough—but not too much. Too much mixing can result in tough cookies.**

# Gluten-Free Cream Cheese Cutout Cookies

**PREP TIME:** 35 Minutes   **START TO FINISH:** 35 Minutes   *1½ dozen cookies*

½ cup powdered sugar

3 oz (from 8-oz package) gluten-free cream cheese, softened

⅓ cup butter, softened

3 tablespoons shortening

1 teaspoon gluten-free vanilla

1 egg yolk

1½ cups Bisquick™ Gluten Free mix
Additional powdered sugar

1 container (1 lb) vanilla creamy ready-to-spread frosting, if desired

**1** Heat oven to 375°F. Lightly grease cookie sheet with shortening.

**2** In large bowl, stir ½ cup powdered sugar, the cream cheese, butter, shortening, vanilla and egg yolk with spoon until well blended. Stir in Bisquick mix until dough forms.

**3** Divide dough in half. On work surface sprinkled with additional powdered sugar, roll one-half of dough until ¼ inch thick. Cut with 2-inch flower-shaped cookie cutter (or desired shape). On cookie sheet, place cutouts 1 inch apart (use metal spatula to transfer from work surface to cookie sheet). Repeat with remaining dough.

**4** Bake 6 to 8 minutes or until edges are light golden brown. Cool 2 minutes; carefully remove from cookie sheet to cooling rack. Cool completely before frosting.

**1 Cookie:** Calories 120; Total Fat 8g (Saturated Fat 3.5g, Trans Fat 0.5g); Cholesterol 25mg; Sodium 140mg; Total Carbohydrate 11g (Dietary Fiber 0g); Protein 1g **Exchanges:** ½ Starch, 1½ Fat **Carbohydrate Choices:** 1

## Make-Ahead Magic
**Store tightly wrapped, unfrosted baked cookies in the freezer up to 2 months, ready for the kids to frost and decorate.**

## Cooking Gluten Free?
**Always read labels to make sure each recipe ingredient is gluten free. Products and ingredient sources can change.**

# Butter Cookies with Lemon Royal Icing

**PREP TIME:** 1 Hour 30 Minutes **START TO FINISH:** 2 Hours 45 Minutes *32 cookies*

## COOKIES

- ¾ cup butter, softened
- ¾ cup granulated sugar
- 1 egg
- 1 tablespoon finely grated lemon peel
- 2 tablespoons lemon juice
- 2½ cups all-purpose flour
- 1 teaspoon baking soda
- ¼ teaspoon salt

## LEMON ROYAL ICING

- 3 cups powdered sugar
- 2 tablespoons meringue powder
- 5 teaspoons lemon juice
- 4 to 5 tablespoons water

## DECORATIONS, IF DESIRED

- Colored sugars
- Candy sprinkles

1 In large bowl, beat butter and granulated sugar with electric mixer on medium speed until creamy. On low speed, beat in egg, lemon peel and 2 tablespoons lemon juice. Stir in flour, baking soda and salt until well blended.

2 Divide dough into 4 equal parts; flatten each part into ½-inch-thick round. Wrap each in waxed paper or plastic wrap; refrigerate 30 minutes.

3 Heat oven to 350°F. Remove 1 round of dough at a time from refrigerator. Between sheets of floured waxed paper or plastic wrap, roll dough until ¼ to ⅜ inch thick. Cut with 3-inch cookie cutters in various shapes. On ungreased cookie sheets, place cutouts 1 inch apart.

4 Bake 10 to 12 minutes or just until edges are golden. Cool 1 to 2 minutes; remove from cookie sheets to cooling racks. To make cookies for hanging, use toothpick or end of plastic straw to carefully poke a hole in the top of each cookie while cookies are still hot. Cool 10 to 15 minutes before frosting.

5 In medium bowl, stir together powdered sugar and meringue powder. Stir in 5 teaspoons lemon juice and enough of the 4 to 5 tablespoons water to make a thin icing. Transfer ½ cup of the icing to small bowl; set aside. Using a flexible pastry brush, paint cookies to the edges with icing. Place on cooling rack to dry completely, about 30 minutes.

6 Beat reserved icing with electric mixer on high speed 5 to 7 minutes or until peaks form. Spoon into decorating bag or resealable bag with one corner cut off; pipe designs onto glazed cookies. Before icing dries, sprinkle with decorations, and tap off excess. Dry thoroughly on cooling rack. Thread cookies with narrow ribbon for hanging.

**1 Cookie:** Calories 140; Total Fat 4.5g (Saturated Fat 3g, Trans Fat 0g); Cholesterol 15mg; Sodium 100mg; Total Carbohydrate 24g (Dietary Fiber 0g); Protein 1g **Exchanges:** 1½ Other Carbohydrate, 1 Fat **Carbohydrate Choices:** 1½

## Make-Ahead Magic
These cookies store well. Once frostings are set (including the decorations), place cookies between layers of cooking parchment or waxed paper, plastic wrap or foil, and freeze up to 2 months.

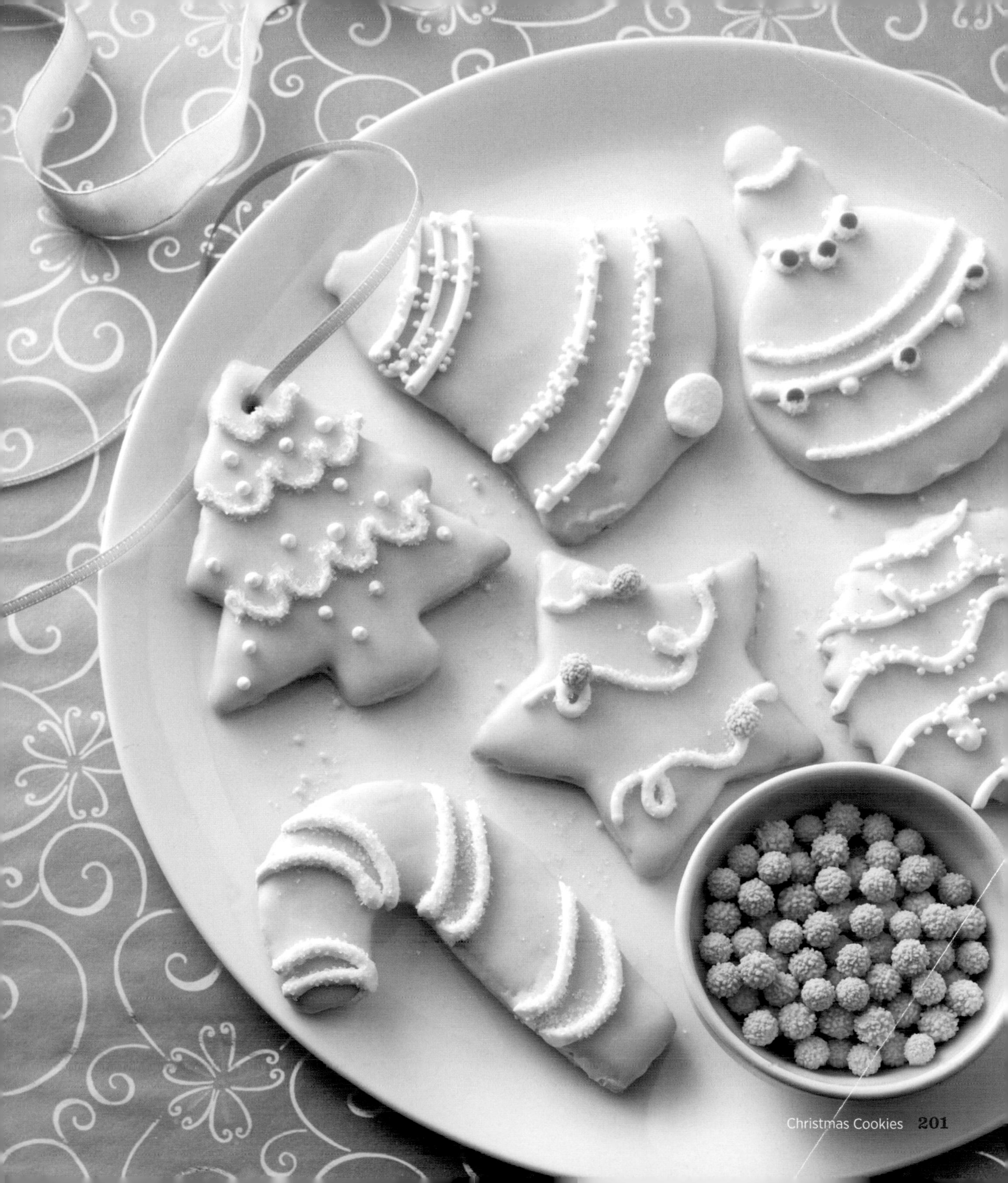

# Sparkling Lemon Snowflakes

**PREP TIME:** 1 Hour 30 Minutes   **START TO FINISH:** 1 Hour 50 Minutes   *6 dozen cookies*

## COOKIES
- ¾ cup butter, softened
- ¾ cup granulated sugar
- 2 teaspoons grated lemon peel
- 1 egg
- 2¼ cups all-purpose flour
- ¼ teaspoon salt

## GLAZE
- 2 cups powdered sugar
- 2 tablespoons lemon juice
- 2 tablespoons water
- ¼ cup coarse white sparkling sugar

1 Heat oven to 350°F. In large bowl, beat butter and granulated sugar with electric mixer on medium speed until light and fluffy. Add lemon peel and egg; beat until well blended. On low speed, beat in flour and salt until well blended.

2 On floured surface, roll dough until ⅛ inch thick. Cut with lightly floured 2½- to 3-inch snowflake-shaped cookie cutter. On ungreased cookie sheets, place cutouts 2 inches apart.

3 Bake 8 to 10 minutes or until cookies just begin to brown. Remove from cookie sheets to cooling racks. Cool completely, about 20 minutes.

4 In small bowl, mix powdered sugar, lemon juice and water. Using small metal spatula, spread glaze over tops of cookies; sprinkle with sparkling sugar. Let glaze dry before storing in airtight container.

**1 Cookie:** Calories 60; Total Fat 2g (Saturated Fat 1g, Trans Fat 0g); Cholesterol 10mg; Sodium 25mg; Total Carbohydrate 9g (Dietary Fiber 0g); Protein 0g **Exchanges:** ½ Other Carbohydrate, ½ Fat **Carbohydrate Choices:** ½

## Kitchen Secrets
**If you don't have a snowflake-shaped cookie cutter, you can use either a star-shaped or scalloped-edge cutter, and then cut small triangles and pieces out of the center to form snowflakes.**

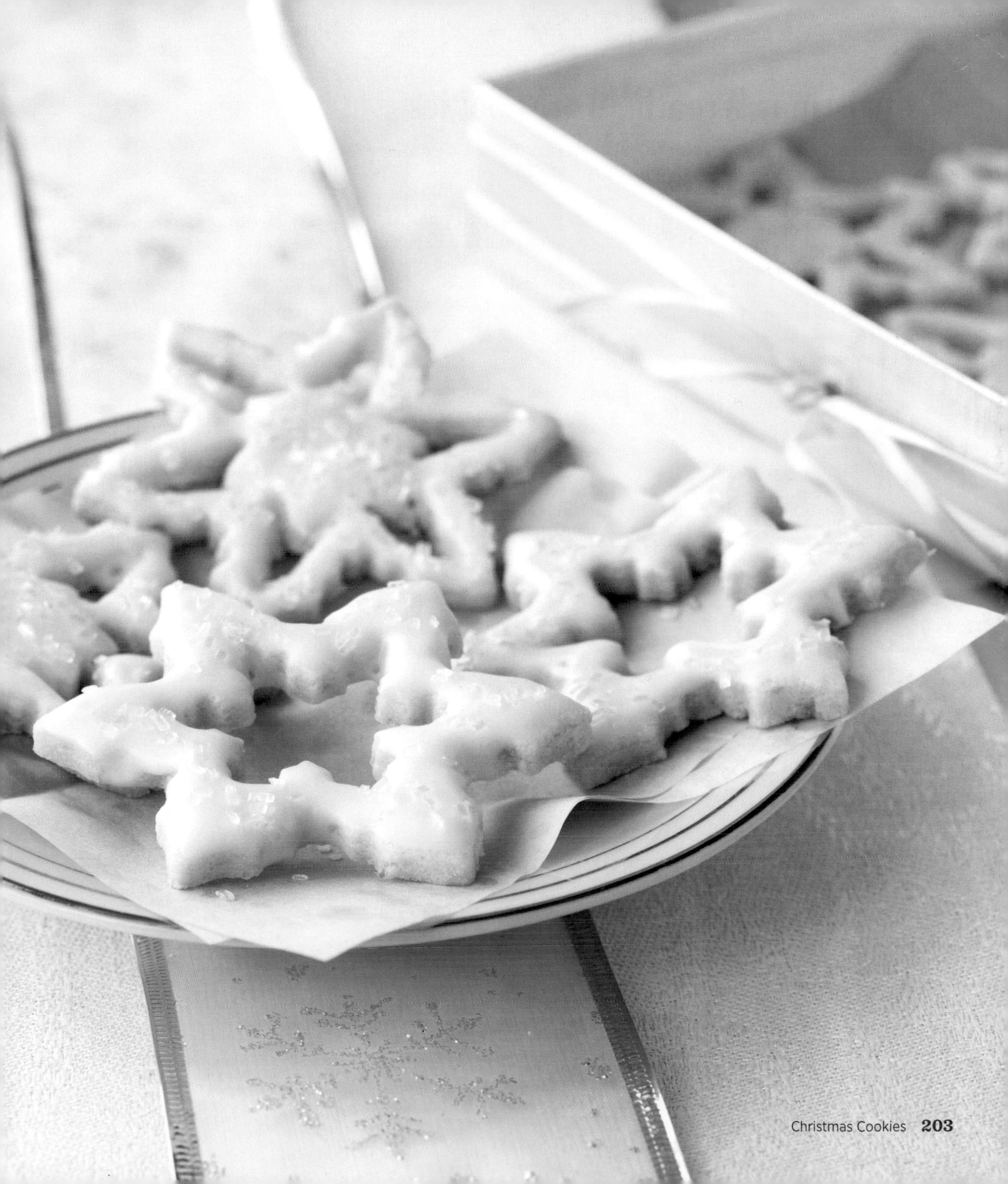

# Christmas Wreath Sugar Cookies

**PREP TIME:** 1 Hour 10 Minutes    **START TO FINISH:** 2 Hours 45 Minutes    *2½ dozen cookies*

½ cup butter, softened
¼ cup sour cream
¾ cup granulated sugar
1 egg
2 tablespoons grated lime peel
1 tablespoon lime juice
1 teaspoon vanilla
2½ cups all-purpose flour
½ teaspoon baking soda
¼ teaspoon salt
1 cup powdered sugar
2 to 3 tablespoons lime juice
Colored sugar or candy sprinkles, if desired

**1** In large bowl, beat butter, sour cream and granulated sugar with electric mixer on medium speed until creamy. Add egg, lime peel, 1 tablespoon lime juice and the vanilla; beat until smooth. On low speed, beat in flour, baking soda and salt until dough forms. Gather dough into ball; divide in half. Shape each half into a disk; wrap in plastic wrap. Refrigerate 1 hour.

**2** Heat oven to 375°F. Place pastry cloth on work surface; sprinkle with flour. With floured cloth-covered rolling pin, roll 1 disk of dough until ⅛ inch thick. Cut with floured 3-inch fluted cutter. With 1-inch scalloped or fluted canapé cutter, cut out center of each circle.

**3** On ungreased cookie sheet, place wreath cutouts 1 inch apart. Cut each small cutout in half; brush backs of small cutouts with water and place on wreaths for bows. Repeat with second disk of dough.

**4** Bake 6 to 8 minutes or until edges start to brown. Remove from cookie sheet to cooling rack; cool completely.

**5** In small bowl, mix powdered sugar and 2 tablespoons of the lime juice with whisk. Stir in remaining 1 tablespoon lime juice, 1 teaspoon at a time, until glaze is thin. Working with a few cookies at a time, brush glaze over cookies and immediately decorate with sugars or sprinkles. Let stand until set. Store in layers with waxed paper between.

**1 Cookie:** Calories 110; Total Fat 3.5g (Saturated Fat 2g, Trans Fat 0g); Cholesterol 15mg; Sodium 65mg; Total Carbohydrate 17g (Dietary Fiber 0g); Protein 1g **Exchanges:** ½ Starch, ½ Other Carbohydrate, ½ Fat **Carbohydrate Choices:** 1

 **Kitchen Secrets** Silicone brushes work very well for brushing the glaze onto the cookies. They can be purchased in most kitchen stores or kitchen sections of department stores.

# Peppermint Swirls

**PREP TIME:** 1 Hour   **START TO FINISH:** 1 Hour   *4 dozen cookies*

1 cup butter, softened
⅓ cup powdered sugar
1 teaspoon vanilla
2 cups all-purpose flour
¼ teaspoon peppermint extract
¼ teaspoon red food color
2 tablespoons granulated sugar

1 Heat oven to 350°F. In large bowl, beat butter, powdered sugar and vanilla with electric mixer on medium speed, or mix with spoon until well blended. Stir in flour.

2 Divide dough in half. Stir peppermint extract and food color into one half of dough. Divide red dough and plain dough in half. On generously floured surface, shape each piece of dough into 12-inch-long rope. Place 2 ropes, 1 red and 1 plain, side-by-side; twist ropes together. Repeat with remaining dough.

3 Cut twisted ropes into ½-inch pieces; shape each into ball. On ungreased cookie sheets, place balls 1 inch apart. In small bowl, place granulated sugar. Dip bottom of glass in granulated sugar, and flatten each ball to about ¼ inch thick.

4 Bake 7 to 9 minutes or until set. Remove from cookie sheets to cooling racks.

**1 Cookie:** Calories 60; Total Fat 4g (Saturated Fat 2g, Trans Fat 0g); Cholesterol 10mg; Sodium 25mg; Total Carbohydrate 5g (Dietary Fiber 0g); Protein 1g **Exchanges:** ½ Other Carbohydrate, ½ Fat **Carbohydrate Choices:** 0

## Make-Ahead Magic

**You can make and freeze these cookies up to 12 months ahead! Place baked, cooled cookies in a freezer-storage container. Cover and freeze up to 12 months. For softer cookies, thaw covered in container at room temperature 1 to 2 hours. For crisper cookies, remove from container to thaw.**

# Almond Angel Cookies

**PREP TIME:** 1 Hour 45 Minutes    **START TO FINISH:** 4 Hours    *4 dozen cookies*

1 cup butter, softened
1 cup granulated sugar
2 tablespoons milk
1 teaspoon vanilla
½ teaspoon almond extract
¼ teaspoon salt
2½ cups all-purpose flour
2 tablespoons yellow
  decorating sugar
2 tablespoons blue
  decorating sugar
96 small pretzel twists
2 tablespoons sliced almonds
1 tube (4.25 oz) yellow
  decorating icing
1 tube (4.25 oz) pink
  decorating icing

1   In large bowl, beat butter with electric mixer on medium-high speed until light and fluffy. Add granulated sugar; beat until creamy. Stir in milk, vanilla, almond extract and salt. Stir in flour until well mixed.

2   Measure ½ cup of dough into small resealable food-storage plastic bag; refrigerate. Divide remaining dough in half; roll each into 6-inch log. Put the decorating sugars in separate shallow dishes. Roll 1 log in yellow sugar; roll other log in blue sugar. Wrap logs separately in plastic wrap or waxed paper. Refrigerate until firm, at least 2 hours.

3   Heat oven to 350°F. For each cookie, place 2 pretzels with flat sides touching on ungreased large cookie sheets; place 3 inches apart. Unwrap logs; cut into 48 (¼-inch) slices. (If dough cracks, let stand at room temperature a few minutes.) Fold in opposite sides at top of each slice to make triangular-shaped body; place each slice on top of 2 pretzels so double loops of pretzels form angel wings at each side. Press lightly into pretzels. Using reserved dough from plastic bag, roll ½ teaspoon dough into ball; place at top for head. Press 2 sliced almonds into dough to make songbook.

4   Bake 11 to 14 minutes or until edges are firm and just begin to brown. Cool 2 to 3 minutes; remove from cookie sheets to cooling racks. Cool completely, about 15 minutes.

5   Pipe yellow icing onto cookies to make eyes and hair. Pipe pink icing to draw mouths. Let stand until set.

**1 Cookie:** Calories 110; Total Fat 5g (Saturated Fat 2.5g, Trans Fat 0g); Cholesterol 10mg; Sodium 85mg; Total Carbohydrate 16g (Dietary Fiber 0g); Protein 1g **Exchanges:** 1 Other Carbohydrate, 1 Fat **Carbohydrate Choices:** 1

## Festive Touch
Use this recipe for the project at a kids' holiday party or even a gift exchange. You could bake the cookies up to 3 days in advance and store them in loosely covered containers to leave the decorating for the party. It's fun to create together!

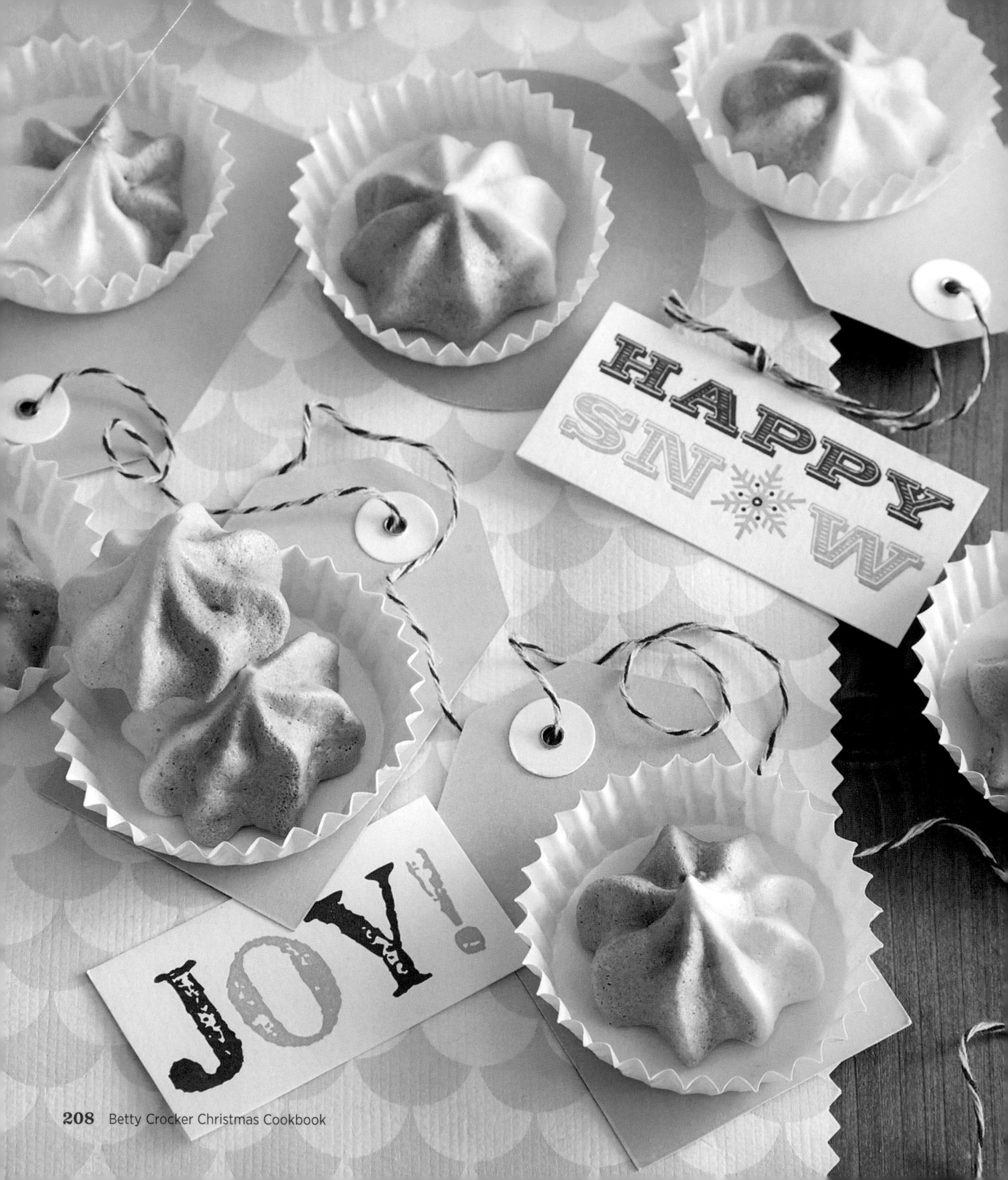
HAPPY
SNOW
JOY!

# Peppermint Meringues

**PREP TIME:** 20 Minutes   **START TO FINISH:** 5 Hours 5 Minutes   *5 dozen cookies*

3 egg whites, at room temperature
¼ teaspoon cream of tartar
¼ teaspoon peppermint extract
⅛ teaspoon salt
½ cup sugar
¼ teaspoon red food color

1 Heat oven to 175°F. Line 2 large cookie sheets with cooking parchment paper.

2 In large bowl, beat egg whites and cream of tartar with electric mixer on medium speed until soft peaks form. Beat in peppermint extract and salt. Gradually add sugar, 2 tablespoons at a time, beating on high speed until stiff glossy peaks form and sugar is dissolved. Spoon half of meringue into medium bowl; add food color. Beat until well blended.

3 In large decorating bag fitted with #827 star tip, place spoonfuls of white and red meringue side by side, alternating colors and working up from tip of bag. Do not mix colors together. Onto cookie sheets, pipe meringue into 1-inch mounds.

4 Bake 3 hours or until meringues are dry to the touch. Turn oven off; leave meringues in oven with door closed 1 hour. Finish cooling at room temperature, about 45 minutes. Remove meringues from parchment paper. Store tightly covered at room temperature.

**1 Cookie:** Calories 10; Total Fat 0g (Saturated Fat 0g, Trans Fat 0g); Cholesterol 0mg; Sodium 10mg; Total Carbohydrate 2g (Dietary Fiber 0g); Protein 0g **Exchanges:** Free **Carbohydrate Choices:** 0

# Eggnog Spritz Cookies

**PREP TIME:** 45 Minutes    **START TO FINISH:** 1 Hour 15 Minutes    *4 dozen cookies*

### COOKIES

 1 pouch (17.5 oz) sugar cookie mix
½ cup butter, melted
 1 egg
½ cup all-purpose flour
 1 teaspoon rum extract
¼ teaspoon ground nutmeg

### ICING

½ cup powdered sugar
1½ teaspoons milk
¼ teaspoon rum extract
  Red and green sugars, if desired

**1** Heat oven to 375°F. In large bowl, stir together cookie mix, butter, egg, flour, 1 teaspoon rum extract and the nutmeg until soft dough forms.

**2** Fit cookie press with desired template. Fill cookie press with dough; press cookies onto ungreased cookie sheets.

**3** Bake 6 to 8 minutes or until set. Cool 1 minute; remove from cookie sheets to cooling racks. Cool completely, about 30 minutes.

**4** In small bowl, stir powdered sugar, milk and ¼ teaspoon rum extract until icing is smooth and thin enough to drizzle. Drizzle over cookies. Sprinkle with colored sugars. Let stand until set.

**1 Cookie:** Calories 70; Total Fat 3g (Saturated Fat 2g, Trans Fat 0g); Cholesterol 10mg; Sodium 40mg; Total Carbohydrate 11g (Dietary Fiber 0g); Protein 0g **Exchanges:** 1 Other Carbohydrate, ½ Fat **Carbohydrate Choices:** 1

**Make-Ahead Magic** **Baked, cooled cookies can be tightly wrapped and stored in the freezer up to 6 months.**

# Cinnamon Cardinal Cookies

**PREP TIME:** 1 Hour 20 Minutes   **START TO FINISH:** 1 Hour 50 Minutes   *4 dozen cookies*

½ cup butter, softened

½ cup packed light brown sugar

1 teaspoon vanilla

2 cups all-purpose flour

¼ teaspoon baking soda

1½ teaspoons ground cinnamon or cardamom

⅓ cup whipping cream

48 miniature chocolate chips

Red, black and yellow decorating sugar crystals

1. In large bowl, beat butter and brown sugar with electric mixer on medium speed until light and fluffy; stir in vanilla. In small bowl, stir together flour, baking soda and cinnamon. On low speed, beat flour mixture into butter mixture alternately with whipping cream. Divide dough in half; wrap in plastic wrap. Refrigerate until firm, about 30 minutes.

2. Heat oven to 350°F. Lightly grease 2 large cookie sheets with shortening or cooking spray.

3. On lightly floured surface, roll one portion of dough until about ⅛ inch thick. Cut with 3-inch floured cardinal-shaped cookie cutter. On cookie sheets, place cutouts 2 inches apart. Repeat with second portion of dough.

4. Place chocolate chip on each bird for eye. Sprinkle top of back, crown, tail and wing of each bird with red sugar crystals; neck and eye with black sugar crystals; and beak with yellow sugar crystals. Leave bottom breast of bird without sugar.

5. Bake 6 to 8 minutes or until light brown and set. Remove from cookie sheets to cooling racks.

**1 Cookie:** Calories 50; Total Fat 2.5g (Saturated Fat 1.5g, Trans Fat 0g); Cholesterol 5mg; Sodium 25mg; Total Carbohydrate 6g (Dietary Fiber 0g); Protein 0g **Exchanges:** ½ Other Carbohydrate, ½ Fat **Carbohydrate Choices:** ½

## Kitchen Secrets

**If you don't have a cardinal-shaped cookie cutter, trace the outline of a cardinal from a coloring book or bird book onto waxed paper; or find one online, print it and cut it out. Place the pattern on the dough, and use a small paring knife to cut around it.**

# Giant Christmas Tree Cookie

**PREP TIME:** 15 Minutes   **START TO FINISH:** 1 Hour   *20 servings*

1 pouch (17.5 oz) sugar cookie mix
⅓ cup butter, softened
1 egg
   Green gel food color
1 container (12 oz) fluffy
   white whipped ready-to-
   spread frosting
   Small candies and candy
   sprinkles, if desired

**1** Heat oven to 375°F. Line 15x10x1-inch pan with foil.

**2** In medium bowl, stir cookie mix, butter and egg until soft dough forms. With moistened fingers, press dough in bottom of pan.

**3** Bake 10 to 14 minutes or until light golden brown. Cool completely, about 30 minutes.

**4** Cut tree shape from baked cookie. Cut star for top of tree from cookie scraps. Stir food color into frosting. Decorate cookie tree with frosting, candies and sprinkles.

**1 Serving:** Calories 210; Total Fat 9g (Saturated Fat 3.5g, Trans Fat 2g); Cholesterol 15mg; Sodium 110mg; Total Carbohydrate 30g (Dietary Fiber 0g); Protein 1g **Exchanges:** 2 Other Carbohydrate, 2 Fat **Carbohydrate Choices:** 2

**Make-Ahead Magic** You can bake the cookie tree the day before decorating. Cover with plastic wrap or foil until you're ready for the fun to begin!

**Festive Touch** Cut a star for the top of the tree from the scraps left after cutting the tree shape. You could also cut squares or rectangles for "gifts" to place under the tree on the serving platter.

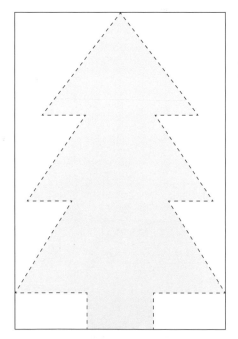

Copy shape on 11x17-inch paper; cut out. Trace shape on cardboard; cut out. Place cardboard shape on cookie to use as a guide for cutting.

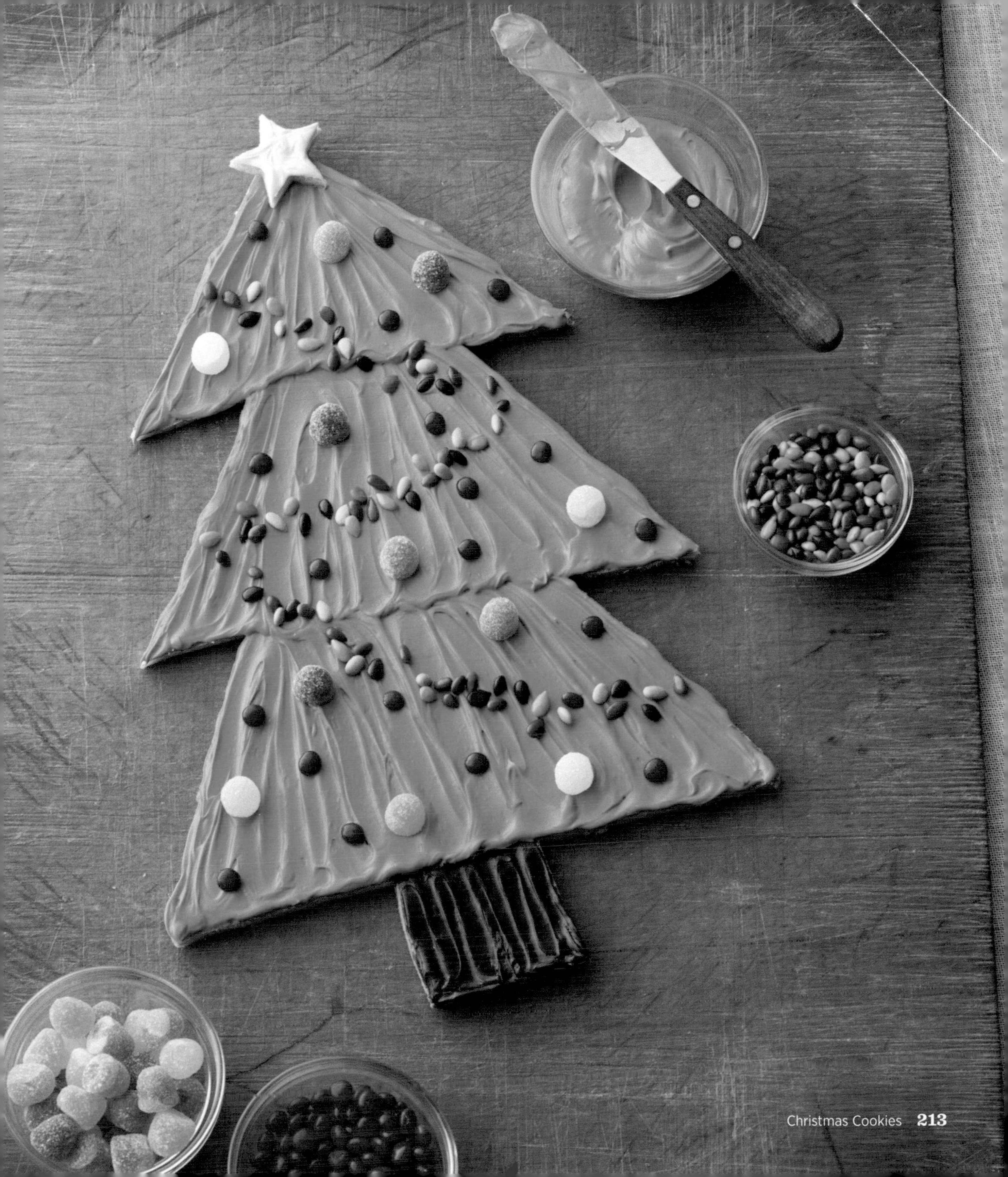

# Giant Gingerbread House Cookie

**PREP TIME:** 35 Minutes    **START TO FINISH:** 1 Hour 15 Minutes    *12 servings*

1 pouch (17.5 oz) gingerbread cookie mix

½ cup butter, softened

1 tablespoon water

1 egg

1 container (1 lb) vanilla creamy ready-to-spread frosting

Assorted candies (gumdrops, peppermints, candy canes, red cinnamon candies, candy sprinkles), if desired

**1** Heat oven to 350°F. Line 15x10x1-inch pan with cooking parchment paper.

**2** Make cookie mix as directed on pouch, using butter, water and egg. Roll dough in pan to about ¼ inch thick.

**3** Bake 10 to 12 minutes or until edges are set and golden brown. Cool 5 minutes. Use pizza cutter to cut gingerbread house shape from cookie. Cool completely.

**4** Use frosting and candies to decorate gingerbread house as desired. Use any excess cookie pieces as decoration. Cut into pieces to serve.

**1 Serving:** Calories 380; Total Fat 16g (Saturated Fat 8g, Trans Fat 0g); Cholesterol 35mg; Sodium 360mg; Total Carbohydrate 57g (Dietary Fiber 0g); Protein 2g **Exchanges:** ½ Starch, 3½ Other Carbohydrate, 3 Fat **Carbohydrate Choices:** 4

---

# Gingerbread House Decorating Ideas

Decorating a gingerbread house can be as unique as you are! Here are some great ideas for decorating your house. You can purchase your favorites or snoop around your cupboards and find foods that would work.

**ROOF**

Bite-size frosted mini wheat cereal

Chocolate flat candy bars

Colorful flat candies

Crackers

Fruit slices candy

Gumdrop halves or slices

Pretzel sticks or rods

Small cookies, such as vanilla wafers

**DOOR**

Candy bar

Graham cracker

Oval-shaped flat cookies (cut off one end, for bottom of door)

Sugar wafers

**CHIMNEY**

Candy sticks or straight candy canes

Chocolate chips

Chocolate rocks

Jelly beans (especially tan, brown, black and speckled)

Sugar ice-cream cone, cut lengthwise in half

**WREATH**

Green holly and red ball decors, arranged in a circle

Gumdrops

Peppermint candy

Round or flower-shaped cookie with hole in center

Small or tiny round candies arranged in a circle

**OTHER DECORATIONS**

Candy canes

Frosted animal crackers

Licorice nibs or ropes

Malted milk balls

Sprinkles

Square chewy candy

Whole almonds

# Simple Turtle Cookie Cups

**PREP TIME:** 30 Minutes  **START TO FINISH:** 1 Hour 15 Minutes  *3 dozen cookie cups*

1 pouch (17.5 oz) double chocolate chunk cookie mix

3 tablespoons vegetable oil

1 tablespoon water

1 egg

36 round milk chocolate–covered chewy caramels, unwrapped

36 pecan halves

**1** Heat oven to 375°F. Place miniature paper baking cup in each of 36 mini muffin cups.

**2** In large bowl, stir together cookie mix, oil, water and egg until soft dough forms. Shape dough into 36 (1¼-inch) balls; place in muffin cups.

**3** Bake 8 to 9 minutes or until edges are set. Immediately press caramel into center of each cookie cup. Cool 2 minutes. Top with pecan halves. Cool completely, about 30 minutes. Remove from pans with narrow spatula.

**1 Cookie Cup:** Calories 110; Total Fat 5g (Saturated Fat 2g, Trans Fat 0g); Cholesterol 5mg; Sodium 75mg; Total Carbohydrate 15g (Dietary Fiber 0g); Protein 1g **Exchanges:** 1 Other Carbohydrate, 1 Fat **Carbohydrate Choices:** 1

**Festive Touch** Bake these cookie cups in holiday-themed mini paper baking cups.

# Gluten-Free Peanut Butter Cookie Cups

**PREP TIME:** 45 Minutes    **START TO FINISH:** 1 Hour 30 Minutes    *5 dozen cookie cups*

1 box (19 oz) gluten-free chocolate chip cookie mix
1 egg
½ cup butter, softened
1 teaspoon vanilla
½ cup creamy peanut butter
60 miniature chocolate-covered peanut butter cup candies, unwrapped

1 Heat oven to 375°F. Place mini paper baking cup in each of 24 mini muffin cups.

2 In large bowl, stir together cookie mix, egg, butter and vanilla with spoon. Stir in peanut butter. Shape about two-fifths of the dough into 24 (1-inch) balls. Place 1 ball in each muffin cup.

3 Bake 9 to 11 minutes or just until lightly browned. Immediately press peanut butter cup candy into center of each cookie. Cool 5 minutes before removing from pan to cooling rack. Repeat with remaining dough and candies to make 36 more cookie cups.

**1 Cookie Cup:** Calories 100; Total Fat 5g (Saturated Fat 2g, Trans Fat 0g); Cholesterol 10mg; Sodium 80mg; Total Carbohydrate 11g (Dietary Fiber 0g); Protein 1g **Exchanges:** ½ Starch, ½ Other Carbohydrate, 1 Fat **Carbohydrate Choices:** 1

# Piña Colada Rum Cups

**PREP TIME:** 35 Minutes    **START TO FINISH:** 1 Hour 5 Minutes    *3 dozen cookie cups*

### COOKIE CUPS

¾ cup butter, softened

1 cup granulated sugar

1 egg

¼ teaspoon rum extract

2 cups all-purpose flour

1 teaspoon baking soda

1 teaspoon cream of tartar

½ teaspoon salt

### FILLING

3 cups powdered sugar

⅓ cup butter, softened

⅛ teaspoon rum extract

1 to 2 tablespoons milk

1 can (8 oz) crushed pineapple, drained, patted dry

2 tablespoons shredded coconut, toasted

1 Heat oven to 350°F. Spray 36 mini muffin cups with cooking spray.

2 In medium bowl, beat ¾ cup butter and the granulated sugar with electric mixer on medium speed 2 minutes or until smooth and creamy. Beat in egg and ¼ teaspoon rum extract until well blended. On low speed, beat in flour, baking soda, cream of tartar and salt about 1 minute or until dough forms.

3 Shape dough into 36 (1¼-inch) balls. Place 1 ball in each muffin cup.

4 Bake 10 to 12 minutes or until set and edges are light golden brown. Using end of wooden spoon handle, press 1-inch-deep indentation in center of each cookie to form a cup. Run knife around edges of cookie cups to loosen. Cool completely, about 15 minutes. Remove from pans to cooling racks.

5 In large bowl, beat powdered sugar and ⅓ cup butter with electric mixer on low speed until well blended. Add ⅛ teaspoon rum extract and 1 tablespoon milk; beat until smooth and spreadable, adding additional milk, 1 teaspoon at a time, if needed for desired consistency. Stir in pineapple.

6 Spoon about 2 teaspoons filling into each cookie cup. Sprinkle with coconut. Store on plate in refrigerator, loosely covered with plastic wrap.

**1 Cookie Cup:** Calories 140; Total Fat 6g (Saturated Fat 3.5g, Trans Fat 0g); Cholesterol 20mg; Sodium 115mg; Total Carbohydrate 22g (Dietary Fiber 0g); Protein 1g **Exchanges:** 1½ Other Carbohydrate, 1 Fat **Carbohydrate Choices:** 1½

## Make-Ahead Magic

Make and bake the cookie cups as directed. Place cooled unfilled cups in plastic storage container or resealable freezer plastic bag; keep frozen up to 2 months. Thaw at room temperature about 30 minutes or until completely thawed. Fill as directed.

## Kitchen Secrets

To toast coconut, heat oven to 350°F. Spread coconut in ungreased shallow pan. Bake uncovered 5 to 7 minutes, stirring occasionally, until golden brown.

# Salted Caramel Pretzel Bars

**PREP TIME:** 20 Minutes    **START TO FINISH:** 1 Hour 50 Minutes    *48 bars*

### CRUST
- 1⅓ cups all-purpose flour
- ½ cup granulated sugar
- ½ cup butter, softened

### CARAMEL LAYER
- 1 cup packed brown sugar
- 1 cup butter
- ¼ cup light corn syrup
- 1 can (14 oz) sweetened condensed milk (not evaporated)
- 1 teaspoon vanilla
- 1 bag (7.2 oz) original pretzel crisps

### TOPPING
- 2 cups semisweet chocolate chips (about 12 oz)
- 1 teaspoon coarse (kosher or sea) salt

1  Heat oven to 350°F. Spray 13x9-inch pan with cooking spray.

2  In large bowl, mix crust ingredients until crumbly. Press in bottom of pan. Bake 12 to 15 minutes or until light golden brown. Cool 15 minutes.

3  Meanwhile, in 2-quart saucepan, heat brown sugar, 1 cup butter, the corn syrup and condensed milk to boiling over medium heat, stirring frequently. Boil 5 minutes, stirring constantly. Remove from heat. Stir in vanilla.

4  Arrange one layer of pretzels over crust. Pour half of the caramel mixture over pretzels. Immediately arrange another layer of pretzels over caramel layer. Pour remaining caramel over pretzels. Coarsely crush remaining pretzels.

5  In small microwavable bowl, microwave chocolate chips uncovered on High 1 to 2 minutes, stirring every 30 seconds, until chips are softened and can be stirred smooth. Pour and evenly spread melted chocolate over caramel layer. Sprinkle with crushed pretzels and salt. Refrigerate about 1 hour or until set. Cut into 8 rows by 6 rows.

**1 Bar:** Calories 180; Total Fat 9g (Saturated Fat 5g, Trans Fat 0g); Cholesterol 20mg; Sodium 135mg; Total Carbohydrate 23g (Dietary Fiber 0g); Protein 1g **Exchanges:** 1½ Other Carbohydrate, 2 Fat **Carbohydrate Choices:** 1½

## Make-Ahead Magic
Bars can be made up to 3 days before serving. Cover and store at room temperature.

## Kitchen Secrets
Because these bars are ultra rich and are cut small, one pan can serve many purposes. Add them to a cookie tray, bring a plate to a neighborhood party or tuck a few into the family's lunch boxes for a special treat.

# Cranberry-Orange Crumble Bars

**PREP TIME:** 20 Minutes  **START TO FINISH:** 40 Minutes  *48 bars*

½ cup granulated sugar
¼ cup orange juice
¼ cup water
2 cups fresh or frozen cranberries
1 tablespoon grated orange peel
½ teaspoon ground cinnamon
¾ cup packed brown sugar
½ cup butter, softened
1½ cups quick-cooking or
old-fashioned oats
1 cup all-purpose flour
¼ teaspoon salt

**1** Heat oven to 400°F. In 1½-quart saucepan, mix granulated sugar, orange juice and water. Heat to boiling. Stir in cranberries, orange peel and cinnamon. Cook over medium heat about 10 minutes, stirring occasionally, until thickened; cool completely.

**2** Meanwhile, in medium bowl, mix brown sugar and butter until well blended. Stir in oats, flour and salt until crumbly. Press half of the crumb mixture in bottom of ungreased 13x9-inch pan. Spread cranberry mixture over crust. Top with remaining crumb mixture; press lightly.

**3** Bake about 20 minutes or until filling is bubbly and topping is light brown. Cut into 8 rows by 6 rows while warm. Serve warm or cool.

**1 Bar:** Calories 60; Total Fat 2g (Saturated Fat 1g, Trans Fat 0g); Cholesterol 5mg; Sodium 25mg; Total Carbohydrate 10g (Dietary Fiber 1g); Protein 1g **Exchanges:** ½ Fruit, ½ Fat **Carbohydrate Choices:** ½

**Festive Touch** Get these not-too-sweet bars ready for your cookie tray by drizzling them with 1 ounce of melted white chocolate. Let it dry before cutting the bars.

**Kitchen Secrets** Line the baking pan with foil to make cleanup and cutting easy.

# German Chocolate–Pecan Pie Bars

**PREP TIME:** 15 Minutes   **START TO FINISH:** 3 Hours 30 Minutes   *24 bars*

1¾ cups all-purpose flour

¾ cup powdered sugar

¾ cup cold butter, cut into pieces

¼ cup unsweetened baking cocoa

1½ cups semisweet chocolate chips (about 9 oz)

¾ cup packed brown sugar

¾ cup light corn syrup

¼ cup butter, melted

3 eggs, slightly beaten

1 cup flaked coconut

3 cups broken pecans, toasted

**1** Heat oven to 350°F. Line bottom and sides of 13x9-inch pan with heavy-duty foil, extending foil 2 to 3 inches over 2 opposite sides of pan; spray foil with cooking spray.

**2** In food processor, place flour, powdered sugar, ¾ cup butter and the cocoa. Cover; process with quick on-and-off pulses until consistency of coarse meal. Press in bottom and ¾ inch up sides of pan.

**3** Bake 15 minutes. Remove from oven; sprinkle chocolate chips over crust. Cool 30 minutes.

**4** In medium bowl, mix brown sugar, corn syrup, melted butter and the eggs with whisk until smooth. Stir in coconut and pecans. Spoon over crust. Bake 25 to 30 minutes or until golden and set. Cool completely in pan on cooling rack, about 1 hour. Refrigerate 1 hour. Use foil to lift out of pan. Cut into 6 rows by 4 rows.

**1 Bar:** Calories 360; Total Fat 22g (Saturated Fat 0g, Trans Fat 0g); Cholesterol 0mg; Sodium 85mg; Total Carbohydrate 0g (Dietary Fiber 3g); Protein 0g **Exchanges:** 1 Starch, 1½ Other Carbohydrate, 4 Fat **Carbohydrate Choices:** 2½

## Kitchen Secrets
To toast pecans, spread in ungreased shallow pan. Bake uncovered at 350°F for 6 to 10 minutes, stirring occasionally, until light brown.

# Cakes
### &
# Desserts

# Candy Cane Bundt Cake

**PREP TIME:** 20 Minutes    **START TO FINISH:** 2 Hours 40 Minutes    *12 servings*

## CAKE

1 box (15.25 oz) white cake mix with pudding
1  cup water
¼ cup vegetable oil
3 egg whites
½ teaspoon red food color
½ teaspoon peppermint extract

## GLAZE

1 cup powdered sugar
1 tablespoon milk or water
½ teaspoon vanilla, if desired

## DECORATION

Crushed candy canes or hard peppermint candies, if desired

**1** Heat oven to 350°F (325°F for dark or nonstick pan). Generously grease 12-cup fluted tube cake pan with shortening; generously sprinkle with flour.

**2** Make cake batter as directed on box, using water, oil and egg whites. Pour about 2 cups batter into pan.

**3** Pour about ¾ cup batter into small bowl; stir in food color and peppermint extract. Carefully pour pink batter over white batter in pan. Carefully pour remaining white batter over pink batter. Bake and cool as directed on box.

**4** In small bowl, mix glaze ingredients. If necessary, stir in additional milk, 1 teaspoon at a time, until smooth and spreadable. Spread over cake. Sprinkle crushed candy on top. Store loosely covered.

**1 Serving:** Calories 240; Total Fat 8g (Saturated Fat 2g, Trans Fat 0g); Cholesterol 0mg; Sodium 280mg; Total Carbohydrate 41g (Dietary Fiber 0g); Protein 2g **Exchanges:** 1 Starch, 1½ Other Carbohydrate, 1½ Fat **Carbohydrate Choices:** 3

## Make-Ahead Magic
You can bake the cake ahead, but do not add the glaze. Wrap in plastic wrap and store in the freezer up to 3 months. To thaw, loosen wrap and let stand at room temperature. Continue as directed in Step 4.

## Kitchen Secrets
Fluted tube cake pans can be a challenge to grease. Try this: Place a dab of shortening on the outside of a small food-storage plastic bag. Slip the bag on your hand and rub shortening on the inside of the pan. Repeat with more shortening until every nook and cranny is greased. Give the inside of the pan a good sprinkling with flour, shake the excess from the pan, and your baked cake will slip right out!

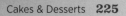

# Hot Chocolate Bundt Cake

**PREP TIME:** 30 Minutes   **START TO FINISH:** 4 Hours 25 Minutes   *14 servings*

## CAKE

- 2 teaspoons unsweetened baking cocoa
- 1 cup water
- ¾ cup unsalted butter, cut into pieces
- ¾ cup vegetable oil
- 4 oz bittersweet baking chocolate, finely chopped
- 1½ cups sugar
- 3 cups all-purpose flour
- ¾ cup sweet ground chocolate & cocoa premium powder
- 2½ teaspoons baking soda
- ½ teaspoon salt
- 3 eggs, at room temperature
- ¾ cup buttermilk
- 1 tablespoon vanilla

## BITTERSWEET CHOCOLATE GANACHE

- ⅓ cup whipping cream
- 2 tablespoons unsalted butter
- 4 oz bittersweet baking chocolate, finely chopped

## GARNISH

- 1 cup marshmallow creme (from 7-oz jar)
- Bittersweet chocolate curls, if desired

**1** Heat oven to 350°F. Lightly grease 12-cup fluted tube cake pan with shortening; sprinkle with the unsweetened cocoa.

**2** In 3-quart saucepan, stir water, ¾ cup butter, the oil and 4 oz bittersweet chocolate. Cook over low heat 8 to 10 minutes, stirring constantly, until chocolate is melted and mixture is smooth. Remove from heat. Stir in sugar until blended. Cool 10 minutes.

**3** In medium bowl, mix flour, ground chocolate and cocoa, baking soda and salt. Add eggs, one at a time, to cooled chocolate mixture, beating with whisk just until blended after each addition. Add flour mixture alternately with buttermilk, stirring just until blended. Stir in vanilla. Pour batter into pan.

**4** Bake 45 to 50 minutes or until toothpick inserted in center comes out clean. Cool 15 minutes; remove from pan to cooling rack. Cool completely, about 2 hours.

**5** In medium microwavable bowl, microwave ganache ingredients on High 45 to 50 seconds, stirring after 30 seconds, until melted and smooth. Cool 10 minutes or until slightly thickened. Place cake on serving plate; drizzle with ganache. Refrigerate 30 minutes or until set.

**6** Spoon marshmallow creme into resealable food-storage plastic bag; seal bag. Cut off ½-inch corner of bag. Squeeze bag to drizzle marshmallow creme over top of cake, allowing some to drip down side. Garnish with chocolate curls.

**1 Serving:** Calories 550; Total Fat 35g (Saturated Fat 15g, Trans Fat 0g); Cholesterol 0mg; Sodium 340mg; Total Carbohydrate 54g (Dietary Fiber 2g); Protein 7g **Exchanges:** 2 Starch, 1½ Other Carbohydrate, 6½ Fat **Carbohydrate Choices:** 3½

## Kitchen Secrets
To make chocolate curls, place a bar or block of chocolate on waxed paper. Press a vegetable peeler firmly against the chocolate and pull toward you in long, thin strokes. Small curls can be made by using the side of the chocolate bar. Transfer each curl carefully with a toothpick to a waxed paper–lined cookie sheet or directly onto cake.

## Kitchen Secrets
Sweet ground chocolate & cocoa premium powder mix is most likely found near the hot chocolate mixes at your grocery store.

# Butter-Rum Pound Cake

PREP TIME: 20 Minutes    START TO FINISH: 3 Hours    *16 servings*

1 box (15.25 oz) butter recipe yellow cake mix with pudding

1 box (4-serving size) vanilla instant pudding and pie filling mix

¾ cup water

⅓ cup sour cream

¼ cup butter, softened

¼ cup dark rum

1 teaspoon grated orange peel

4 eggs

½ cup vanilla creamy ready-to-spread frosting (from 1-lb container)

2 teaspoons dark rum

¼ cup chopped pecans

1 Heat oven to 325°F. Grease and flour 10-inch angel food (tube) cake pan or 12-inch fluted tube cake pan, or spray with baking spray with flour.

2 In large bowl, beat cake mix, pudding mix, water, sour cream, butter, ¼ cup rum, the orange peel and eggs with electric mixer on low speed 30 seconds; beat on medium speed 2 minutes. Spread batter in pan.

3 Bake 45 to 55 minutes or until toothpick inserted in center comes out clean. Cool 15 minutes; remove from pan to cooling rack. Cool completely, about 1 hour 30 minutes.

4 In small microwavable bowl, microwave frosting uncovered on Medium (50%) 15 seconds. Stir in 2 teaspoons rum. Spread over top of cake, allowing some to drizzle down side. Sprinkle with pecans. Store loosely covered.

**1 Serving:** Calories 230; Total Fat 9g (Saturated Fat 4g, Trans Fat 0.5g); Cholesterol 65mg; Sodium 340mg; Total Carbohydrate 35g (Dietary Fiber 0g); Protein 2g **Exchanges:** 1 Starch, 1½ Other Carbohydrate, 1½ Fat **Carbohydrate Choices:** 2

## Kitchen Secrets
If you don't have rum on hand or prefer not to use it, substitute water for the ¼ cup rum in the cake, and ½ teaspoon rum extract for the 2 teaspoons rum in the frosting.

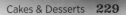

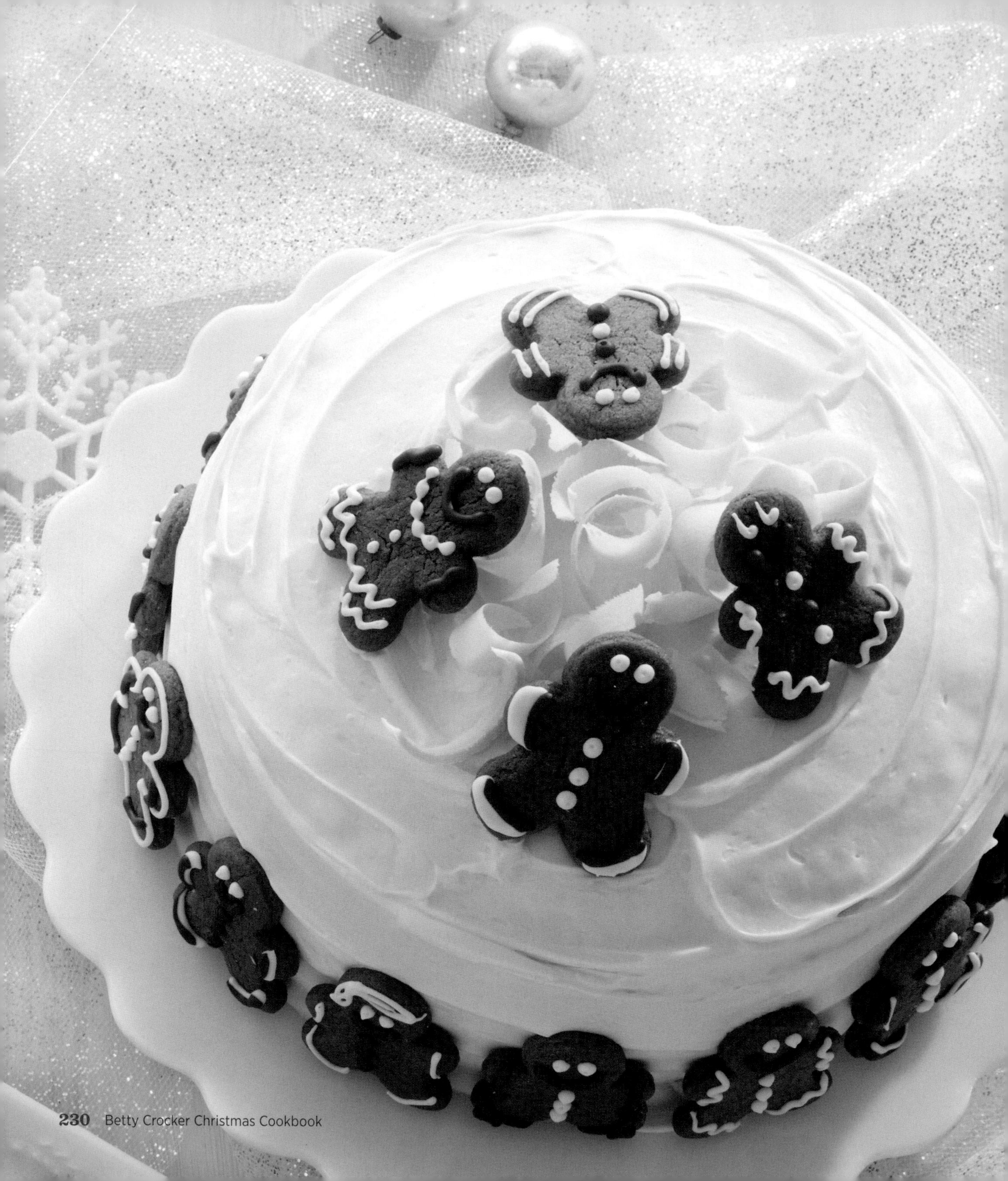

# Holiday Gingerbread Cookie Cake

**PREP TIME:** 1 Hour   **START TO FINISH:** 3 Hours 25 Minutes   *14 servings*

### LAYER CAKE

- 1 box (15.25 oz) devil's food cake mix with pudding
- 1¼ cups water
- ½ cup vegetable oil
- 3 eggs
- 2 teaspoons ground ginger
- 1½ teaspoons ground cinnamon
- 2 containers (12 oz each) fluffy white or vanilla whipped ready-to-spread frosting
- 1 oz vanilla-flavored candy coating (almond bark), shaved

### GINGERBREAD PEOPLE

- 1 pouch (17.5 oz) gingerbread cookie mix
- Butter, water and egg called for on cookie mix pouch
- 1 pouch (7 oz) white cookie icing
- 1 pouch (7 oz) red cookie icing

1  Heat oven to 350°F (325°F for dark or nonstick pans). Grease bottoms and sides of 2 (8-inch) round cake pans with shortening or cooking spray.

2  In large bowl, beat cake mix, water, oil, eggs, ginger and cinnamon with electric mixer on medium speed 2 minutes, scraping bowl occasionally. Divide batter evenly between pans (2 cups each). Bake 30 to 35 minutes or until toothpick inserted in center comes out clean. Cool 10 minutes; remove from pans to cooling racks. Cool completely, about 30 minutes.

3  Heat oven to 375°F (350°F for dark or nonstick cookie sheets). In medium bowl, stir cookie mix, butter, water and egg until soft dough forms. (If dough is too sticky to roll out, cover and refrigerate 15 minutes.)

4  On lightly floured surface, roll dough until ¼ inch thick. Cut with 1-inch gingerbread boy or girl cookie cutter. On ungreased cookie sheets, place cutouts 2 inches apart. Bake 7 to 9 minutes or until edges are set. Cool 1 minute; remove from cookie sheets to cooling racks. Cool completely. Decorate 18 cookies with white and red cookie icing. Reserve remaining cookies for another use.

5  On serving plate, place one cake layer, top side down. Spread with about ½ cup frosting; top with second cake layer, top side up. Using metal spatula, frost side and top of cake with thin layer of frosting to make a crumb coat; refrigerate 30 minutes. Remove from refrigerator; frost side and top of cake with second layer of frosting.

6  Sprinkle top of cake with shaved almond bark; insert decorated cookies in top of cake and around side.

**1 Serving (1 Cake Slice and 1 Cookie):** Calories 570; Total Fat 26g (Saturated Fat 9g, Trans Fat 2g); Cholesterol 65mg; Sodium 520mg; Total Carbohydrate 80g (Dietary Fiber 0g); Protein 3g **Exchanges:** 1 Starch, 4½ Other Carbohydrate, 5 Fat **Carbohydrate Choices:** 5

**Make-Ahead Magic** Bake, cool and decorate the gingerbread cookies the day before you make the cake, and serve the cake on the same day you make it for the best texture of the cookies.

**Kitchen Secrets** Use a vegetable peeler to shave the almond bark.

# Bûche de Noël

**PREP TIME:** 40 Minutes   **START TO FINISH:** 1 Hour 25 Minutes   *10 servings*

### CAKE

- 3 eggs
- 1 cup granulated sugar
- ⅓ cup water
- 1 teaspoon vanilla
- ¾ cup all-purpose flour
- 1 teaspoon baking powder
- ¼ teaspoon salt

### FILLING

- 1 cup whipping cream
- 2 tablespoons granulated sugar
- 1½ teaspoons instant coffee granules or crystals

### CHOCOLATE BUTTERCREAM FROSTING

- ⅓ cup unsweetened baking cocoa
- ⅓ cup butter, softened
- 2 cups powdered sugar
- 1½ teaspoons vanilla
- 1 to 2 tablespoons hot water

**1** Heat oven to 375°F. Line 15x10x1-inch pan with foil; grease foil with shortening or cooking spray.

**2** In medium bowl, beat eggs with electric mixer on high speed about 5 minutes or until very thick and lemon colored. On low speed, gradually beat in 1 cup granulated sugar. Beat in ⅓ cup water and 1 teaspoon vanilla. Gradually add flour, baking powder and salt, beating just until batter is smooth. Pour into pan, spreading to corners.

**3** Bake 12 to 15 minutes or until toothpick inserted in center comes out clean. Immediately loosen cake from edges of pan; invert onto towel generously sprinkled with powdered sugar. Carefully remove foil. Trim off stiff edges of cake if necessary. While hot, carefully roll cake and towel from narrow end. Cool on cooling rack at least 30 minutes.

**4** In chilled medium bowl, beat filling ingredients on high speed until stiff peaks form. Unroll cake; remove towel. Spread filling over cake. Roll up cake.

**5** In medium bowl, beat cocoa and butter with electric mixer on low speed until well blended. Beat in powdered sugar. Beat in 1½ teaspoons vanilla and enough of the hot water, one teaspoon at a time, until frosting is smooth and spreadable.

**6** For tree stump, cut off a 2-inch diagonal slice from one end of cake. Attach stump to one long side using 1 tablespoon frosting. Frost cake with remaining frosting. With tines of fork, make strokes in frosting to look like tree bark.

**1 Serving:** Calories 390; Total Fat 16g (Saturated Fat 9g, Trans Fat 0.5g); Cholesterol 100mg; Sodium 190mg; Total Carbohydrate 57g (Dietary Fiber 1g); Protein 4g **Exchanges:** 1 Starch, 3 Other Carbohydrate, 3 Fat **Carbohydrate Choices:** 4

## Make-Ahead Magic You can make this cake up to 2 days in advance. Cover and refrigerate until ready to serve.

## Festive Touch Decorate your yule log with beautiful sugared cranberries and rosemary sprigs. Thin light corn syrup with a little bit of water. Dip fresh cranberries and fresh rosemary sprigs, one at a time, in mixture, rolling to coat completely; shake off excess. Roll in granulated sugar. Let stand until set. Arrange around log on serving platter or on top of log. Chopped pistachios would also make a nice garnish sprinkled over the frosting.

Cakes & Desserts **233**

# avenly Chocolate Soufflé Cake

**PREP TIME:** 30 Minutes   **START TO FINISH:** 2 Hours 25 Minutes   *12 servings*

## CAKE

- 1⅔ cups semisweet chocolate chunks
- ½ cup butter
- ½ cup all-purpose flour
- 4 eggs, separated
- ¼ teaspoon cream of tartar
- ½ cup granulated sugar

## CHOCOLATE SAUCE

- ⅓ cup semisweet chocolate chunks
- 3 tablespoons granulated sugar
- ¼ cup evaporated fat-free milk (from 5-oz can)
- ½ teaspoon butter

## SWEETENED WHIPPED CREAM

- 1 cup whipping cream
- 2 tablespoons powdered sugar
- ½ teaspoon vanilla

  Crushed hard peppermint candies, if desired

1  Heat oven to 325°F. Grease bottom and side of 9-inch springform pan with shortening.

2  In 2-quart saucepan, heat 1 cup of the chocolate chunks and ½ cup butter over medium heat, stirring occasionally, until melted. Cool 5 minutes. Stir in flour until smooth. Stir in egg yolks until well blended.

3  In large bowl, beat egg whites and cream of tartar with electric mixer on high speed until foamy. Beat in ½ cup granulated sugar, 1 tablespoon at a time, until soft peaks form. Fold about one-fourth of the egg whites in bowl into chocolate mixture; fold that mixture into egg whites. Spread in pan. Sprinkle remaining ⅔ cup chocolate chunks evenly over top.

4  Bake 35 to 40 minutes or until toothpick inserted in center comes out clean (top will appear dry and cracked). Cool 10 minutes. Remove side of pan; leave cake on pan bottom. Cool completely on cooling rack, about 1 hour.

5  Just before serving, in 1-quart saucepan, heat ⅓ cup chocolate chunks, 3 tablespoons granulated sugar and the milk over medium heat, stirring constantly, until chocolate is melted and mixture boils. Remove from heat; stir in ½ teaspoon butter.

6  In chilled small bowl, beat whipping cream, powdered sugar and vanilla with electric mixer on high speed until stiff peaks form. Drizzle cake slices with chocolate sauce. Serve with whipped cream. Sprinkle with candies.

**1 Serving:** Calories 390; Total Fat 25g (Saturated Fat 15g, Trans Fat 0.5g); Cholesterol 110mg; Sodium 105mg; Total Carbohydrate 36g (Dietary Fiber 2g); Protein 4g **Exchanges:** 1½ Starch, 1 Other Carbohydrate, 5 Fat **Carbohydrate Choices:** 2½

## Kitchen Secrets

**Milk chocolate–coated toffee bits, or chopped chocolate-covered English toffee candy bars, can be used in place of the peppermint candies.**

# Tiramisu

**PREP TIME:** 25 Minutes   **START TO FINISH:** 4 Hours 25 Minutes   *9 servings*

1 container (8 oz) mascarpone
  cheese or 1 package (8 oz)
  cream cheese, softened
½ cup powdered sugar
2 tablespoons light rum or
  ½ teaspoon rum extract
1 cup whipping cream
1 package (3 oz) ladyfingers
½ cup cold brewed espresso
  or strong coffee
2 teaspoons unsweetened
  baking cocoa

1  In large bowl, beat cheese and powdered sugar with electric mixer
   on medium speed until smooth. On low speed, beat in rum; set aside.

2  In chilled small bowl, beat whipping cream on high speed until stiff peaks
   form. Fold into cheese mixture.

3  Split ladyfingers horizontally in half. Arrange half of the ladyfingers,
   cut side up, on bottom of ungreased 8-inch square or 9-inch round pan.
   Drizzle ¼ cup of the espresso over ladyfingers. Spread half of the cheese
   mixture over ladyfingers.

4  Arrange remaining ladyfingers, cut side up, on cheese mixture. Drizzle
   with remaining ¼ cup espresso. Spread with remaining cheese mixture.

5  Sift or sprinkle cocoa over top. Cover; refrigerate at least 4 hours or until
   filling is firm but no longer than 24 hours. Store covered in refrigerator.

**1 Serving:** Calories 260; Total Fat 21g (Saturated Fat 13g, Trans Fat 0.5g); Cholesterol 80mg; Sodium 35mg;
Total Carbohydrate 14g (Dietary Fiber 0g); Protein 2g **Carbohydrate Choices:** 1

## Kitchen Secrets Look for mascarpone in the cheese case in large supermarkets, specialty cheese shops and gourmet food stores.

# Cake Ball Ornaments

**PREP TIME:** 1 Hour 15 Minutes  **START TO FINISH:** 3 Hours  *45 cake balls*

1 box (15.25 oz) German chocolate cake mix with pudding

1 cup buttermilk

½ cup vegetable oil

3 eggs

2 tablespoons unsweetened baking cocoa

1 bottle (1 oz) red food color

1 cup cream cheese creamy ready-to-spread frosting (from 1-lb container)

2 cups green candy melts or coating wafers, melted

2 cups red candy melts or coating wafers, melted

1 cup white candy melts or coating wafers, melted

90 pieces Frosted Cheerios™ cereal (about ⅓ cup)

**1** Heat oven to 350°F. Spray 13x9-inch pan with cooking spray. In large bowl, beat cake mix, buttermilk, oil, eggs, cocoa and food color with electric mixer on medium speed 2 minutes, until smooth. Pour into pan.

**2** Bake 25 to 30 minutes or until toothpick inserted in center comes out clean. Cool completely in pan on cooling rack.

**3** Line cookie sheet with waxed paper. Crumble cake into large bowl. Add frosting; mix well. Shape into 45 (1¼-inch) balls. Place on cookie sheet; freeze 15 minutes. Transfer to refrigerator.

**4** Dip half of balls in melted green candy and other half in melted red candy; tap off excess. Return to cookie sheet; let stand until set, about 30 minutes.

**5** Spoon melted white candy into resealable food-storage plastic bag; cut off tiny corner of bag. Pipe designs on cake balls; let stand until set. Gently press 1 cereal piece on top of each cake ball, attaching with white candy. Pipe dot of candy on cereal piece; attach another cereal piece upright in center for ornament hook.

**1 Cake Ball:** Calories 240; Total Fat 12g (Saturated Fat 6g, Trans Fat 0g); Cholesterol 0mg; Sodium 110mg; Total Carbohydrate 32g (Dietary Fiber 0g); Protein 1g **Exchanges:** ½ Starch, 1½ Other Carbohydrate, 2½ Fat **Carbohydrate Choices:** 2

## Festive Touch

**Fill a decorative bowl or platter with these creative cake balls, and use it as a centerpiece for your holiday table. Your guests will delight in being able to eat them! Packaged in a small box, they also make a cute edible gift.**

## Festive Touch

**Use other colors of candy melts to change the look of these balls, like we did for the cover of the book.**

# Reindeer Cupcakes

**PREP TIME:** 1 Hour 5 Minutes   **START TO FINISH:** 2 Hours 5 Minutes   *24 cupcakes*

### CHOCOLATE CUPCAKES

| | |
|---|---|
| 2 | cups all-purpose flour |
| 1¼ | teaspoons baking soda |
| 1 | teaspoon salt |
| ¼ | teaspoon baking powder |
| 1 | cup hot water |
| ⅔ | cup unsweetened baking cocoa |
| ¾ | cup shortening |
| 1½ | cups granulated sugar |
| 2 | eggs |
| 1 | teaspoon vanilla |

### FROSTING

| | |
|---|---|
| ½ | cup butter, softened |
| 3 | oz unsweetened baking chocolate, melted, cooled |
| 3 | cups powdered sugar |
| 2 | teaspoons vanilla |
| 3 to 4 | tablespoons milk |

### DECORATIONS

| | |
|---|---|
| | Chocolate candy sprinkles |
| 24 | large pretzel twists |
| 24 | miniature marshmallows |
| 24 | small green gumdrops |
| 24 | red cinnamon candies |

**1** Heat oven to 350°F. Place paper baking cup in each of 24 regular-size muffin cups.

**2** In medium bowl, mix flour, baking soda, salt and baking powder; set aside. In small bowl, mix hot water and cocoa until dissolved; set aside.

**3** In large bowl, beat shortening with electric mixer on medium speed 30 seconds. Gradually add granulated sugar, about ¼ cup at a time, beating well after each addition. Beat 2 minutes longer. Add eggs, one at a time, beating well after each addition. Beat in 1 teaspoon vanilla. Alternately add flour mixture and cocoa mixture, beating on low speed just until blended. Divide batter evenly among muffin cups, filling each two-thirds full.

**4** Bake 20 to 25 minutes or until toothpick inserted in center comes out clean. Cool 5 minutes. Remove from pans to cooling racks; cool completely.

**5** In large bowl, mix butter and chocolate. Stir in powdered sugar. Beat in 2 teaspoons vanilla and 3 tablespoons milk until smooth and spreadable. If frosting is too thick, beat in remaining milk, 1 teaspoon at a time. (If frosting becomes too thin, beat in a small amount of powdered sugar.) Frost cupcakes. Sprinkle candy sprinkles over tops of cupcakes.

**6** For each cupcake, cut pretzel twist in half; poke into cupcake for reindeer antlers. Cut miniature marshmallow in half; arrange on cupcake for eyes. Center gumdrop below marshmallow halves for nose. Place red cinnamon candy below gumdrop for mouth.

**1 Frosted Cupcake (Undecorated):** Calories 360; Total Fat 13g (Saturated Fat 6g, Trans Fat 0g); Cholesterol 25mg; Sodium 410mg; Total Carbohydrate 55g (Dietary Fiber 2g); Protein 4g **Exchanges:** 1 Starch, 2½ Other Carbohydrate, 2½ Fat **Carbohydrate Choices:** 3½

## Make-Ahead Magic
Baked, cooled cupcakes can be frozen in an airtight container or resealable freezer plastic bag up to 4 months. Frost and decorate the frozen cupcakes—they'll thaw while you're decorating!

## Kitchen Secrets
Save time by substituting 1 box devil's food cake mix with pudding for the Chocolate Cupcakes and 1 container (1 pound) chocolate creamy ready-to-spread frosting for the Frosting. Bake and cool cupcakes as directed on box, then decorate as directed.

# Elf Hat Cupcakes

**PREP TIME:** 45 Minutes    **START TO FINISH:** 1 Hour 45 Minutes    *24 cupcakes*

1 box (15.25 oz) chocolate fudge
   cake mix with pudding

1¼ cups water

½ cup vegetable oil

3 eggs

¼ cup assorted candy sprinkles

3 containers (1 lb each) vanilla
   creamy ready-to-spread frosting

Red, green and blue gel
food color

1  Heat oven to 350°F (325°F for dark or nonstick pans). Place paper baking cup in each of 24 regular-size muffin cups.

2  In large bowl, beat cake mix, water, oil and eggs with electric mixer on medium speed 2 minutes, scraping bowl occasionally. Divide batter evenly among muffin cups, filling each two-thirds full.

3  Bake 14 to 19 minutes or until toothpick inserted in center comes out clean. Cool 10 minutes; remove from pans to cooling racks. Cool completely, about 30 minutes.

4  Place candy sprinkles in shallow bowl. Fill large resealable food-storage plastic bag with 1¼ cups frosting; cut off tiny bottom corner. Pipe frosting in a circle one time around outside edge of cupcake. Dip edge of frosting into sprinkles. Reserve remaining frosting in bag for pom-poms.

5  Among 3 small bowls, evenly divide remaining frosting (about 1⅓ cups each). Tint frosting in bowls with food colors: 1 red, 1 green and 1 blue. Place frosting in 3 small resealable food-storage plastic bags; cut off tiny bottom corner of each bag. Pipe red frosting, starting on inside edge of white frosting and spiraling up toward center to form a hat; continue red piping on 7 additional cupcakes. Repeat piping with green and blue frosting with remaining 16 cupcakes (8 cupcakes each). Pipe a small dab of reserved untinted frosting on top of each hat for pom-pom.

**1 Cupcake:** Calories 390; Total Fat 19g (Saturated Fat 6g, Trans Fat 0g); Cholesterol 25mg; Sodium 280mg; Total Carbohydrate 54g (Dietary Fiber 0g); Protein 1g **Exchanges:** 3½ Other Carbohydrate, 4 Fat **Carbohydrate Choices:** 3½

**Festive Touch** For a more decorative look when piping the frosting, use decorating bags with tips.

**Kitchen Secrets** Not a fan of chocolate? Try yellow cake mix for a different flavor.

# Espresso Cupcakes

**PREP TIME:** 1 Hour 15 Minutes   **START TO FINISH:** 2 Hours   *24 cupcakes*

### CHOCOLATE CUPCAKES

2 cups all-purpose flour

1 tablespoon instant espresso coffee powder or granules

1¼ teaspoons baking soda

1 teaspoon salt

¼ teaspoon baking powder

1 cup hot water

⅔ cup unsweetened baking cocoa

¾ cup shortening

1½ cups granulated sugar

2 eggs

1 teaspoon vanilla

### FILLING

1 container (8 oz) mascarpone cheese

2 teaspoons milk

2 teaspoons instant espresso coffee powder or granules

1 cup powdered sugar

### FROSTING

4 oz semisweet baking chocolate, finely chopped

6 tablespoons butter, softened

3 tablespoons milk

1 teaspoon instant espresso coffee powder or granules

½ teaspoon vanilla

Dash salt

3 cups powdered sugar

1. Heat oven to 350°F. Place paper baking cup in each of 24 regular-size muffin cups.

2. In medium bowl, mix flour, 1 tablespoon espresso powder, the baking soda, salt and baking powder; set aside. In small bowl, mix hot water and cocoa until dissolved; set aside.

3. In large bowl, beat shortening with electric mixer on medium speed 30 seconds. Gradually add granulated sugar, about ¼ cup at a time, beating well after each addition. Beat 2 minutes longer. Add eggs, one at a time, beating well after each addition. Beat in vanilla. Alternately add flour mixture and cocoa mixture, beating on low speed just until blended. Divide batter evenly among muffin cups, filling each two-thirds full.

4. Bake 20 to 25 minutes or until toothpick inserted in center comes out clean. Cool 5 minutes. Remove from pans to cooling racks; cool completely.

5. Meanwhile, in medium bowl, beat filling ingredients with electric mixer on medium speed until smooth. Spoon mixture into decorating bag fitted with ¼-inch (#9) writing tip.

6. To fill each cupcake, insert tip of bag into center of cooled cupcake; gently squeeze bag until cupcake expands slightly but does not burst (each cupcake should be filled with about 1 tablespoon filling).

7. In small microwavable bowl, microwave chocolate uncovered on High 45 seconds. Stir; continue microwaving and stirring in 15-second increments until melted. Cool slightly, about 5 minutes.

8. In another medium bowl, beat butter, 3 tablespoons milk, 1 teaspoon espresso powder, the vanilla and salt with electric mixer on low speed until well blended. Beat in 3 cups powdered sugar, 1 cup at a time, until smooth. Stir in melted chocolate until blended. Spoon mixture into decorating bag fitted with ¾-inch (#824) star tip. Pipe frosting over tops of cupcakes. Store covered in refrigerator.

**1 Cupcake:** Calories 340; Total Fat 16g (Saturated Fat 7g, Trans Fat 0g); Cholesterol 35mg; Sodium 210mg; Total Carbohydrate 46g (Dietary Fiber 1g); Protein 2g **Exchanges:** 1 Starch, 2 Other Carbohydrate, 3 Fat **Carbohydrate Choices:** 3

## Festive Touch
Sprinkle the frosted cupcakes with grated chocolate or mini chocolate chips, or top each with a chocolate-covered espresso coffee bean.

## Kitchen Secrets
Save time by using 1 box chocolate fudge cake mix with pudding instead of the Chocolate Cupcakes. Make cake as directed, using water, oil and eggs called for on box, and stir in 1 tablespoon instant espresso coffee powder or granules. Bake and cool as directed on box. Fill and frost as directed in Steps 5 through 8.

# Pistachio–Vanilla Bean Cheesecake

**PREP TIME:** 25 Minutes    **START TO FINISH:** 8 Hours 30 Minutes    *16 servings*

### SUGAR CONE CRUST

9 sugar-style ice cream cones with pointed ends, crushed (1 cup)

1 cup pistachio nuts, finely chopped

¼ cup butter, melted

1 tablespoon sugar

### CHEESECAKE

4 packages (8 oz each) cream cheese, cut into cubes and softened

⅔ cup sugar

½ cup sour cream

1 tablespoon vanilla

Seeds of 2 vanilla beans

4 eggs

⅓ cup pistachio nuts, coarsely chopped

1 Heat oven to 325°F. In medium bowl, mix crust ingredients. Press in bottom and slightly up side of ungreased 9-inch springform pan.

2 In food processor, place cream cheese, ⅔ cup sugar, the sour cream, vanilla and vanilla bean seeds. Cover; process until smooth. Add eggs. Cover; process until well blended, scraping bowl occasionally. Spread over crust.

3 Bake 1 hour 20 minutes or until center is set. Cool on cooling rack 15 minutes. Carefully run small metal spatula or knife around side of pan to loosen cheesecake. Remove side of pan; cool 30 minutes.

4 Refrigerate uncovered at least 6 hours or until chilled. Store covered in refrigerator 3 to 5 days. Before serving, sprinkle ⅓ cup pistachios around top edge of cheesecake.

**1 Serving:** Calories 390; Total Fat 30g (Saturated Fat 15g, Trans Fat 1g); Cholesterol 120mg; Sodium 270mg; Total Carbohydrate 21g (Dietary Fiber 1g); Protein 7g **Exchanges:** 1½ Other Carbohydrate, 1 High-Fat Meat, 4½ Fat **Carbohydrate Choices:** 1½

## Festive Touch

**During the holiday season, red-colored pistachios are sometimes available. If you like, try using both red and green pistachios in this cheesecake.**

## Kitchen Secrets

**You can crush the sugar cones by placing them in a resealable food-storage plastic bag and crushing them with a rolling pin.**

## Kitchen Secrets

**To remove seeds from a vanilla bean, cut the bean in half lengthwise. Run the blade of a knife across the inside of the bean, gathering seeds on the edge of the knife.**

# Peppermint Cupcake Tree

**PREP TIME:** 45 Minutes    **START TO FINISH:** 1 Hour 45 Minutes    *24 cupcakes*

## PEPPERMINT CUPCAKES

- 2¾ cups all-purpose flour
- 1 tablespoon baking powder
- ½ teaspoon salt
- ¾ cup butter, softened
- 1⅔ cups granulated sugar
- 5 egg whites
- 2½ teaspoons vanilla
- 1¼ cups milk
- ½ cup peppermint crunch baking chips (from 10-oz bag)
- 1 teaspoon all-purpose flour

## FROSTING

- 6 cups powdered sugar
- ⅔ cup butter, softened
- 1 tablespoon vanilla
- ½ teaspoon green paste food color
- 3 to 4 tablespoons milk
  Assorted holiday candies and sprinkles, if desired

1. Heat oven to 350°F. Place paper baking cup in each of 24 regular-size muffin cups.

2. In medium bowl, mix 2¾ cups flour, the baking powder and salt. In large bowl, beat ¾ cup butter with electric mixer on medium speed 30 seconds. Gradually add granulated sugar, ⅓ cup at a time, beating well after each addition. Beat 2 minutes. Add egg whites, a little at a time, beating well after each addition. Beat in 2½ teaspoons vanilla. Alternately add flour mixture and 1¼ cups milk, beating on low speed just until blended.

3. Toss baking chips with 1 teaspoon flour; stir into batter. Divide evenly among muffin cups, filling each two-thirds full.

4. Bake 20 to 23 minutes or until toothpick inserted in center comes out clean. Cool 5 minutes; remove from pans to cooling racks. Cool completely, about 30 minutes.

5. In large bowl, beat powdered sugar and ⅔ cup butter with electric mixer on low speed until well blended. Add 1 tablespoon vanilla, the food color and 3 tablespoons milk; beat until smooth and creamy. Stir in additional milk, 1 teaspoon at a time, until desired consistency. Spoon frosting into decorating bag fitted with large #1 star tip. Pipe a swirl of frosting on top of each cupcake.

6. On 12-inch serving plate, arrange 9 of the cupcakes. On top of cupcakes, stack three more layers—6 cupcakes, 5 cupcakes and 3 cupcakes—with 1 cupcake on top, to form tree. Decorate with candies and sprinkles.

**1 Cupcake:** Calories 360; Total Fat 13g (Saturated Fat 8g, Trans Fat 0g); Cholesterol 30mg; Sodium 220mg; Total Carbohydrate 58g (Dietary Fiber 0g); Protein 3g **Exchanges:** 1 Starch, 3 Other Carbohydrate, 2½ Fat **Carbohydrate Choices:** 4

## Make-Ahead Magic
Get a jump on preparing your tree by baking and freezing the cupcakes in advance. Freeze unfrosted cupcakes in airtight container up to 1 month. Thaw uncovered at room temperature before continuing as directed in Steps 5 and 6.

## Festive Touch
This fun cupcake tree is not only delicious to eat but makes a great centerpiece for any holiday gathering.

## Kitchen Secrets
To stabilize the cupcake tree, cut 24 (1½-inch) rounds from poster board. Place 1 round under each cupcake as you assemble the tree.

# Start a New Tradition

**What is it about traditions that seem to bind us closer together? Everyone always ends up in the kitchen anyway—why not try one of these new kitchen-centered ways to have fun together, and maybe it will become an annual event.**

## Girls' Night In

Invite your besties over for a night of gab and giggles. Keep it casual with a few appetizers and sweet treats with a festive beverage. Mix it up by using holiday plates with funny cocktail napkins.

Cranberry, Pomegranate and Caramelized Onion
    Flatbread (page 22)

Baked Sweet Potato–Zucchini Tots (page 32)

Bowls of olives and nuts

Piña Colada Rum Cups (page 218)

Pomegranate-Orange Sangria (page 35)

## Family-Time Movie Night

Spend the evening together whipping up a few family-friendly munchies, and then gather around the TV for your traditional favorite holiday movie.

Cheesy Ranch Chex Mix (page 33)

Sliced apples and clusters of grapes

Easy Gingerdoodle Cookies (page 170)

Eggnog-Toffee Milkshakes (page 50)

## Cooking-Together Date Night

Have another couple over, or keep it to just the two of you. Take turns playing your favorite Christmas carols as you prepare and enjoy each course together. Stop occasionally for a dance around the kitchen!

Fire-Roasted Tomato and Olive Bruschetta (page 19)

Berry-Rosemary Margaritas (page 43)

Roasted Brined Duck with Cranberry-Chipotle Glaze (page 90)

Mashed or baked potatoes

Holiday Romaine Salad (page 132)

Red wine, such as Merlot or Malbec

Heavenly Chocolate Soufflé Cake (page 234)

Coffee

## Kids' Indoor S'mores Pops Party

Have a group of kiddos over for a make-and-eat party. Create the pops, adding other bowls of sprinkles and small candies to dip them in. Let the kids devour their creations, and then play a fun holiday-themed game. Check out online resources for ideas.

Holiday S'mores Pops (page 252)

Alpine Mint Hot Chocolate (page 45)

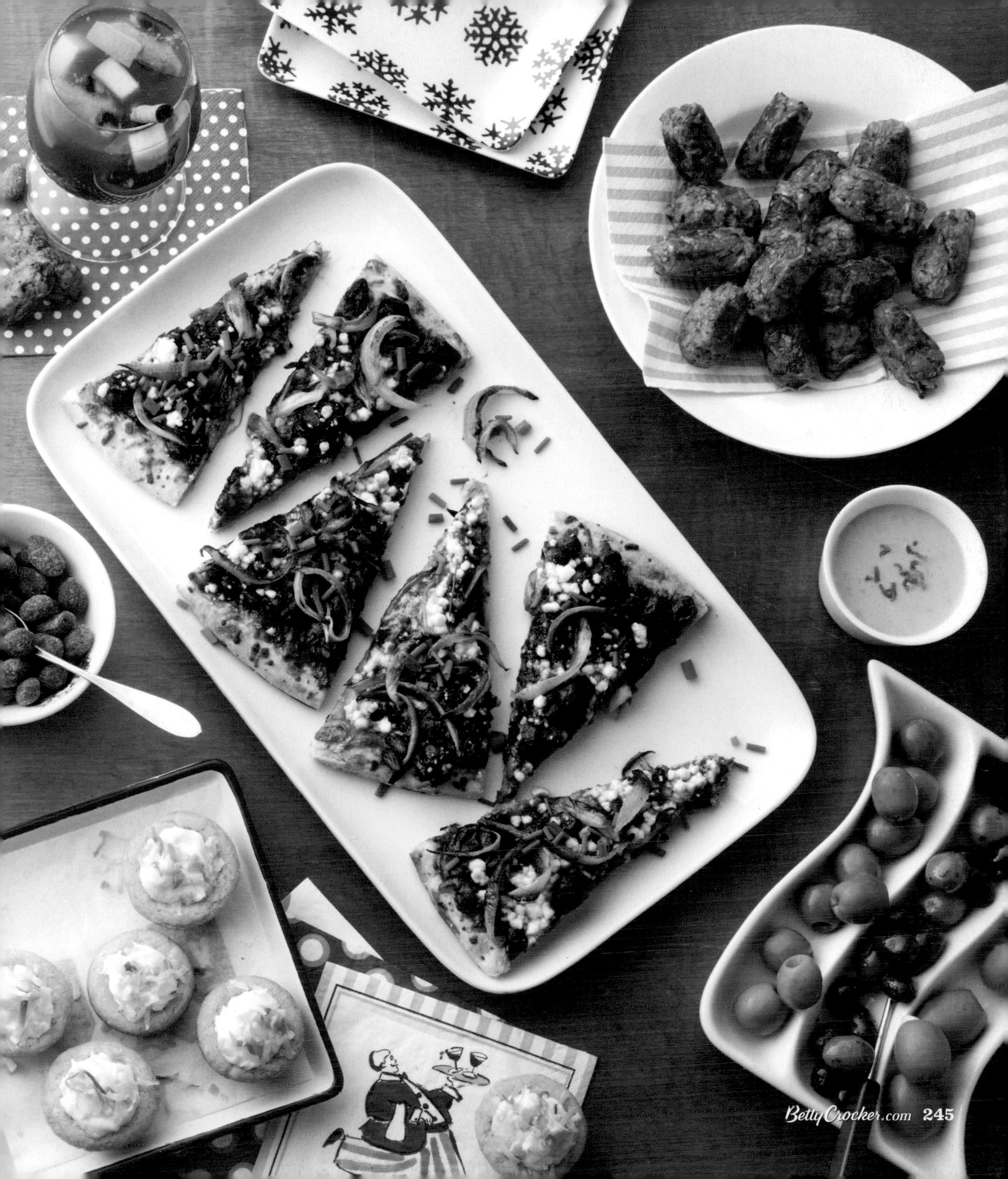

# Mini Red Velvet Cheesecakes

**PREP TIME:** 20 Minutes    **START TO FINISH:** 3 Hours    *16 mini cheesecakes*

24 thin chocolate wafer cookies, crushed (1¼ cups)

3 tablespoons butter, melted

2 packages (8 oz each) plus 4 oz cream cheese, softened

1 cup granulated sugar

¼ cup unsweetened baking cocoa

2 teaspoons vanilla

2 tablespoons red food color

3 eggs

½ cup whipping cream

1 tablespoon granulated or powdered sugar

Chocolate curls, if desired

**1** Heat oven to 350°F. Place foil baking cup in each of 16 regular-size muffin cups. Mix cookie crumbs and butter; divide evenly among muffin cups. Using back of spoon, firmly press mixture in bottoms of baking cups.

**2** In large bowl, beat cream cheese with electric mixer on medium speed until smooth. Gradually beat in 1 cup granulated sugar and the cocoa until fluffy. Beat in vanilla and food color. Beat in eggs, one at a time, until well blended. Divide batter evenly among baking cups (cups will be almost full).

**3** Bake 20 to 25 minutes or until centers are firm. Cool 15 minutes (centers will sink). Remove from pans. Refrigerate at least 1 hour. Cover; refrigerate at least 1 hour longer.

**4** In chilled small bowl, beat whipping cream and 1 tablespoon sugar with electric mixer on high speed until stiff peaks form. Just before serving, peel off baking cups. Top cheesecakes with whipped cream and chocolate curls. Store cheesecakes in a deep plastic or glass storage container with lid in the refrigerator.

**1 Mini Cheesecake:** Calories 290; Total Fat 19g (Saturated Fat 11g, Trans Fat 0.5g); Cholesterol 95mg; Sodium 210mg; Total Carbohydrate 23g (Dietary Fiber 0g); Protein 4g **Exchanges:** ½ Starch, ½ Other Carbohydrate, ½ Milk, 3 Fat **Carbohydrate Choices:** 1½

## Make-Ahead Magic
These little cheesecakes freeze beautifully! Wrap tightly and freeze up to 5 months. Thaw in the original wrapping in the refrigerator 2 to 4 hours.

## Kitchen Secrets
To make chocolate curls, place a bar or block of chocolate on waxed paper. Press a vegetable peeler firmly against the chocolate and pull toward you in long, thin strokes. Small curls can be made by using the side of the chocolate bar. Transfer each curl carefully with a toothpick to a waxed paper–lined cookie sheet or directly onto cheesecake.

# Spiced Rum–White Chocolate Fondue

**PREP TIME:** 5 Minutes    **START TO FINISH:** 5 Minutes    *6 servings*

2 cups white vanilla baking chips (about 12 oz)

¼ cup whipping cream

¼ cup Caribbean spiced rum cream liqueur

⅛ teaspoon pumpkin pie spice

Assorted fruit, such as apple slices, whole strawberries, sliced bananas and orange sections

1 In medium microwavable bowl, microwave white baking chips and whipping cream uncovered on High 40 to 60 seconds, stirring every 20 seconds, until chips are softened and mixture can be stirred smooth. Stir in liqueur.

2 Pour mixture into fondue pot. Sprinkle pumpkin pie spice over fondue; use knife to swirl spice into fondue. Keep warm over low heat. Spear fruit with forks and dip into fondue.

**1 Serving (¼ Cup Fondue and 6 Fruit Pieces):** Calories 350, Total Fat 18g (Saturated Fat 14g, Trans Fat 0g); Cholesterol 15mg; Sodium 135mg; Total Carbohydrate 39g (Dietary Fiber 0g); Protein 4g **Carbohydrate Choices:** 2½

## Festive Touch Try other dippers, such as cubed Spiced Apple Bread (page 145), the doughnut holes from Chocolate-Hazelnut Doughnuts (page 148), cubed pound cake, crisply fried bacon pieces, caramels, pretzels, crisp rice cereal treats or marshmallows.

## Kitchen Secrets Don't throw out any leftover fondue! Try it on the rocks or splashed into a cup of coffee for a special dessert treat.

# Holiday S'mores Pops

**PREP TIME:** 30 Minutes    **START TO FINISH:** 50 Minutes    *8 pops*

¾ cup coarsely crushed graham crackers (6 rectangles)

1 bottle (1.3 oz) red and green candy sprinkles

1 cup dark chocolate chips (about 6 oz)

¼ cup hazelnut spread with cocoa

16 jumbo marshmallows

8 candy sticks or lollipop sticks

1   Line 8-inch square pan with waxed paper. In separate small bowls, place graham cracker crumbs and candy sprinkles.

2   In small microwavable bowl, microwave chocolate chips and hazelnut spread uncovered on High 1 minute to 1 minute 30 seconds, stirring twice, until chips are softened and mixture can be stirred smooth. Dip 1 marshmallow about one-fourth into melted chocolate on both flat ends, letting excess drip off. Dip top end of marshmallow in graham crackers; dip bottom end of marshmallow into sprinkles. Insert 1 candy stick into marshmallow.

3   Repeat with second marshmallow. Insert the same stick halfway into second marshmallow (with crumb side up).

4   Repeat with remaining marshmallows and candy sticks to make 7 more pops. Place pops, candy stick facing up, in pan. Refrigerate 20 minutes or until set.

**1 Pop:** Calories 320; Total Fat 12g (Saturated Fat 6g, Trans Fat 0g); Cholesterol 0mg; Sodium 60mg; Total Carbohydrate 53g (Dietary Fiber 2g); Protein 2g **Exchanges:** ½ Starch, 3 Other Carbohydrate, 2½ Fat **Carbohydrate Choices:** 3½

## Kitchen Secrets
These pops are so easy to make—you can plan to give them on the same day, so the marshmallows are ultra-fresh. To store, keep pops in an airtight container at room temperature up to 3 days.

## Kitchen Secrets
You can find candy sticks at specialty gift stores, candy stores or online. Lollipop sticks can be found where candy-making supplies are sold.

Also pictured, Marshmallow Mug Mates (page 279)

# Hot Chocolate Popovers

**PREP TIME:** 15 Minutes    **START TO FINISH:** 1 Hour
*12 popovers*

## POPOVERS

- 1½ cups all-purpose flour
- 2 tablespoons unsweetened baking cocoa
- ½ teaspoon salt
- 4 eggs
- 1½ cups milk
- 3 tablespoons butter, melted
- 12 large marshmallows

## ICING

- ⅓ cup dark chocolate chips
- ¼ teaspoon vegetable oil

1 Heat oven to 450°F. Spray 12 regular-size muffin cups with cooking spray. Heat pan in oven 2 to 3 minutes.

2 In small bowl, mix flour, cocoa and salt. In medium bowl, beat eggs and milk with whisk. Add flour mixture and melted butter; beat with whisk just until blended (do not overbeat). Divide batter evenly among muffin cups (cups will be almost full).

3 Bake 20 minutes. Reduce oven temperature to 350°F; bake 15 to 18 minutes longer or until tops of popovers are dry. Immediately press 1 marshmallow in center of each popover. Bake 2 minutes longer or until marshmallows are soft. Remove from muffin cups to serving platter.

4 In small microwavable bowl, microwave chocolate chips and oil on High 30 to 60 seconds, stirring every 15 seconds, until melted and smooth. Drizzle over popovers. Serve warm or at room temperature.

**1 Popover:** Calories 180; Total Fat 7g (Saturated Fat 3.5g, Trans Fat 0g); Cholesterol 75mg; Sodium 160mg; Total Carbohydrate 23g (Dietary Fiber 1g); Protein 5g **Exchanges:** 1 Starch, ½ Other Carbohydrate, 1½ Fat **Carbohydrate Choices:** 1½

## Kitchen Secrets Easily pour the popover batter into the muffin cups by pouring it into a large liquid measuring cup first.

# Cheerios Christmas Trees

**PREP TIME:** 45 Minutes    **START TO FINISH:** 1 Hour 45 Minutes
*18 trees*

- 6 cups Honey Nut Cheerios™ cereal
- 4½ cups miniature marshmallows
- 6 tablespoons butter
- Green gel food color
- Red cinnamon candies or sliced gumdrops

1 Line cookie sheet with waxed paper. Pour cereal into 4-quart bowl; set aside.

2 In 3-quart saucepan, heat marshmallows and butter over low heat, stirring constantly, until smooth. Remove from heat. Stir in food color until mixture is evenly colored. Pour over cereal and stir until evenly coated.

3 For each tree, using hands lightly sprayed with cooking spray, shape about ¼ cup cereal mixture into Christmas tree on cookie sheet.

4 Press candies into trees to decorate. Refrigerate until firm, about 1 hour. Store loosely covered up to 2 days.

**1 Tree:** Calories 130; Total Fat 4.5g (Saturated Fat 2.5g, Trans Fat 0g); Cholesterol 10mg; Sodium 110mg; Total Carbohydrate 21g (Dietary Fiber 1g); Protein 1g **Exchanges:** 1½ Other Carbohydrate, 1 Fat **Carbohydrate Choices:** 1½

## Festive Touch Personalize the trees with guests' names using decorator icing, and use as creative place cards! Or add a garland on each tree with icing.

# Pomegranate-Vanilla Panna Cotta

**PREP TIME:** 30 Minutes    **START TO FINISH:** 2 Hours 40 Minutes    *8 servings*

### POMEGRANATE LAYER

- 2 teaspoons unflavored gelatin
- 1 cup pomegranate juice
- 2 tablespoons sugar
- 1 tablespoon pomegranate-flavored liqueur

### VANILLA LAYER

- 1 envelope unflavored gelatin
- 1½ cups milk
- ⅔ cup sugar
- Seeds from 1 vanilla bean
- 1½ cups whipping cream

1 In 1-quart saucepan, sprinkle 2 teaspoons gelatin over pomegranate juice; let stand 5 minutes to soften. Heat over low heat about 30 seconds or just until gelatin is dissolved. Stir in 2 tablespoons sugar; heat until sugar is dissolved, stirring constantly. Remove from heat; stir in liqueur. Cool to room temperature.

2 Meanwhile, in 2-quart saucepan, sprinkle envelope of gelatin over milk; let stand 5 minutes to soften. Heat over low heat, stirring frequently, about 2 minutes or just until gelatin is dissolved. Stir in ⅔ cup sugar and the vanilla seeds. Continue stirring over low heat about 2 minutes longer or until sugar is dissolved (mixture should not boil or steam). Remove from heat; stir in whipping cream with whisk. Strain mixture through fine-mesh strainer.

3 Place cooling rack in refrigerator. While holding stemmed glass (such as champagne flute or parfait glass) at an angle, pour about 2 tablespoons vanilla mixture into glass. Carefully place glass in refrigerator, keeping angle by propping stem on rack and leaning glass against side of refrigerator. Repeat, filling 7 more glasses as directed. Refrigerate 30 minutes or until firm. Keep remaining vanilla mixture at room temperature.

4 Carefully pour about 2 tablespoons pomegranate mixture into each glass, keeping same angle. Return to refrigerator for 30 minutes or until firm.

5 Carefully pour remaining vanilla mixture over pomegranate layer, holding glasses upright. Refrigerate on flat surface at least 1 hour but no longer than 24 hours.

**1 Serving:** Calories 260; Total Fat 15g (Saturated Fat 9g, Trans Fat 0.5g); Cholesterol 55mg; Sodium 45mg; Total Carbohydrate 28g (Dietary Fiber 0g); Protein 3g **Carbohydrate Choices:** 2

## Festive Touch Garnish these lovely desserts with a few pomegranate seeds.

## Kitchen Secrets To remove seeds from a vanilla bean, cut the bean in half lengthwise. Run the blade of a knife across the inside of the bean, gathering seeds on the edge of the knife.

## Kitchen Secrets The vanilla bean seeds give a beautiful speckled appearance to the dessert and assure a rich vanilla flavor in the panna cotta. If you like, 2 teaspoons vanilla extract may be substituted for the vanilla bean—there's no need to strain the milk mixture then.

# Chocolate Bark–Caramel Trifle

**PREP TIME:** 30 Minutes   **START TO FINISH:** 8 Hours   *20 servings*

### CHOCOLATE BARK

- ½ lb bittersweet baking chocolate, coarsely chopped
- ½ lb semisweet baking chocolate, coarsely chopped
- ½ cup chopped almonds, toasted
- ½ cup finely chopped dried apricots
- 2 tablespoons coarsely chopped dried cranberries or cherries

### CHOCOLATE FILLING

- 2 boxes (4-serving size each) chocolate instant pudding and pie filling mix
- 4 cups half-and-half
- 2½ cups whipping cream
- 1 jar (11.5 oz) salted caramel topping
- 1 lb pound cake or white cake, cut into ¾-inch cubes
- ¼ cup almond- or orange-flavored liqueur

**1** Line cookie sheet with cooking parchment paper. In large microwavable bowl, heat bittersweet and semisweet chocolate uncovered on High about 2 minutes, stirring every 15 seconds, until melted and smooth.

**2** Spread melted chocolate onto cookie sheet until about ½ inch thick. Sprinkle evenly with almonds, apricots and cranberries; press lightly into chocolate. Let stand at room temperature 1 hour 30 minutes to 2 hours or until firm.

**3** Cut or break half of the bark into large shards, 1 to 2 inches long. Place in covered container; set aside in cool place until serving time. Coarsely chop remaining bark.

**4** In large bowl, beat pudding mixes and half-and-half with whisk until smooth, about 2 minutes. Stir in the chopped bark; set aside. In chilled medium bowl, beat whipping cream with electric mixer on high speed until stiff peaks form. Gently fold in ½ cup of the caramel topping.

**5** Spoon 3 cups of the pudding mixture into trifle bowl or other large serving bowl. Arrange half of the cake cubes on pudding; gently press into the pudding. Drizzle with 2 tablespoons of the liqueur and 2 cups of the whipped cream mixture. Repeat layers with remaining pudding mixture, cake cubes, liqueur and whipped cream mixture. Cover; refrigerate at least 6 hours but no longer than 24 hours.

**6** Arrange reserved bark shards on top of trifle; drizzle with remaining caramel sauce.

**1 Serving (⅔ Cup):** Calories 520; Total Fat 33g (Saturated Fat 19g, Trans Fat 0.5g); Cholesterol 90mg; Sodium 280mg; Total Carbohydrate 49g (Dietary Fiber 4g); Protein 7g **Carbohydrate Choices:** 3

## Festive Touch Save some of the shards of chocolate reserved for the top to serve on the side instead. Add a dusting of unsweetened baking cocoa or powdered sugar to individual serving plates before serving the trifle.

## Kitchen Secrets No time to make the chocolate bark? Substitute 16 ounces of premium chocolate-nut or chocolate-nut-fruit candy bars.

## Kitchen Secrets To toast almonds, sprinkle in ungreased skillet. Cook over medium heat 5 to 7 minutes, stirring occasionally until nuts begin to brown, then stirring constantly until nuts are light brown.

# Mini Churro–Salted Caramel Cream Puffs

**PREP TIME:** 45 Minutes   **START TO FINISH:** 1 Hour 45 Minutes   *28 cream puffs*

### CREAM PUFFS

- ½ cup butter, cut into small pieces
- 1 cup water
- 1 cup all-purpose flour
- 4 eggs

### COATING

- ¼ cup granulated sugar
- 1 teaspoon ground cinnamon
- 3 tablespoons butter, melted

### FILLING

- 1 cup whipping cream
- ¼ cup powdered sugar
- 2 tablespoons caramel topping
- ½ teaspoon coarse (kosher or sea) salt

### ICING

- ¼ cup dark chocolate chips
- ¼ teaspoon vegetable oil

1 Heat oven to 400°F. In 2-quart saucepan, heat ½ cup butter and the water over high heat, stirring occasionally, until boiling rapidly. Stir in flour; reduce heat to low. With wooden spoon, beat vigorously about 1 minute or until mixture forms a ball; remove from heat.

2 Add eggs, one at a time, beating vigorously after each addition until mixture is smooth and glossy. Onto ungreased cookie sheets, drop dough by 28 level tablespoonfuls about 3 inches apart.

3 Bake 25 to 30 minutes or until puffed and golden. Remove from cookie sheets to cooling racks; prick side of each puff with tip of sharp knife to release steam. Cool away from drafts 30 minutes.

4 Line work surface with cooking parchment paper. In small bowl, mix granulated sugar and cinnamon. Roll cream puffs, one at a time, in melted butter; shake off excess. Roll in cinnamon-sugar. Place on paper. Using serrated knife, cut off top third of each puff; reserve tops.

5 In medium bowl, beat whipping cream with electric mixer on high speed until soft peaks form. Add powdered sugar and caramel topping; beat on high speed until stiff peaks form. Fold in salt.

6 Spoon or pipe about 1 tablespoon filling into each cream puff. Cover with reserved tops.

7 In small microwavable bowl, microwave chocolate chips and oil uncovered on High 30 to 60 seconds, stirring every 15 seconds, until melted and smooth. Drizzle over cream puffs.

**1 Cream Puff:** Calories 120; Total Fat 8g (Saturated Fat 5g, Trans Fat 0g); Cholesterol 50mg; Sodium 75mg; Total Carbohydrate 9g (Dietary Fiber 0g); Protein 1g **Exchanges:** ½ Starch, 1½ Fat **Carbohydrate Choices:** ½

## Make-Ahead Magic
**Make dough as directed; drop by tablespoonfuls onto cookie sheet lined with cooking parchment paper. Freeze until firm. Place frozen dough in an airtight container or resealable freezer plastic bag; freeze up to 2 months. To bake, place frozen puffs on cookie sheets sprayed with cooking spray, and bake as directed.**

## Make-Ahead Magic
**After filling, cream puffs can be refrigerated up to 3 hours. Drizzle with chocolate just before serving.**

## Festive Touch
**For a more decadent cream puff, drizzle with 2 tablespoons caramel topping in addition to the chocolate icing.**

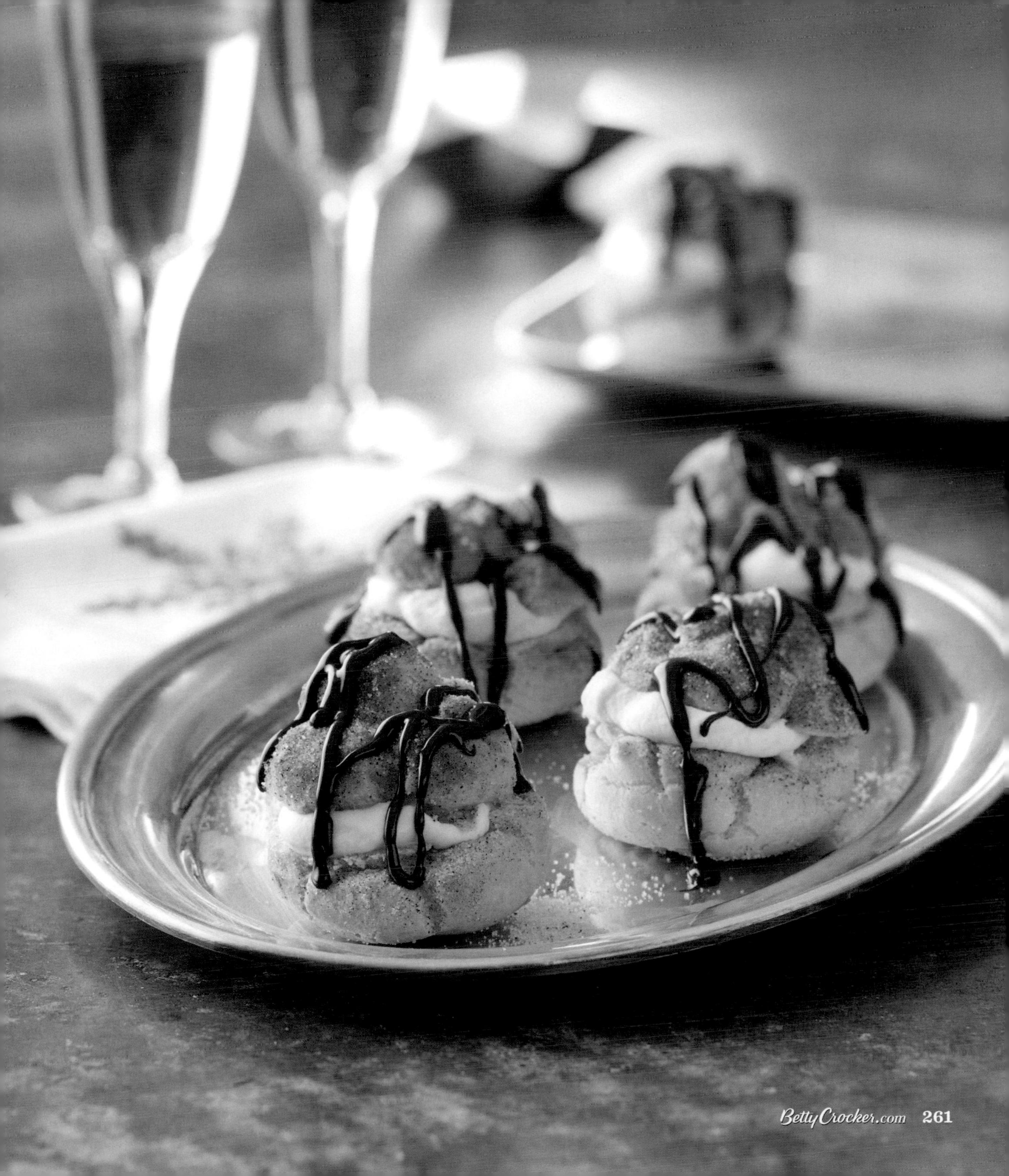

# Gifts
## from the
# Kitchen

# Sugar-and-Spice Body Scrub

**PREP TIME:** 10 Minutes   **START TO FINISH:** 10 Minutes
*4 (½ pint) jars*

- 2 cups packed brown sugar
- 1 cup coconut oil
- 1 cup coarse (kosher or sea) salt
- 2 teaspoons pumpkin pie spice or apple pie spice

1 In medium bowl, mix brown sugar and oil until well blended. In small bowl, mix salt and pie spice.

2 Spoon ¼ cup brown sugar mixture into bottom of each jar; add 2 tablespoons salt mixture. Repeat layers. Cover jars with lids. Store at room temperature up to 3 months.

3 To use, spoon about 1 teaspoonful of scrub at a time into wet hand or washcloth. Apply to skin (avoid eye area) in circular motion. Rinse with warm water; pat dry.

## Festive Touch
**Decorate the lid of the jar with holiday fabric. Use raffia or twine to tie a small spoon to the jar for mixing and scooping; look for ice cream sample spoons at party stores.**

## Festive Touch
**For even more Christmas color, add some green or red decorator sugar to the salt mixture.**

## Kitchen Secrets
**This scrub is layered in jars for a pretty effect, but be sure you include a note to spoon out some of both the brown sugar and salt layers when using.**

# Kiwi-Yogurt Facial Mask

**PREP TIME:** 10 Minutes   **START TO FINISH:** 4 Hours 10 Minutes   *2 (4 oz) jars*

- 1 kiwifruit, peeled, coarsely chopped
- ¼ cup Greek plain yogurt (not low-fat or fat-free)
- 2 tablespoons honey
- 1 tablespoon quick-cooking oats
- 1 tablespoon flaxseed

1 In mini food processor, place kiwi, yogurt and honey. Cover; process until blended. Divide mixture between 2 jars.

2 Top each jar with half of the oats and half of the flaxseed. Cover; refrigerate undisturbed at least 4 hours.

3 To use, stir oat mixture into yogurt mixture. Spoon about 2 tablespoons mixture into hands and gently apply to face (avoid eye area). Let stand 5 to 10 minutes; rinse thoroughly with warm water.

## Make-Ahead Magic
**The jars can be stored in the refrigerator up to 5 days.**

## Festive Touch
**Make cute labels listing the ingredients and directions to affix to the jar. Include a small wooden paddle or shallow spoon for a nice touch.**

## Kitchen Secrets
**It's important to allow the jars to cool at least 4 hours for the mixture to get thick enough so the pretty layers won't mix before you give them as gifts.**

# Dried Fruit and Nut Corncakes in a Jar

**PREP TIME:** 25 Minutes  **START TO FINISH:** 25 Minutes
*5 servings*

### CORNCAKE MIX
 1 cup all-purpose flour
 1 teaspoon baking powder
 ¼ teaspoon salt
 ⅓ cup yellow cornmeal
 ¼ cup chopped dried cherries or cranberries
 ¼ cup chopped walnuts or almonds
 ¼ cup chopped dried apricots
 2 tablespoons packed brown sugar

### CORNCAKES
 ¾ cup milk
 ¼ cup vegetable oil
 ¼ teaspoon vanilla
 1 egg
   Maple syrup, if desired

1 In small bowl, mix flour, baking powder and salt. In 1-pint jar, layer half of the flour mixture, the cornmeal, cherries, walnuts and apricots. Top with brown sugar; press sugar down to form firm layer over apricots. Top with remaining flour mixture; cover with lid. Store the mix in a cool, dry place up to 1 month.

2 In small bowl, beat milk, oil, vanilla and egg. Empty contents of jar into medium bowl; make well in center. Pour wet ingredients into well; mix until just blended.

3 Heat griddle or skillet over medium heat (350°F). For each corncake, pour about ¼ cup batter onto hot griddle. Cook 2 to 4 minutes, turning once, until puffed and dry around edges. Serve with syrup.

**1 Serving (2 Corncakes):** Calories 350; Total Fat 17g (Saturated Fat 3g, Trans Fat 0g); Cholesterol 40mg; Sodium 250mg; Total Carbohydrate 43g (Dietary Fiber 2g); Protein 7g **Exchanges:** 2 Starch, 1 Other Carbohydrate, 3 Fat **Carbohydrate Choices:** 3

### Festive Touch
Cover the jar lid with colorful holiday fabric. Add a gift tag listing the wet ingredients needed to make the corncakes and the directions for mixing and cooking them.

# Giftable Jars of Muesli

**PREP TIME:** 10 Minutes  **START TO FINISH:** 1 Hour
*12 (8 oz) jars*

 1 cup pecan halves
 1 cup hazelnuts (filberts)
 ¾ cup pumpkin seeds (pepitas)
 7 cups old-fashioned oats
 1 cup flaked coconut
 ¾ cup wheat bran
 ¾ cup wheat germ
 ¼ cup chia seed

1 Heat oven to 350°F. In ungreased shallow pan, spread pecans and hazelnuts in single layer on one side. Spread pumpkin seeds on other side of pan. Bake about 5 minutes, stirring occasionally, until light brown. Remove from pan; cool. Coarsely chop nuts; place in large bowl. Add pumpkin seeds; set aside.

2 Meanwhile, spread oats and coconut in same shallow pan. Bake 12 to 15 minutes or until lightly browned, stirring 2 to 3 times to prevent burning.

3 Add oats, coconut, wheat bran, wheat germ and chia seed to nut mixture in bowl; toss to mix. Cool completely, about 30 minutes.

4 Divide muesli evenly among jars, about 1 cup in each.

**1 Serving (½ Jar):** Calories 230; Total Fat 12g (Saturated Fat 2.5g, Trans Fat 0g); Cholesterol 0mg; Sodium 10mg; Total Carbohydrate 23g (Dietary Fiber 5g); Protein 7g **Exchanges:** 1 Starch, ½ Other Carbohydrate, ½ High-Fat Meat, 1½ Fat **Carbohydrate Choices:** 1½

### Festive Touch
Place labels on jars with these directions: Mix ½ cup muesli with ½ cup yogurt and ½ cup fruit (fresh or frozen). Drizzle with honey or agave nectar or syrup. Use decorative cards attached with ribbon, or design sticky labels to adhere to the jars.

# Jeweled Fruitcake

**PREP TIME:** 15 Minutes   **START TO FINISH:** 4 Hours   *32 servings*

2 cups dried apricots (11 oz)

2 cups pitted dates (12 oz)

1½ cups Brazil nuts (8 oz)

1 cup red and green candied
pineapple, chopped (7 oz)

1 cup red and green maraschino
cherries, drained (12 oz)

¾ cup all-purpose flour

¾ cup sugar

½ teaspoon baking powder

½ teaspoon salt

1½ teaspoons vanilla

3 large eggs

1 Heat oven to 300°F. Line 9x5- or 8x4-inch loaf pan with foil; grease foil
with shortening.

2 In large bowl, mix all ingredients. Spread in pan.

3 Bake about 1 hour 45 minutes or until toothpick inserted in center comes
out clean. If necessary, cover with aluminum foil during last 30 minutes
of baking to prevent excessive browning.

4 Remove fruitcake from pan (with foil) to cooling rack. For a glossy top,
immediately brush with light corn syrup. Cool completely, about 2 hours.
Wrap tightly and store in refrigerator up to 2 months.

**1 Serving:** Calories 160; Total Fat 5g (Saturated Fat 1g, Trans Fat 0g); Cholesterol 15mg; Sodium 55mg;
Total Carbohydrate 26g (Dietary Fiber 2g); Protein 2g **Exchanges:** 1 Starch, ½ Fruit, 1 Fat **Carbohydrate Choices:** 2

## Festive Touch

**The fruitcake makes a beautiful
gift! Wrap in clear cellophane
with a ribbon to let its own
beauty be the decoration. You
can add the storage information
to a gift tag.**

## Festive Touch

**If you like, brush cake occasionally
with brandy, rum or bourbon
during storage. It adds a rich
mellow flavor to fruitcake.**

## Festive Touch

**For *Petite Jeweled Fruitcakes*,
place foil cupcake liner in each
of 24 medium-size muffin cups.
Divide batter evenly among cups
(about ⅓ cup each). Bake 35 to
40 minutes or until toothpick
inserted in center comes out
clean. Remove from pans to
cooling racks; cool completely.**

# Cranberry-Apple Nut Bread

**PREP TIME:** 15 Minutes     **START TO FINISH:** 2 Hours 50 Minutes     *1 loaf (12 slices)*

¾ cup sugar
½ cup vegetable oil
1 egg
1 cup shredded peeled apple
   (about 1 medium)
1½ cups all-purpose flour
½ teaspoon baking soda
½ teaspoon baking powder
½ teaspoon salt
¾ cup chopped walnuts
½ cup dried cranberries
1 tablespoon sugar
½ teaspoon ground cinnamon

**1** Heat oven to 350°F. Grease bottom only of 8x4- or 9x5-inch loaf pan with shortening.

**2** In large bowl, mix ¾ cup sugar, the oil and egg. Stir in apple, flour, baking soda, baking powder and salt. Stir in walnuts and cranberries. Pour batter into pan. In small bowl, mix 1 tablespoon sugar and the cinnamon; sprinkle over batter.

**3** Bake 45 to 55 minutes or until toothpick inserted in center comes out clean. Cool 10 minutes. Run table knife or metal spatula along sides of pan to loosen loaf; remove from pan to cooling rack. Cool completely, about 1 hour 30 minutes.

**1 Slice:** Calories 270; Total Fat 15g (Saturated Fat 2g, Trans Fat 0g); Cholesterol 15mg; Sodium 180mg; Total Carbohydrate 32g (Dietary Fiber 1g); Protein 3g **Exchanges:** 1 Starch, 1 Other Carbohydrate, 3 Fat **Carbohydrate Choices:** 2

## Make-Ahead Magic
This bread will become more flavorful and easier to slice after refrigerating for 24 hours, plus it keeps well stored in the fridge or freezer. Wrap cooled loaf tightly in plastic wrap or foil, and refrigerate up to 1 week. Or place wrapped loaf in a resealable freezer plastic bag, and freeze up to 3 months.

## Kitchen Secrets
To easily shred the apple, use a medium-size hand grater or the large grater attachment of your food processor.

# Peanut Butter Cookie Truffles

**PREP TIME:** 55 Minutes  **START TO FINISH:** 2 Hours 10 Minutes  *48 truffles*

1 pouch (17.5 oz) peanut butter cookie mix

3 tablespoons vegetable oil

1 tablespoon water

1 egg

4 oz (half of 8-oz package) cream cheese, cut into cubes, softened

½ cup creamy peanut butter

2 cups semisweet chocolate chips (about 12 oz)

2 tablespoons shortening

¼ cup finely chopped cocktail peanuts

**1** Heat oven to 375°F. Make and bake cookies as directed on pouch, using oil, water and egg. Cool completely, at least 15 minutes.

**2** In food processor, place half of the cookies. Cover; process until fine crumbs form. Remove and set aside. Repeat with remaining cookies. Return first batch of crumbs to food processor. Add cream cheese and peanut butter. Cover; process 1 to 2 minutes or until well combined and mixture can be pressed into a ball.

**3** Line cookie sheet with waxed paper. Shape peanut butter mixture into 48 (1¼-inch) balls; place on cookie sheet. Refrigerate 15 minutes.

**4** In medium microwavable bowl, microwave chocolate chips and shortening uncovered on High 1 minute to 1 minute 30 seconds, stirring every 30 seconds, until chips are softened and mixture can be stirred smooth.

**5** Using 2 forks, dip and roll chilled cookie balls, one at a time, in melted chocolate. Return to cookie sheet; immediately sprinkle top with chopped peanuts. (If chocolate has cooled too much, reheat 10 to 20 seconds or until mixture can be stirred smooth.) Refrigerate truffles about 10 minutes or until coating is set. Store covered in refrigerator.

**1 Truffle:** Calories 119; Total Fat 8g (Saturated Fat 3g, Trans Fat 0g); Cholesterol 3mg; Sodium 40mg; Total Carbohydrate 12g (Dietary Fiber 1g); Protein 2g **Exchanges:** 1 Starch, 1½ Fat **Carbohydrate Choices:** 1

## Make-Ahead Magic **Freeze truffles in airtight containers with waxed paper between layers up to 3 months.**

## Kitchen Secrets **For even easier dipping, take two plastic forks, cut out center two tines, and use to dip the cookie balls in chocolate.**

## Kitchen Secrets **No food processor? Place half of the cookies in 1-gallon resealable food-storage plastic bag. Seal bag; crush cookies with rolling pin into small crumbs, breaking up larger pieces with hands if necessary. Place crumbs in large bowl. Repeat with remaining cookies; add to crumbs in large bowl. Add cream cheese and peanut butter. Beat with electric mixer on low speed 1 to 2 minutes or until mixture is well combined, starts to come together and can be formed into a ball. Continue as directed in Step 3.**

# Candy Bar Brownie Bombs

**PREP TIME:** 55 Minutes  **START TO FINISH:** 3 Hours  *35 candies*

1 box (18.3 oz) fudge brownie mix
½ cup vegetable oil
3 tablespoons water
3 eggs
1 pouch (8 oz) unwrapped candy bar bites
2¼ cups semisweet chocolate chips (about 13 oz)
2 tablespoons shortening

1. Heat oven to 350°F. Line 13x9-inch pan with nonstick foil, allowing foil to extend 2 inches over opposite sides of pan. Make brownie batter as directed on box, using oil, water and eggs. Spread in pan.

2. Bake 24 to 26 minutes or until toothpick inserted 2 inches from side of pan comes out clean. (Do not overbake.) Cool completely in pan on cooling rack, about 1 hour.

3. Use foil to lift brownie from pan; pull back foil from edges. Trim ⅛ inch off edges of brownie. (Discard trimmings, or save for another use, such as to top ice cream or pudding.) Cut into 7 rows by 5 rows, making 35 squares.

4. Line cookie sheet with cooking parchment paper. Place 1 brownie square in palm of your hand, and press with fingers of other hand to flatten. Place 1 candy in center of flattened brownie piece; wrap brownie gently around candy, pressing into a ball. Place on cookie sheet. Repeat with remaining brownie squares and 34 of the candies. Refrigerate 15 minutes.

5. Finely chop remaining candy; set aside. In medium microwavable bowl, microwave chocolate chips and shortening uncovered on High 1 minute to 1 minute 30 seconds, stirring every 30 seconds, until chips are softened and mixture can be stirred smooth.

6. Using 2 forks, dip and roll chilled balls, one at a time, in melted chocolate. Return to cookie sheet; immediately top with chopped candy. (If chocolate has cooled too much, reheat 10 to 20 seconds or until mixture can be stirred smooth.) Refrigerate brownie bombs about 20 minutes or until coating is set. Store covered in refrigerator up to 1 week.

**1 Candy:** Calories 148; Total Fat 7g (Saturated Fat 3g, Trans Fat 0g); Cholesterol 1mg; Sodium 55mg; Total Carbohydrate 21g (Dietary Fiber 1g); Protein 2g **Exchanges:** ½ Starch, 1 Other Carbohydrate, 2 Fat **Carbohydrate Choices:** 1½

## Kitchen Secrets
**Customize your brownie bites! Try one or a combination of your favorite candies available in unwrapped mini size, such as milk chocolate-covered peanut caramel and nougat; chocolate-covered peanut butter cup candies; or chocolate-covered crispy peanut-buttery candies.**

# Chocolate-Mint Pinwheels

**PREP TIME:** 30 Minutes   **START TO FINISH:** 3 Hours 20 Minutes   *4 dozen cookies*

1 pouch (17.5 oz) sugar cookie mix
½ cup butter, softened
1 egg
¼ cup unsweetened baking cocoa
2 tablespoons all-purpose flour
½ teaspoon mint extract
2 to 3 drops green food color

**1** In large bowl, stir cookie mix, butter and egg until dough forms. Divide dough in half. Stir cocoa into one half. Stir flour, mint extract and food color into other half. Place chocolate dough on 17x12-inch sheet of waxed paper. Top dough with second sheet of waxed paper. Roll dough to 12x7-inch rectangle. Repeat with green dough.

**2** Remove top sheet of waxed paper from both doughs. Using waxed paper to lift green dough, invert onto chocolate dough. Gently press layered dough to 14x8-inch rectangle. Remove top sheet of waxed paper. Starting at one long side, use bottom sheet of waxed paper to help roll doughs up together tightly. Wrap tightly in waxed paper; freeze at least 2 hours or until very firm.

**3** Heat oven to 375°F. Unwrap dough; cut into ¼-inch slices. On ungreased cookie sheet, place slices 2 inches apart. Bake 9 to 11 minutes or until set. Cool 2 minutes; remove from cookie sheet to cooling rack.

**1 Cookie:** Calories 21; Total Fat 2g (Saturated Fat 1g, Trans Fat 0g); Cholesterol 9mg; Sodium 2mg; Total Carbohydrate 1g (Dietary Fiber 0g); Protein 0g **Exchanges:** Free **Carbohydrate Choices:** ½

**Make-Ahead Magic** Cookie dough can be covered and refrigerated up to 24 hours before baking.

**Festive Touch** Put a different spin on these cookies by reversing the chocolate and mint dough layers.

**Kitchen Secrets** Each time you slice a cookie, roll the dough one-quarter turn to prevent flattening on one side.

# Gingerbread Cookies with Royal Icing

**PREP TIME:** 1 Hour 40 Minutes   **START TO FINISH:** 3 Hours 40 Minutes   *5 dozen cookies*

### COOKIES

- ½ cup butter, softened
- ½ cup packed brown sugar
- ½ cup molasses
- ⅓ cup cold water
- 3½ cups all-purpose flour
- 2 teaspoons baking soda
- 2 teaspoons ground ginger
- ½ teaspoon ground allspice
- ½ teaspoon ground cinnamon
- ¼ teaspoon salt
- ¼ teaspoon ground cloves

### ROYAL ICING

- 1 tablespoon meringue powder
- 2 tablespoons cold water
- 1 cup powdered sugar
- Granulated sugar or sanding sugar, if desired

**1** In large bowl, beat butter, brown sugar, molasses and cold water with electric mixer on medium speed until well mixed, or mix with wooden spoon. (Mixture may look curdled.) Stir in remaining cookie ingredients until soft dough forms. Wrap in plastic wrap; refrigerate at least 2 hours or until firm.

**2** Heat oven to 350°F. Lightly spray cookie sheets with cooking spray. On floured surface, roll dough until ⅛ inch thick. Cut with floured 3½- by 2½-inch gingerbread boy or girl cookie cutter. On cookie sheets, place cutouts 2 inches apart. Reroll dough, and cut additional cookies.

**3** Bake 10 to 12 minutes or until no indentation remains when lightly touched. Immediately remove from cookie sheets to cooling racks. Cool completely, about 30 minutes.

**4** In medium bowl, beat meringue powder and cold water with electric mixer on medium speed until stiff peaks form. Gradually beat in powdered sugar until soft peaks form, about 1 minute. Spoon icing into decorating bag fitted with medium round tip; pipe icing over cookies. Sprinkle with granulated sugar. Let stand until icing is set, about 5 minutes.

**1 Cookie:** Calories 60; Total Fat 1.5g (Saturated Fat 1g, Trans Fat 0g); Cholesterol 0mg; Sodium 65mg; Total Carbohydrate 12g (Dietary Fiber 0g); Protein 0g **Exchanges:** ½ Other Carbohydrate, ½ Fat **Carbohydrate Choices:** 1

### Make-Ahead Magic
**Secrets Make these adorable cookies up to 3 months in advance. Place frosted cookies in resealable freezer plastic bags with waxed paper between layers. Remove from freezer bags to thaw at room temperature.**

### Kitchen Secrets
**Royal Icing is the perfect icing to use when packaging and sending cookies. Once it dries, it can't get smudged! Add the sugar immediately after piping on the icing so the icing will hold the decorations in place.**

### Kitchen Secrets
**When baking cookies in batches, cool the cookie sheets 10 minutes before reusing.**

# Pink Peppermint Whoopie Pies

**PREP TIME:** 45 Minutes   **START TO FINISH:** 1 Hour 25 Minutes   *1½ dozen sandwich cookies*

## COOKIES

1 **cup granulated sugar**
½ **cup butter, softened**
½ **cup buttermilk**
2 **teaspoons vanilla**
1 **egg**
2 **oz unsweetened baking chocolate, melted, cooled**
1¾ **cups all-purpose flour**
½ **teaspoon baking soda**
½ **teaspoon salt**

## CREAMY MARSHMALLOW FILLING

3 **cups powdered sugar**
1 **jar (7 oz) marshmallow creme**
¾ **cup butter, softened**
6 to 7 **teaspoons milk**
6 **drops red food color**

## DECORATION

**Crushed hard peppermint candies or candy canes**

**1** Heat oven to 400°F. Grease cookie sheets with shortening or cooking spray, or line with cooking parchment paper or silicone baking mat.

**2** In large bowl, beat granulated sugar, ½ cup butter, the buttermilk, vanilla, egg and chocolate with electric mixer on medium speed, or mix with spoon, until well blended. Stir in flour, baking soda and salt. Onto cookie sheets, drop dough by rounded tablespoonfuls 2 inches apart.

**3** Bake 8 to 10 minutes or until almost no indentation remains when lightly touched in center. Immediately remove from cookie sheets to cooling racks. Cool completely, about 30 minutes.

**4** In large bowl, beat filling ingredients with electric mixer on medium speed about 2 minutes or until light and fluffy.

**5** For each whoopie pie, spread slightly less than 3 tablespoons filling on bottom of one cookie; top with second cookie, bottom side down. Gently press together; sprinkle edge of filling with crushed candies. Store in airtight container.

**1 Sandwich Cookie:** Calories 350; Total Fat 15g (Saturated Fat 9g, Trans Fat 0.5g); Cholesterol 45mg; Sodium 230mg; Total Carbohydrate 51g (Dietary Fiber 1g); Protein 2g **Exchanges:** ½ Starch, 3 Other Carbohydrate, 3 Fat **Carbohydrate Choices:** 3½

## Kitchen Secrets

For *Chocolate Chip Whoopee Pies,* fold ½ cup miniature semisweet chocolate chips into the filling. For *Toffee Whoopee Pies,* fold ½ cup chocolate-coated toffee bits into the filling.

# Marshmallow Mug Mates

**PREP TIME:** 35 Minutes   **START TO FINISH:** 50 Minutes   *24 mug mates*

24 small candy canes

24 large marshmallows

1½ cups dark chocolate chips
(about 9 oz)

1 package (4.67 oz) thin
rectangular crème de menthe
chocolate candies (28 pieces),
unwrapped, finely chopped

**1** Line large cookie sheet with cooking parchment paper. Insert candy cane in center of flat side of each marshmallow to within ½ inch from bottom.

**2** In medium microwavable bowl, microwave chocolate chips uncovered on High 45 to 60 seconds, stirring every 15 seconds, until chips are softened and can be stirred smooth.

**3** Using candy cane for handle, dip 1 marshmallow into melted chocolate to coat; sprinkle side with chopped candies. Place on cookie sheet. Repeat with remaining candy canes, marshmallows, melted chocolate and candies. Refrigerate about 15 minutes or until chocolate is set, up to 3 days.

**1 Mug Mate:** Calories 110; Total Fat 4g (Saturated Fat 3.5g, Trans Fat 0g); Cholesterol 0mg; Sodium 30mg; Total Carbohydrate 17g (Dietary Fiber 0g); Protein 1g **Exchanges:** 1 Other Carbohydrate, 1 Fat **Carbohydrate Choices:** 1

## Festive Touch

**For a fun hostess gift, pair these mug mates with hot cocoa mix and a festive holiday mug.**

# Snowy Bourbon Balls

**PREP TIME:** 30 Minutes   **START TO FINISH:** 30 Minutes   *48 candies*

1 box (12 oz) vanilla wafer cookies, finely crushed

1 cup chopped pecans or walnuts

¾ cup powdered sugar

2 tablespoons unsweetened baking cocoa

½ cup bourbon

2½ tablespoons light corn syrup

Additional powdered sugar

**1** In large bowl, mix cookie crumbs, pecans, ¾ cup powdered sugar and the cocoa, stirring well.

**2** In small bowl, mix bourbon and corn syrup until blended. Pour bourbon mixture over cookie mixture; stir until blended.

**3** Shape into 1-inch balls; roll in additional powdered sugar.

**1 Candy:** Calories 70; Total Fat 3g (Saturated Fat 0g, Trans Fat 0g); Cholesterol 0mg; Sodium 25mg; Total Carbohydrate 9g (Dietary Fiber 0g); Protein 0g **Carbohydrate Choices:** ½

**Make-Ahead Magic** **Store bourbon balls tightly covered at room temperature up to 2 weeks.**

**Kitchen Secrets** **Try rolling all or half of these tasty treats in unsweetened baking cocoa instead of powdered sugar.**

# Cranberry-Pistachio Cookies

**PREP TIME:** 45 Minutes   **START TO FINISH:** 45 Minutes   *4 dozen cookies*

1 pouch (17.5 oz) sugar cookie mix

1 box (4-serving size) pistachio instant pudding and pie filling mix

¼ cup all-purpose flour

½ cup butter, melted

2 eggs

1 cup dry-roasted salted pistachio nuts, chopped

½ cup dried cranberries, chopped

1. Heat oven to 350°F. In large bowl, stir cookie mix, pudding mix and flour. Stir in butter and eggs until soft dough forms. Add nuts and cranberries; mix well.

2. Onto ungreased cookie sheets, drop dough using small cookie scoop or teaspoon 2 inches apart. Press with fingers to slightly flatten.

3. Bake 9 to 11 minutes or until edges are light golden brown. Cool 2 minutes; remove from cookie sheets to cooling racks. Store cooled cookies tightly covered at room temperature.

**1 Cookie:** Calories 90; Total Fat 4.5g (Saturated Fat 1.5g, Trans Fat 0g); Cholesterol 15mg; Sodium 85mg; Total Carbohydrate 12g (Dietary Fiber 0g); Protein 1g **Exchanges:** 1 Other Carbohydrate, 1 Fat **Carbohydrate Choices:** 1

## Kitchen Secrets
Use a food processor to quickly chop the nuts and cranberries.

# Dulce de Leche–Coffee Dipped Pears

**PREP TIME:** 10 Minutes   **START TO FINISH:** 1 Hour 10 Minutes   *6 servings*

½ cup chopped chocolate-covered espresso coffee beans

1 can (13.4 oz) dulce de leche (caramelized sweetened condensed milk)

1 tablespoon coffee-flavored liqueur

6 red or green firm but ripe pears with stems

1 Line cookie sheet with waxed or cooking parchment paper. In shallow bowl, place coffee beans.

2 In 1-quart saucepan, stir together dulce de leche and liqueur. Heat over low heat, stirring constantly, 5 minutes or until smooth. Remove from heat.

3 Holding stem, dip bottom half of each pear into caramel mixture; shake off excess. Roll in coffee beans. Place on cookie sheet. Drizzle any remaining caramel mixture over pears (rewarm, if necessary). Refrigerate 1 hour or until set. Store loosely covered in refrigerator up to 1 week.

**1 Serving:** Calories 390; Total Fat 9g (Saturated Fat 5g, Trans Fat 0g); Cholesterol 20mg; Sodium 95mg; Total Carbohydrate 70g (Dietary Fiber 6g); Protein 6g **Exchanges:** 1 Fruit, 3 Other Carbohydrate, 1 Milk **Carbohydrate Choices:** 4½

## Festive Touch For variety, dip the caramel pears in other toppings. Chocolate candy sprinkles, mini chocolate chips, crushed chocolate wafers or graham crackers would all be delicious!

## Kitchen Secrets Before dipping pears, check that they will stand upright. If not, cut a thin slice from bottom of pear so it has a flat surface.

## Kitchen Secrets Not a coffee fan? Substitute chopped toasted hazelnuts (filberts) for the coffee beans and hazelnut liqueur for the coffee-flavored liqueur.

# Elf Chow

**PREP TIME:** 20 Minutes    **START TO FINISH:** 4 Hours 50 Minutes    *18 servings*

12 cups popped popcorn

2 cups roasted whole almonds

2 cups small pretzel twists

1 cup red and green candy-coated chocolate candies

1 cup packed brown sugar

¾ cup butter

½ cup light corn syrup

1 teaspoon baking soda

½ teaspoon salt

½ teaspoon vanilla

¾ cup dark chocolate chips

½ teaspoon vegetable oil

½ cup white vanilla baking chips

½ cup crushed hard peppermint candies

**1** Heat oven to 250°F. Lightly spray large roasting pan with cooking spray. In roasting pan, mix popcorn, almonds, pretzels and chocolate candies; set aside.

**2** In 2-quart saucepan, heat brown sugar, butter and corn syrup to boiling over medium heat. Boil 8 to 10 minutes, stirring occasionally. Remove from heat; stir in baking soda, salt and vanilla until well mixed. Pour over popcorn mixture; toss until coated.

**3** Bake 1 hour, stirring every 15 minutes. Immediately spread on waxed or cooking parchment paper. Cool 30 minutes.

**4** Meanwhile, in small microwavable bowl, microwave dark chocolate chips and ¼ teaspoon of the oil on High 30 to 60 seconds, stirring every 15 seconds, until melted and smooth. Drizzle over popcorn mixture.

**5** In another small microwavable bowl, microwave white baking chips and remaining ¼ teaspoon oil on High 30 to 40 seconds, stirring every 15 seconds, until melted and smooth. Drizzle over popcorn mixture. Sprinkle with peppermint candies. Let stand 3 to 4 hours or until chocolate is set. Store in airtight container.

**1 Serving (1 Cup):** Calories 450; Total Fat 25g (Saturated Fat 10g, Trans Fat 0g); Cholesterol 25mg; Sodium 270mg; Total Carbohydrate 50g (Dietary Fiber 3g); Protein 5g **Exchanges:** 1½ Starch, 2 Other Carbohydrate, 5 Fat **Carbohydrate Choices:** 3

**Make-Ahead Magic** **This recipe can be made up to 4 days in advance. Store in an airtight container or resealable food-storage plastic bags.**

**Festive Touch** **This eye-catching, sweet-and-salty snack mix would make a great hostess gift. Place chow in holiday food-safe tins or decorative bags tied with a ribbon.**

# Marzipan Snow People

PREP TIME: 45 Minutes    START TO FINISH: 45 Minutes    *8 snow people*

1 package (7 or 8 oz) marzipan
   or almond paste
56 slivered almonds (about
   2 tablespoons)
8 chocolate-covered peppermint
   patties (1.5 oz), unwrapped
   Multicolored candy sprinkles
2 rolls chewy fruit snack in 3-foot
   rolls, any flavor (from 4.5-
   oz box)
8 small gumdrops

1  Roll marzipan into log shape; divide into 8 portions. Divide each portion into 1 large (1¼-inch) ball, 1 medium (1-inch) ball and 1 small (¾-inch) ball.

2  For each snow person, insert 1 slivered almond halfway (upright) into center of peppermint patty. Place large ball over almond, gently pushing downward to attach to peppermint patty for base. Insert 2 almonds into center of large ball; attach medium ball, gently pushing down. Gently insert 1 almond into center of medium ball; place small ball over almond, gently pushing down to attach.

3  Using toothpick, make holes in face of snowman for eyes and nose. Insert 1 brown candy sprinkle into each hole to look like eyes. Insert 1 sprinkle into hole to look like nose. Make holes for buttons and insert sprinkles. Insert 2 almonds partway on either side of middle ball to look like arms.

4  Unroll fruit snacks. For scarves, cut 8 (5x½-inch) strips. Fold each strip in half horizontally, leaving 1 inch on each end unfolded; make small cuts at ends for fringe. Wrap around neck, slightly overlapping at shoulder. To make bases of hats, cut 8 (¾-inch diameter) rounds of fruit snack; place 1 on each snowman's head. Insert almond halfway (upright) down into center. Cut off and discard ⅛ inch off bottom of gumdrop; flatten bottom slightly. Attach onto slivered almond to finish hat.

**1 Snow Person:** Calories 190; Total Fat 8g (Saturated Fat 1g, Trans Fat 0g); Cholesterol 0mg; Sodium 10mg; Total Carbohydrate 27g (Dietary Fiber 2g); Protein 3g **Exchanges:** 2 Other Carbohydrate, ½ Very Lean Meat, 1½ Fat **Carbohydrate Choices:** 2

## Festive Touch  These snow people make adorable place cards! Cut flags from small pieces of paper, write guests' names on them and attach with toothpicks.

## Kitchen Secrets  If the marzipan is hard or crumbly, gently knead in a small amount of corn syrup, 1 teaspoon at a time, until desired softness.

# Buckeye Fudge

**PREP TIME:** 15 Minutes    **START TO FINISH:** 2 Hours 45 Minutes    *64 pieces*

3 cups peanut butter chips
   (about 18 oz)
1 can (14 oz) sweetened
   condensed milk
   (not evaporated)
½ cup creamy peanut butter
⅓ cup finely chopped
   cocktail peanuts
1 cup dark chocolate chips
   (about 6 oz)
½ cup whipping cream

1  Line 9-inch square pan with foil; spray foil with cooking spray.

2  In large microwavable bowl, microwave peanut butter chips uncovered on Medium (50%) in 1-minute increments 3 to 4 minutes, stirring well after each minute, until melted and smooth.

3  Stir in condensed milk, peanut butter and peanuts until blended. (Mixture will be thick.) Press evenly in pan. Refrigerate 30 minutes.

4  In small microwavable bowl, microwave chocolate chips and whipping cream uncovered on High 1 minute to 1 minute 30 seconds, stirring every 30 seconds, until smooth. Spread evenly over chilled fudge. Refrigerate 2 hours or until chocolate is set.

5  Use foil to lift fudge from pan. Cut into 8 rows by 8 rows. Store covered in refrigerator.

**1 Piece:** Calories 107; Total Fat 6g (Saturated Fat 2g, Trans Fat 0g); Cholesterol 4mg; Sodium 47mg; Total Carbohydrate 12g (Dietary Fiber 1g), Protein 2g **Exchanges:** ½ Other Carbohydrate, ½ Fat **Carbohydrate Choices:** ½

**Make-Ahead Magic** Fudge can be stored in the refrigerator up to 1 week.

**Kitchen Secrets** Peanut butter chips can be very heat sensitive, so it is important to reduce the power level when melting them in the microwave.

**Kitchen Secrets** To easily line pan with foil, turn pan upside down. Tear off a piece of foil longer than the pan. Smooth foil around pan bottom, then remove. Turn pan over, and gently fit shaped foil into pan. When fudge is cooled completely, lift out of pan by foil "handles," peel back foil and cut fudge into pieces.

# Caramel-Rum Fudge

**PREP TIME:** 20 Minutes    **START TO FINISH:** 2 Hours 20 Minutes    *64 pieces*

¾ cup sugar

¼ cup water

1 tablespoon fresh lemon juice

⅓ cup whipping cream

4½ tablespoons butter

2 cans (14 oz each) sweetened condensed milk (not evaporated)

4 cups semisweet chocolate chips (about 24 oz)

¼ cup dark rum

¼ teaspoon salt

1 Line 9-inch square pan with cooking parchment paper; grease paper with shortening.

2 In 1-quart saucepan, heat sugar, water and lemon juice to boiling over medium-high heat. Boil 8 to 10 minutes or until sugar begins to brown. (Do not stir.) Stir in whipping cream and 2 tablespoons of the butter; remove from heat. Let stand, stirring constantly, until caramel is no longer bubbling.

3 In large microwavable bowl, microwave condensed milk and chocolate chips uncovered on High 3 minutes, stirring after every minute. Stir in rum, remaining 2½ tablespoons butter and the salt. Immediately pour into pan. Immediately pour caramel over chocolate mixture; gently swirl with knife. Cover; refrigerate 2 to 4 hours.

4 Use paper to lift fudge from pan. Cut into 8 rows by 8 rows; rewrap in cooking parchment paper. Store in refrigerator.

**1 Piece:** Calories 120; Total Fat 5g (Saturated Fat 3.5g, Trans Fat 0g); Cholesterol 10mg; Sodium 35mg; Total Carbohydrate 16g (Dietary Fiber 0g); Protein 1g **Carbohydrate Choices:** 1

## Make-Ahead Magic

**Store fudge covered in the refrigerator up to 1 week. Remove from the refrigerator 15 minutes before serving.**

## Festive Touch

**Delight your guests by offering a piece of this grown-up fudge with dessert coffee or an after-dinner drink.**

# S'more Bark

**PREP TIME:** 10 Minutes   **START TO FINISH:** 1 Hour 10 Minutes   *24 pieces*

4   cups milk chocolate chips
    (about 24 oz)

6   graham cracker rectangles,
    coarsely crushed

2   cups miniature marshmallows

**1** Line cookie sheet with waxed paper. In medium microwavable bowl, microwave chocolate chips uncovered on High 2 minutes, stirring once, until chips are softened and can be stirred smooth. Stir in half of the crushed graham crackers and 1 cup of the marshmallows.

**2** On cookie sheet, spread mixture to ¼-inch thickness. Sprinkle remaining crushed graham crackers and 1 cup marshmallows over top; press in lightly. Refrigerate 1 hour or until chocolate has hardened. Break into 2 inch pieces. Store tightly covered in refrigerator up to one week.

**1 Piece:** Calories 180; Total Fat 9g (Saturated Fat 5g, Trans Fat 0g); Cholesterol 0mg; Sodium 40mg; Total Carbohydrate 23g (Dietary Fiber 1g); Protein 2g **Exchanges:** 1½ Other Carbohydrate, 1½ Fat **Carbohydrate Choices:** 1½

## Festive Touch

This easy-to-make confection is a nice addition to your holiday cookie tray, and it also makes a great gift for a teacher or your mail carrier or newspaper carrier. Place bark in a holiday-themed cellophane bag, and tie with a ribbon.

## Kitchen Secrets

This bark can also be made with semisweet or bittersweet chocolate chips instead of the milk chocolate chips.

# Cappuccino-Walnut Toffee

**PREP TIME:** 35 Minutes    **START TO FINISH:** 1 Hour 40 Minutes    *30 pieces*

1¼  cups butter
1  cup granulated sugar
⅓  cup packed light brown sugar
1  tablespoon full-flavor (dark) molasses
2  teaspoons instant espresso coffee powder or granules
½  teaspoon ground cinnamon
¼  teaspoon salt
⅓  cup water
2  cups chopped walnuts, toasted
1  cup milk chocolate chips (about 6 oz)
1  cup white vanilla baking chips (about 6 oz)

1   Butter 15x10-inch pan. In heavy 3½-quart saucepan, melt 1¼ cups butter over medium heat. Stir in granulated sugar, brown sugar, molasses, coffee powder, cinnamon, salt and water. Cook, stirring constantly, to 290°F on candy thermometer or until small amount of mixture dropped into cup of very cold water separates into threads that are hard but pliable.

2   Remove from heat; stir in walnuts. Quickly pour mixture into pan and spread in even layer. Immediately sprinkle chocolate and white chips over top; let stand 5 minutes. Swirl melted chips using offset spatula.

3   Cover; refrigerate 1 hour or until firm. Break toffee into pieces. Serve cold or at room temperature. Store tightly covered.

**1 Piece:** Calories 230; Total Fat 17g (Saturated Fat 9g, Trans Fat 0g); Cholesterol 0mg; Sodium 100mg; Total Carbohydrate 20g (Dietary Fiber 1g); Protein 2g **Exchanges:** 1½ Other Carbohydrate, 3½ Fat **Carbohydrate Choices:** 1½

## Make-Ahead Magic Tightly covered toffee can be stored in the refrigerator up to 7 days.

## Festive Touch Want to bring something unique to a cookie exchange? This twist on toffee is sure to be a hit. Package it in decorative food boxes available at party or cake supply stores or online.

## Kitchen Secrets To toast walnuts, sprinkle in ungreased skillet. Cook over medium heat 5 to 7 minutes, stirring frequently until nuts begin to brown, then stirring constantly until nuts are light brown.

# Chocolate-Drizzled Lace Brittle

**PREP TIME:** 25 Minutes   **START TO FINISH:** 1 Hour 55 Minutes   *24 pieces*

¼ cup butter
½ cup sugar
¼ cup light corn syrup
⅓ cup all-purpose flour
½ cup finely chopped almonds
1 teaspoon vanilla
½ cup semisweet chocolate chips

**1** Heat oven to 375°F (350°F for dark or nonstick pan). Line cookie sheet with cooking parchment paper.

**2** In 2-quart saucepan, melt butter over medium heat. Stir in sugar and corn syrup. Reduce heat to medium-low. Heat to boiling, stirring constantly, until sugar is dissolved. Remove from heat. Stir in flour, almonds and vanilla until blended. Quickly spread mixture into 11x10-inch rectangle on cookie sheet.

**3** Bake 10 minutes or until brittle spreads thin and is deep golden brown. Cool 5 minutes; remove from cookie sheet to cooling rack. Cool completely, about 15 minutes.

**4** In small microwavable bowl, microwave chocolate chips uncovered on High 30 to 60 seconds, stirring once, until chips are softened and can be stirred smooth. Spoon melted chocolate into small resealable food-storage plastic bag; seal bag. Cut off tiny corner of bag. Squeeze bag to drizzle chocolate over brittle. Let stand 1 hour or until chocolate is firm. Break into irregular pieces. Store in tightly covered container up to 2 weeks.

**1 Piece:**Calories 90; Total Fat 4.5g (Saturated Fat 2g, Trans Fat 0g); Cholesterol 5mg; Sodium 20mg; Total Carbohydrate 11g (Dietary Fiber 0g); Protein 1g **Exchanges:** ½ Starch, 1 Fat **Carbohydrate Choices:** 1

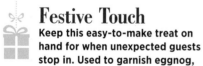

## Festive Touch
**Keep this easy-to-make treat on hand for when unexpected guests stop in. Used to garnish eggnog, ice cream or cake with whipped cream, it can make almost anything seem special!**

## Kitchen Secrets
**This delicate brittle is much easier and quicker to make than the traditional nut candy.**

# Metric Conversion Guide

## VOLUME

| U.S. Units | Canadian Metric | Australian Metric |
|---|---|---|
| ¼ teaspoon | 1 mL | 1 ml |
| ½ teaspoon | 2 mL | 2 ml |
| 1 teaspoon | 5 mL | 5 ml |
| 1 tablespoon | 15 mL | 20 ml |
| ¼ cup | 50 mL | 60 ml |
| ⅓ cup | 75 mL | 80 ml |
| ½ cup | 125 mL | 125 ml |
| ⅔ cup | 150 mL | 170 ml |
| ¾ cup | 175 mL | 190 ml |
| 1 cup | 250 mL | 250 ml |
| 1 quart | 1 liter | 1 liter |
| 1½ quarts | 1.5 liters | 1.5 liters |
| 2 quarts | 2 liters | 2 liters |
| 2½ quarts | 2.5 liters | 2.5 liters |
| 3 quarts | 3 liters | 3 liters |
| 4 quarts | 4 liters | 4 liters |

## WEIGHT

| U.S. Units | Canadian Metric | Australian Metric |
|---|---|---|
| 1 ounce | 30 grams | 30 grams |
| 2 ounces | 55 grams | 60 grams |
| 3 ounces | 85 grams | 90 grams |
| 4 ounces (¼ pound) | 115 grams | 125 grams |
| 8 ounces (½ pound) | 225 grams | 225 grams |
| 16 ounces (1 pound) | 455 grams | 500 grams |
| 1 pound | 455 grams | 0.5 kilogram |

**Note:** The recipes in this cookbook have not been developed or tested using metric measures. When converting recipes to metric, some variations in quality may be noted.

## MEASUREMENTS

| Inches | Centimeters |
|---|---|
| 1 | 2.5 |
| 2 | 5.0 |
| 3 | 7.5 |
| 4 | 10.0 |
| 5 | 12.5 |
| 6 | 15.0 |
| 7 | 17.5 |
| 8 | 20.5 |
| 9 | 23.0 |
| 10 | 25.5 |
| 11 | 28.0 |
| 12 | 30.5 |
| 13 | 33.0 |

## TEMPERATURES

| Fahrenheit | Celsius |
|---|---|
| 32° | 0° |
| 212° | 100° |
| 250° | 120° |
| 275° | 140° |
| 300° | 150° |
| 325° | 160° |
| 350° | 180° |
| 375° | 190° |
| 400° | 200° |
| 425° | 220° |
| 450° | 230° |
| 475° | 240° |
| 500° | 260° |

# Index

# Recipe Testing and Calculating Nutrition Information

## RECIPE TESTING:

- Large eggs and 2% milk were used unless otherwise indicated.

- No fat-free, low-fat, low-sodium or lite products were used unless indicated.

- No nonstick cookware or bakeware was used unless otherwise indicated. No dark-colored, black or insulated bakeware was used.

- When a pan is specified, a metal pan was used; a baking dish or pie plate means ovenproof glass was used.

- An electric hand mixer was used for mixing only when mixer speeds are specified.

## CALCULATING NUTRITION:

- The first ingredient was used wherever a choice is given, such as ⅓ cup sour cream or plain yogurt.

- The first amount was used wherever a range is given, such as 3- to 3½-pound whole chicken.

- The first serving number was used wherever a range is given, such as 4 to 6 servings.

- "If desired" ingredients were not included.

- Only the amount of a marinade or frying oil that is absorbed was included.